Connected
THE EMERGENCE OF GLOBAL CONSCIOUSNESS

ROGER D. NELSON

ICRL Press
Princeton, New Jersey

Connected: The Emergence of Global Consciousness
Copyright © 2019 Roger D. Nelson
ISBN: 978-1-936033-35-5

Cover image by Maxiphoto/iStock

Book design by Smythtype

All rights reserved. No part of this publication may be reproduced, transmitted, or stored in a retrieval system or by any means without the permission in writing from the publisher.

For information address:
ICRL Press
468 N. Harrison Street
Princeton, NJ 08540-3530

To my wife, Lefty, who has been my friend and counselor and patient muse for all my adult life. She is the "sage" I refer to and defer to when it comes to the most human of matters. It is she who observed long ago that there's no loss if psi is explained as an experimenter effect. After all, she said, we can all be experimenters.

Table of Contents

Foreword by Dean Radin 9
Prologue 11
Introduction 13

Part One: The EGG Story 21
Chapter 1: Starting Points 23
Chapter 2: Interconnections 27
Chapter 3: Seeing the Path 33
Chapter 4: Development 37
Chapter 5: Design by Coincidence 39
Chapter 6: Hatching the EGG 47
Chapter 7: Encouraging Results 53

Part Two: The Instrument 55
Chapter 8: Intention Affects RNGs 57
Chapter 9: Random Event Generator 71
Chapter 10: The FieldREG Experiment 81
Chapter 11: The EGG Network 93
Chapter 12: Bringing It All Together 101
Chapter 13: Suitable Measures 107
Chapter 14: The Art of Science 117

Part Three: The Results 129

Chapter 15: Event Categories and Results 133
    15.1 Terror attacks and war 135
    15.2 Natural disasters...149
    15.3 Celebration and sharing..153
    15.4 Compassion and empathy 158
    15.5 Cosmic and social abstractions.............................162
    15.6 Powerful interest 166
    15.7 Deliberate focus 171

Chapter 16: The Bottom Line 179
Chapter 17: Deeper Analysis 185
Chapter 18: Independent Subsets...201
Chapter 19: Characterizing Event Categories................................209
Chapter 20: Structural Analysis...217
Chapter 21: Modeling and Theory 229
    21.1 Modeling based on data 231
    21.2 Speculative Notions and Models 246

Part Four: Interpretation and Meaning 257

Chapter 22: Extracting Meaning...261
Chapter 23: And Then? 275
Chapter 24: Implications of the Evidence......................................279
Chapter 25: Reflections..289
Chapter 26: What We Can Do 295
Chapter 27: Poetic History...299
Chapter 28: Love to the Earth 309

Acknowledgments 313
Appendix..315
Endnotes..321
Index 331

Personal experiences of interconnection, such as falling in love or losing ourselves in the beauty of a sunset, remind us all that we are not alone, imprisoned in our skin and skulls.

Now, just at a time in history when it appears to be essential for us to work together, we see evidence of a shared consciousness beginning to appear on a global scale.

Foreword

In a key scene in the first *Star Wars* movie, Obi-Wan Kenobi is traveling in a spaceship when he suddenly staggers, as if in pain. Luke Skywalker sees this and asks, "Are you all right? What's wrong?" With some effort, Obi-Wan gravely replies, "I felt a great disturbance in the Force, as if millions of voices suddenly cried out in terror and were suddenly silenced. I fear something terrible has happened."

Obi-Wan was referring to the evil Empire's use of a terrifying weapon called the Death Star, which had just been used to destroy the planet Alderaan. Besides acting as a compelling plot point, what's most interesting about this scene is that it didn't need an extensive explanation. Somehow, we all knew what Obi-Wan meant and what he felt.

This strange *knowing* raises a series of intriguing questions: Is a "disturbance in the Force" just an engaging fictional fancy? Or is it real? And is there a way to objectively detect it so we don't have to rely on Obi-Wan to inform us that something terrible just happened elsewhere in the galaxy? These are fundamental questions about the woof and warp of the universe, and about the role that consciousness plays in the complex tapestry we call reality.

Perhaps the most sophisticated instrument we've developed to probe the nature of reality is the Large Hadron Collider (LHC) at CERN, in Switzerland. The LHC is the world's largest and highest-energy machine. In each experiment, it's run for thousands of hours, probing ever deeper into the nature of the physical world by causing trillions upon trillions of collisions of elementary particles. The collective picture wrought by all those data points tells us how the physical world is constructed.

So far, the LHC has confirmed to an almost unbelievably precise degree what our mathematical models have predicted. This is a magnificent achievement, but it's also a little suspicious. A few lumps of neural tissue managed to dream up a purely symbolic representation of reality. Then, some other lumps of neural tissue pondered that representation and felt it had merit. So, it was tested in the world's most expensive physics project, and the results were essentially identical to what the tissue lumps had predicted. How is that possible? Those must have been some awfully clever neurons, because they not only dreamt up amazingly accurate symbolic models of reality, they also described their own deep structure, millions of time smaller even than a single neuron.

Or could there be another reason? Could the collective attention of tens of thousands of LHC physicists and engineers somehow have manipulated the physical world to *manifest* what they wanted to see? After all, billions of dollars and thousands of careers depend on the success of that project. Running the LHC is said to cost $23 million a year just for the electric bill. And the cost of the search for the Higgs Boson, just one of the many LHC projects, is estimated to be over $13 billion dollars.

What if the CERN LHC is revealing a "disturbance in the Force" more along the lines of what Obi-Wan described, rather than just corroborating a mindless model of the physical world? And what if there were another sort of LHC, an instrument designed to probe not just physical laws, but say, the Laws of Human Coherence, and how those limits interact with the physical world.

We could run our fanciful second LHC to test if the physical world is indeed altered when it "collides" with coherent minds. But unlike the collider in Switzerland, this LHC would cost almost nothing, and yet what it could tell us about reality would be far more important than the one at CERN, because this LHC would tell us if the disturbance in the Force is real. If it is, then we'd be compelled to radically rethink our models of reality.

That second LHC is not just a whimsical fantasy. It's real, it's been quietly collecting data for nearly two decades, and it has reached a conclusion based on those data that's much stronger than the evidence that won the CERN team the Nobel Prize for discovering the Higgs Boson.

The conclusion is that Obi-Wan's sense of a disturbance in the Force is not mere fiction. It's real. This second LHC is called the Global Consciousness Project. And this is its remarkable story.

—*Dean Radin*

Prologue

We are all caught in an inescapable network of mutuality, tied in a single garment of destiny.
—*Dr. Martin Luther King Jr.*

This book is a snapshot of science at the edges of what we know about being human, at the end of the second decade of the 21st century. It is primarily about consciousness—which is paradoxically the most intimate aspect of our personal world, and the most challenging subject confronting our scientific understanding. The background from which we begin is the careful and rigorous research at Princeton University, in the Princeton Engineering Anomalies Research laboratory, on remarkable but little-known aspects of human consciousness. The experiments showed that our consciousness is able to reach across time and space to commune with another consciousness or to change subtle aspects of the world, as in healing, or changing the behavior of random devices. The research was groundbreaking, but also founded on that of other scientists with the curiosity and courage (in the face of opposition and taboos) to look for ways to make the unseen visible.

Refined tools allowed us to step out of the lab to study group consciousness, and that led to a broader question. Might we be able to see indications of a global consciousness, a coalescing global mind? It was a surprising but natural question, reflecting the wisdom of sages from all cultures and ages who have told us that our world, indeed the entire universe, is one unified whole.

That wisdom has had its ups and downs in the last few centuries, as the modern world we inhabit grew strong and clear in its approach to understanding where we live, manifested over the last 100 years as an increasing reliance on physical science. Together with engineering, that science has created the world we live in, or more correctly said, the world we think we live in. It doesn't say much about consciousness, probably because that profound personal aspect of our lives is ephemeral—it is hugely difficult to grasp with the ordinary tools of current science. How can we capture thoughts and emotions with tools designed to measure mass and acceleration? Even the instruments of medicine and psychological science, such as those which detect electrical fields and energy consumption in the brain, fail utterly to show us the sources of creativity or the dimensions of our mental worlds.

This book asks questions that touch on these matters, including the simple-seeming but very challenging, "What is consciousness?" The Global Consciousness Project's research reveals subtle but meaningful structure in what should be random data, collected during periods of time when millions of people share common emotions, suggesting a powerful conclusion: consciousness is instrumental, implying that it is fundamental. It is not just a secondary emanation from the brain, but instead is both part of and independent of the physical substrate of neurons and synapses protected by the skull. Mind has a real and participatory role in the world.

We need to refine scientific and philosophical perspectives on who we are and what makes us endlessly creative and at the same time dangerously destructive—this is a time that is correctly described as critical. The decisions and directions of humanity now and in the next few brief years will determine the fate of our world. We are at a recognizable tipping point where we must select wisely which of many alternative paths we will follow. The world we know is always changing, and every age has its crises. But the changes over which we have some control will determine whether much of the biosphere, including us, will wither and die, or whether we take strides toward becoming the Noosphere described by Teilhard de Chardin, a sheath of intelligence for the earth.

Because we are subtly interconnected, we humans have the potential to become the guiding light of evolution, meaning that we could become conscious agents of growth and a cooperative, intentional force for change guided by principles of compassion and love. Our destiny, according to the wisest of our forebears and many of our far-thinking contemporaries, is conscious evolution. When we grow into our full potential as individual human beings, we will discover that we are all connected as the human species in a global consciousness. We have only to take our part in an essential collaboration that is the next stage of our evolution.

Introduction

We haven't worked on ways to develop a higher social intelligence... Ordinary thought in society is incoherent—it is going in all sorts of directions, with thoughts conflicting and canceling each other out. But if people were to think together in a coherent way, it would have tremendous power.

—David Bohm[1]

It was my good fortune to have an excellent education, the sort that makes it possible to understand the laws of nature deduced and refined by scientists over the past few hundred years. As a result, I'm inclined to give special place to things that can be measured and counted, and I'm a little skeptical about mystical notions and claims of extraordinary powers. But somehow I escaped the full force of that education, which means I still can see anomalies and possibilities suggesting that beyond physics there is more to learn about life and consciousness and spirit. The questions at the edge of what we know about the mind seem to me to be really worthwhile. They are difficult, and thus interesting, but beyond that there is reason to believe they are essential questions, with implications for our very survival on this earth.

Forty years ago I met Teilhard de Chardin's ideas, and I've never forgotten the excitement of his conviction that our purpose is to become a "noosphere" for the earth, a sheath of intelligence covering it like the winds of the atmosphere.[2] He thought it would be thousands of years before there could be a coalescence, before this great global mind might begin to know itself, but this deeply spiritual scientist, a paleontologist, was sure the trends of evidence for this direction and this "Omega" point were clear. By chance, my path brought me to a rarefied combination of inclination and opportunity to look for indications of Teilhard's noosphere with the tools of science. The search is a rich and intriguing story, and the findings along the way have implications for how we view ourselves and what we might be doing to manifest our potentials.

Measurements

The scene is a lab at NYU where I am a graduate student late in the exploratory time of the 1960's. An advanced yogi submits to our measurement process, EEG electrodes all over his head. He produces beta waves like all of us do in the normal waking state of mind, then on demand he reduces the frequency and gives us alpha in a smooth, pure trace, no doubt about it. On instruction, the yogi goes on to produce still lower frequencies we refer to as delta waves. He talks to us about the process, what he is doing and what it means in his world, and then, when asked to generate still lower brain wave frequencies, what we call "theta," he apologizes. "Yes, I can do that for you, but I won't be able to talk to you until later. To enter this condition, I must go away from here."

This is a story that has been told in all cultures. There are aspects of the world we can access only by leaving it behind; there are experiences we can only name in retrospect, and the names we give are curious, surprising the logical mind by calling up images of opposites. The "One" and the "Void," fullness and emptiness, which are not only the same thing, but all there is. In the language of modern science this deep background is beginning to find a place, though only recently, and against considerable resistance. The most powerful physical models of the cosmos require virtual particles and near infinite energies bound in an inaccessible, universal zero-point-field. Some descriptions call for an unknowable "implicate order" behind our tangible world of material objects, and tell of information fields that guide the construction of our reality. The ancient wisdom traditions speak of the source, and poets in all languages ask for guidance to return to love, to the union that is torn by being in the world.

The wisdom and apparent powers of special people are fascinating to most of us, but mysterious. We hardly know what questions to ask in order to learn more. For several decades, Elmer Green focused scientific instruments on healers and yogis, to visualize their brain waves and see what sorts of energies they give off.[3] He looked for and found synchronies between the physiologies of healers and their distant, shielded patients. Elmer believed that the scientific data could help to explain what healers do, and teach us what attitude to take. He built a room with polished copper walls, reflecting a ancient Tibetan teaching device. Integrated into the space was a full panoply of high-tech devices intended to capture the signatures of subtle energy. The healers were asked to do what they do, and then analysts worked to understand the signals borne in the spikes and wiggles of recorded traces from both healer and patient, and from the instrumented environment. The data were bountiful, but it was hard to understand the complex of unusual fields and sharply defined electrical curiosities.

There is much to learn from the details, but as in other scientific efforts to study the extraordinary qualities of mind there is an essential message. The experience of the scientific explorer as well as the shaman is this: our being is not confined inside the skull and skin, but lives in a subtly interconnected world where intentions and consciousness are not abstractions. There are qualities and consequences and correlations we cannot explain without acknowledging a direct participation of mind in the world.

Instrumenting consciousness

Since August, 1998, an international team of researchers has been working with a globally distributed network of detectors responsive to the influence of intentions and emotions.[4] We have been gathering evidence of a global consciousness apparently made from some wondrous assembly of our own extended mind-stuff, melded in ways we hope someday to understand. The science clearly shows that in special moments when our normally separated lives—our thoughts and feelings—come together, the world-spanning instrument registers a change. The findings are most unlikely to be mere coincidence or chance fluctuations, because the correlations found in the research are both reliable and meaningful. They make us think of the synchronicities Carl Jung ascribed to the collective unconscious.[5]

But the correlations we see are different in important ways. They suggest a gathering of independent activities into an unconscious collaboration stimulated by shared perceptions, experiences, and emotions. It is an interaction that we cannot see or feel. It implies an interconnection which, while subtle and inconstant, has the character of the "oneness" we hear about from poets and sages.

On the one hand this is a fabulous suggestion, given the faint indications we can draw from the research, but on the other hand because those indications are scientifically strong, the meaning and import of the suggestion makes it worth our attention.

The research project was conceived in 1997 and born in late 1998 as a world-wide network, collecting data continuously from globally distributed physical random number generators (RNGs). The idea was to make something like an EEG for the world, and the metaphoric similarity led us to call this instrument an ElectroGaiaGram, or EGG. We set about looking for structure in data sequences gathered during great events on the world stage, in an analogy to the way EEG traces are used to see patterns in the activity of a human brain in response to sensory stimuli. The question was whether synchronized thoughts and emotions powered by terrible tragedies or grand celebrations might correspond to departures from expectation in the data. Would the totally random behavior of research-quality instruments show changes correlated with happenings important to human beings? The surprising answer we have found to these questions is yes.

Our RNG network runs like a true random system should overall, but we find structure in data recorded during natural disasters or terrorist attacks, or great celebrations like New Year's. The effects are so subtle that it takes months and years of repeated testing to be sure the correlations are there and to estimate their magnitude. But we now have nearly two decades of work yielding over 500 separate tests, and the bottom line says there is a linkage between global events and deviations found in our data. The odds against chance explanations are more than 1000 billion to one (probability ~ 10^{-13}), and the experimental design excludes spurious sources, so we can safely say there is a real effect, though we do not know yet how it arises.

We are digging deeper into the data, teasing out the factors that matter, and this educates our attempts to develop explanatory models and theories. We still have much work ahead because the suggestions of what we're calling global consciousness don't fit into normal science. Even if we leave out the fact that the structure is related to human interests, there are challenging questions about how the structure we see could possibly arise in random data where there should be no patterning at all. If we add back the fact that we find the unexpected correlations reliably during global events that have meaning for us, and not otherwise, it suggests we should take seriously the idea of mental interactions that have a real presence in the physical world.

There are other more personal and active implications, chief among which is that we are interconnected in subtle ways. We are almost entirely unconscious of this, and there is as yet no clear explanation of how the connections arise or how to understand them, but the evidence is solid—we become a "group" with linkages that change the way we operate, under certain conditions. Circumstances determine the nature of the shared consciousness that encompasses and integrates us as couples, as groups, and sometimes as a global mind. Though we may have differing interpretations of the data, there is good reason to speak of a global consciousness, and I think even better reason to act as if a melding of humans to form a global intelligence is not only in progress, but amenable to our intention to foster it.

What this means, assuming it is true, is that we can consciously evolve; we do have a say in how humanity grows into its future. We can take control of our destiny—and the time for that is ripe.

There is a huge and growing interest in deepening human interconnections, and in shared activities aimed directly at creating a better world. Many of these are practical and political, as in groups working to influence government and businesses to pay more attention to ecosystems and to understand the effects of present decisions on the future health of people and planet. But in addition to these pragmatic, down-to-earth movements, there is another category of cooperation and collaboration. People are organizing worldwide meditations, and using technology to synchronize concerts and dancing and participation in virtual choirs across the world. There are groups and websites and social media gatherings for shared prayer and focused intention based often on esoteric understandings—for example, Valentine's Day, or a Solstice, or the "end of the Mayan calendar." These shared moments of future focus may create a kind of global consciousness, and if so, we should see signs of it in data collected with this question in mind.

There are many aspects of our world that are pressing toward the birth of a potent global awareness The Internet and ever more ubiquitous mobile phones connect us into places that were inaccessible only a couple of decades ago. Radio and television coverage make us one population facing news of big events in the world. There is much written about these trends, enough to make us generally aware of the electronically, technically connected world, but there is another gathering trend that is ultimately deeper and richer. That is what this book is about. We are at the beginning of an awakening long envisioned by seers, which now is becoming visible to science.

I'm getting ahead of the story at this point, but if the data do respond to shared human moments, it would be a good sign in another sense. It would show humanity is growing up, leaving adolescence at last. Or, using a different metaphor, it would show we are beginning to gain control over the reptilian "survival" brain that continues to manifest our primitive past. The needs of the present are different in many ways, but the best simple description is that we have come to a stage of human existence where cooperation and integration are required for us to have a chance of a bright future. (Some would say, any future at all.) Without recognition of our interdependence and our responsibilities to each other and the earth, the way ahead will be difficult. There are lots of pieces in the puzzle of who we are, and the scientific study described here points to one that may surprise. It says we already are interconnected at some deeply unconscious level, and that we are part of an unrecognized collective consciousness. The subtle data suggest that this need not remain a hidden quality—that we can gather intentionally and choose our destiny as an integrated intelligence for the earth.

Humanity is uniquely positioned to avert what appears to be a looming catastrophe of our own making. We are too numerous, and we are too smart for our own good—unless we can learn to use our amazing creativity to solve problems and find better ways to live together with each other and with the environment that sustains us. The networks that connect us electronically are a model for a more subtle kind of interconnection that we need to recognize and understand. We will need the bonds of human compassion to succeed in the tasks ahead, for it is clear we can live together with enough for all only if we find and establish mutual respect.

Purpose

One of the questions I have gotten most often over the years is "Do you have a book about the GCP" Many people would like to know what it is all about, but they find it difficult to get through the large and complex website. It is a combination of descriptive information and the experiment's archive, containing huge amounts of data and automatically generated summaries and displays. The explanations and descriptions of what we are doing are both voluminous and widely distributed in the various contexts where they are most relevant, and there is no linear path through the documentation. In short, the website is challenging at best and difficult for the casual reader to enjoy. It is useful and necessary documentation, but it is too much, except for the few who need to delve deeply and can put in the time.

One motivation for this book is to put the most salient information in one place, ordered so the reader can understand what we are doing. Although it is unusual content for a "readable" book, I think it is important to show a spectrum of examples displaying results over the years. There is ultimately no better way to explain the development of protocols to deal with the great variety of real-world events, while also showing why we think there is some genuine meat on the bones of this experiment.

We need to better understand both our capabilities and our responsibilities. This book is a look at subtle, almost magical means we have for moving toward a better tomorrow. With good fortune, we will activate the power that comes from being interconnected. With focused intent, we can begin the work today.

Part One: The EGG Story

Someday after mastering winds, waves, tides and gravity, we shall harness the energies of love, and then, for the second time in the history of the world, man will discover fire.

—Teilhard de Chardin

The 21st Century is a time of great changes, some long anticipated, others still almost invisible nearly two decades after the millennial transition. Human activities are at the center of sweeping developments that focus on interaction. Our communication systems have blossomed into an approximation of world-wide coverage and a temporal presence that is both continuous and instantaneous. Some changes are less visible to us unless we are in the neighborhood, but they also are global in dimension and effect. Again, their source is human-centric. Great swaths of the rainforests are being decimated for corporate-level agriculture and logging, with the devastation of essential environment for thousands of living creatures. Species are going extinct at an abnormally high rate, faster than ever despite efforts by eco-warriors. Global warming is happening while politicians continue to argue whether it is driven by human activities, and an open eye on international news shows it is impinging on people. The tiny islands of the Maldives rise so little above sea level that the people are making contingency plans; losing mere centimeters of altitude will shrink their land mass significantly. Insurers are quietly eliminating or redesigning flood insurance for coastal areas. The Inuit of the Arctic see their homes sink into thermokarsts as the ice of the tundra melts. The devastation brought to New York City and surrounding coastal communities by hurricane Sandy continues years later to be a presence in thousands of lives.

The earth shifts and changes at a geological pace following a timeline that is normally not perceptible—but now many of its major systems, climate, glaciation, sea temperatures, water chemistry, animal and plant populations, are changing while we watch. You and I are not unaffected by this, for we are part of the world, but special because we have the potential for conscious observation and action. We are participants whether or not we intend to be, and being intentional about it may be the next important human act. This looks possible, and there are signs it is also happening while we watch.

The technological world is ever more fertile, with what seems to be exponential growth both of sophistication and "market" penetration. We have faster, more flexible phones and computers, and the networks that link us are more numerous and increasingly interconnected. Most places on earth where humans live have some level of electronic linkage, especially with mobile phones. The Internet has some untouched spaces still, but they are shrinking at the same astonishing pace that created the world-wide-web in just 15 years. It is hard for us to really grasp the speed of recent developments, even for those of us who saw the birth and watched the growth of these networks. For younger people, of course, the Internet is just there, like air and water. They live and breathe email and instant messaging, and their circle of friends is very likely to include people on the other side of the earth with different skin color and language and religion. Their culture is becoming one of communication, not nationality, and we can hope this implies they will naturally grow toward a culture of cooperation and collaboration. It takes only a little reflection to see that a confluence of forces and trends leading toward crises for humanity will have to be matched by an ability to bring communal, global attention and creativity to the challenges we face keeping a viable home on earth.

Chapter 1: STARTING POINTS

There is almost a sensual longing for communion with others who have a large vision. The immense fulfillment of the friendship between those engaged in furthering the evolution of consciousness has a quality impossible to describe.
—*Pierre Teilhard de Chardin*

Deep in the background of humanity's self-portrait is a kind of shared consciousness that has long been acknowledged by seers but hidden from most of us. Fortunately, it is becoming possible to see this interconnection with increasing clarity. It is developing in parallel with the electronic communication networks, and there is a kind of cross fertilization between them. It may be that the pressures and the apparent dangers of a complex and shrinking world are forcing a greater awareness of our neighbors not only next door, but on the other side of fences, borders, oceans, and most important, across cultural divides.

It is obvious from headlines and newscasts that the world moves in synchrony driven by powerful events. News of terrible accidents, hurricanes and earthquakes, acts of war and terror expands outward to affect the whole planet. We learn about major crises and disasters almost instantly, and we are changed by this. The effects of shared information are widespread and may be profound, bringing us into a broad synchrony that is in one sense new, only possible in our modern world. And yet, the shared emotions and thoughts stimulated in this way are not unique to this age. Emotions are contagious and, as the poets have always said, love binds us and makes us one. Music can transport an audience of individuals into one rapture, and the roar of a crowd congratulating a hard-fought goal is one voice. This is a birthright of being human, and we should take delight in recognizing it. More important, we need to accept it and with that accept each other. It is essential to balance personal needs with connection and community. We might survive as "rugged individualists" but we will forgo an opportunity for greatness if that's the way we choose.

Where we want to go

This is the territory we want to explore. What is the nature and the potential of shared consciousness and emotion, and how can we learn from it? Is there a way to study the deeper levels of interconnection fostered by experiencing the same events? The EGG Project, which is more formally called the Global Consciousness Project or GCP, was formed with such questions in mind. The project has been active for nearly two decades, and has grown naturally to accommodate new insights from the data and the analyses. At the same time, the basic focus on human consciousness and the interconnections that link us across the room or across global distances remain at the center of the project.

This idea of interconnected consciousness is not new, although the means to observe it scientifically have only now become available. In the middle of the last century, Teilhard de Chardin wrote in his beautiful books, *The Phenomenon of Man* and *The Future of Man*,[6] that he could only understand our existence and our nature as purposeful. He argued, poetically and passionately, but with scientific understanding, that we would become an integrated intelligence for the earth—like an atmosphere, but made of thought and feeling. He called this the Noosphere, a layer of knowing that would sheath the Earth. It makes sense, and even seems possible: we only need to decide to accept it as our future.

This is a book describing the Global Consciousness Project: how it works, what it's about, and what we have learned in more than 17 years of research. We begin with a brief overview of findings. They will need background and detail to be properly understood, but I respect the desire to "get to the point." The rest of the book will sharpen that point and put flesh on the bones.

In the smallest nutshell this is what we have learned: *Changes in our random data are correlated with major events that connect human beings on a global scale.* This implies that what we think and feel creates unconscious interconnections that have effects in the world. It suggests the deep unity described by poets and sages. The data show faint harmonies rising out of random noise. We are not aware that this happens; we cannot see it without statistical tools, yet it is easy to imagine these faint connections amplified by conscious intent becoming a force in the world.

Subtle Energy and Information

Intuition and direct experience make us wonder if mind extends beyond the confines of the skull: When I think of my mother, I am suddenly, subtly in Nebraska and I'm tasting home-baked bread. When I fall in love, a new entity is created somewhere in the space between me and this fresh new part of me—and she feels the same deep changes: a slight lessening of personal identity, and a delicate participatory dance that re-creates the time we share and does it in a fresh, new space. Reflection on this magic is hardly possible while we're in the experience, but it has much to teach us about human consciousness.

Science has only reticently engaged such mysteries, and, though we can expect many refinements in the future, we have barely begun to imagine instruments and measures that can give us a (cloudy) picture of subtle qualities of consciousness that only poets knew up to now. We are at the beginning of studies that will tell us more about the extended mind. We will learn what justifies the persistence of ancient practices of prayer and ritual despite the ambiguity of their effects and despite modern "science-based" skepticism.

Now science is making room for research on the hypothesis that when we wish or pray, or hold an intention for something to happen, there is a minute but detectable change in its likelihood—because we set our minds to it. We have begun to talk about mind as a source of information fields and "subtle energy." There are long traditions and deep convictions maintaining that these "energies" can be felt by sensitive people, but such anecdotal sources have not had a scientific ally. Especially in a scientific age, most of us want quantitative and objective evidence for claims about things we cannot see or touch. Very recent developments using electronic devices and computers have given us tools for gathering that evidence. Among these devices are "random number generators" (RNGs or REGs). More later on what they are and how they work, but the essence is, these are devices that show effects of conscious intention or coherence where there should be none. They register manifestations of the extended mind.

Chapter 2: INTERCONNECTIONS

Now, if the cooperation of some thousands of millions of cells in our brain can produce our consciousness, a true singularity, the idea becomes vastly more plausible that the cooperation of humanity, or some sections of it, may determine what Comte calls a Great Being.

—*J.B.S. Haldane*[7]

I was not a "Diana watcher" like so many people in the 1990s, but her death in a high-speed crash in a Paris tunnel brought me to attention. Diana, Princess of Wales, was not just a famous media personality, a beautiful aristocrat, she was also a humanitarian who was using her position and her newsworthiness to tackle the land mine problem around the world. She was making progress, and pushing governments to do something at long last about this scourge of innocents maimed and killed by the left-over detritus of wars. And suddenly she was gone, herself the victim of a deadly accident. I had been thinking about the big events which bring people to a common awareness, and it was obvious that Diana's funeral would engage the attention of hundreds of millions—actual estimates at the time said 2 billion people would be watching or listening, from everywhere in the world. So, I asked my friends who do research like mine, using random number generators, to collect data on the day of the funeral. They sent the data to me and when I put it all together, the result was a strong deviation from chance expectation during the funeral ceremonies.

Most, if not all, ancient traditions have a concept of interconnection and sharing as the natural order. It is typically given a name like "oneness," and in some sense it is the basis of most religions and spiritual disciplines. The meaning is that, although we act as individuals most of the time, we aren't really separate from our culture or our neighbors—we are parts in a whole community. This isn't just about physical proximity. It includes shared understandings and assumptions, and a deep layer of evolutionary basics we cannot directly perceive, but which drive us on the same paths.

The possibility the GCP has been probing is that these commonalities create and sustain a subtle interconnected matrix that is a new entity, a global consciousness composed of our interactions, just as a mind is composed by the interaction of neurons in a brain.

A little outrageous perhaps, but it is an interesting idea. A composite mind that is made of us. The idea isn't mine, to start with, but can be found in every culture in some form, from ancient times to the present. Nature spirits, the gods, the guides tapped by your local shaman, all these are looking toward structures we can't see, but we intuit must be present in the world. I think it is fair to say that we have prayed since the first dawning of introspective and reflective consciousness, and that we have done so with good reason. After all, we still do it, and we are practical beings who have been pretty successful picking the useful behaviors and discarding (sometimes much too slowly) the useless ones.

Of course, this is only a general observation and there are many exceptions, like the tendency to imagine or allow ourselves to be persuaded that war is a sensible way to pursue our ends. But we have been, so far, a successful experiment, and have evolved to become the most powerful agent on our planet. This surely is because we have chosen correctly, voted for the better alternatives more often than not. So, if we continue over the centuries and eons to pray, or to write poetry about the ineffable, or to honor our spiritual understandings, this means something. It suggests we should be looking for ways to document and explore the not-quite-physical entities we think of as mind and spirit.

The territory isn't an easy one, so our aspirations need to be reasonable. It will be best to keep it simple as we explore the somewhat hazy world just beyond the material. The place to start needs to be amenable to tools and constructs that are close at hand. We need tools like those used to deepen our understanding of the physical world, refined for applications at the boundaries of what we know about mind and consciousness. The tools and procedures of science are unexcelled if applied correctly. They can make the difference between conjecture and understanding, and they are capable of converting a vague notion into a solid finding or, conversely, finding that the notion has no substance.

Why are we here?

The perennial question for the college sophomore late at night in the coffee shop with friends engaging real, personal philosophy is about purpose and destiny. Are we an accident, a random fluke? Is there a "source" we might be able to understand out of which everything flows? What is my potential, and where shall I go in the endless future that is starting to unfold before me?

Introspection quickly loops back to discover itself while observing that same self in the act of discovery. At first such complexities are daunting, and we might decide to switch to beer and go partying rather than to confront such impossible things to think about. Is the universe infinite? And if not, what, pray tell, might be outside its finite boundaries? Is there really a past and a future, or are they illusions and artifacts of the present that we can experience? More to the point, what is consciousness? Is it an epiphenomenon, something spurting out of the brain-meat, as so many scientists are willing to say, or is it an independent presence in the world, with direct effects in its environment? These are not easy questions, but they are deeply interesting—and arguably more important than the easier (though hugely expensive) questions of big science: is there a Higgs boson? What was the temperature of the singularity during the first 42 microseconds of the universe...?

What does it matter to any of us if the Higgs boson shows up in the creative smashing of particles at CERN? What will it matter to you and to me living our normal lives if we learn that we are all connected by unseen subtle links? These questions focus on science at its most abstract versus its most personal. We can hope that some part of the huge sums spent on the big science of small particles may be shifted to focus on the very personal science of human consciousness.

Teilhard

I was young when I first read Pierre Teilhard de Chardin's *The Phenomenon of Man*, but this gentle and deeply passionate vision of purpose and possibility for human beings rang true, and settled deep within. Even though it may be premature to expect the full measure of our potential, we are growing fast, and as Teilhard observed long before the age of the Internet, we are becoming one world; we have no other choice.

Carl Jung, Henri Bergson, Bertrand Russell, Teilhard, and others of like mind have suggested also that because humanity is reflective and creative, we can make decisions and take actions that will direct and shape our own evolution. There is little doubt this is true, but we have only begun to sense this power, just in time to take control of ourselves so that we may accelerate the maturation of a "noosphere" or layer of intelligence for the earth. The integrity of our only possible home, this beautiful world, is in great danger from our own destructive and careless misunderstanding. It is time for us to see ourselves growing toward the next stage of humanity. The future of man is reaching toward us, drawing us into an awakening earth mind which can begin healing the wounds of people and planet. We must hope this happens soon, for the spirals of confusion and destruction have been accelerating along with our potential to understand and create solutions.

What evidence is there that we really have the potential to collaborate to replace strife and war and destructive practices with wiser approaches? Recent history does show some improvements. War, despite appearances, is trending downward. But simply watching the news fails to show this. Watching news of international deliberations on climate change isn't very encouraging either, and even optimists wonder if we will get our collective human act together in time to rescue our coastlines, stop desertification of bread-basket farmlands, and save elephants and tigers and orangutans from extinction. We need to foster and encourage human potentials for common action and understanding in order to supplant the aggressive zero-sum models left over from our primitive background. The last few decades have seen increasing and potentially explosive class separations and shocking insensitivity to troubling global issues. We need an overhaul of our evaluative standards to shift from profit-above-all to well-being and compassion as the desiderata for personal and cultural worth. Similarly, we need to switch our attitude to the environment and the planet from a failing but still destructive concept of domination to one of conscious husbandry. Tall orders, but I hope not just pie in the sky.

There is a source we can draw on for some encouragement. It may even be possible through natural feedback for this source to become clearer and more prominent. New science suggests there is a nascent interaction among us, operating on a hidden, unconscious level, which can have direct effects on the physical world. To the extent we come to recognize and understand this deep-lying interconnection, we should see it grow stronger, ultimately making itself apparent to direct perception. As this happens we should see larger effects, focused reflexively and cumulatively on the source itself, making the linkage more potent and meaningful.

Chapter 3: SEEING THE PATH

The second stage is the super-evolution of man, individually and collectively, by use of the refined forms of energy scientifically harnessed and applied in the bosom of the Noosphere, thanks to the coordinated efforts of all men working reflectively and unanimously upon themselves.
—Teilhard de Chardin

Connections

We recognize certain times when we share with others a special, fully interconnected consciousness. When great music thrills us, or we are mutually inspired by an awesome sunset, or when we fall in love, we are transported temporarily into a shared world which is remarkable. This state of true intermingling is rare for most of us, but it is experiential, and that means we know it for what it is; we feel it intimately as real and filled with meaning. When such an experience is past and we return to our normal, separated perceptions, the experience becomes a vulnerable memory and our educated personality may reject the consciousness that knew this deeper connection. Yet, the suspicion remains that there is something of mind that is not just inside our heads. We feel interconnected with each other and the world in a profound and important way. We know at some level that we are not isolated, but interdependent, so that a subtle energy of mine can reach out and mingle with yours, allowing us to share a moment that is important to both of us. If we think of this potential extending beyond the two of us to a world full of living beings, we have the inspiration for a model of global consciousness. Maybe, as Teilhard believed, the world ultimately needs that shared consciousness and is actively growing toward it.

The research described here points to subtle indications that we do live in an interconnected, potentially conscious world, in which we surely play an important role. We have shown immense capacities for both destructive and creative impact, and this implies that the future is ours to mold. It will be a desirable future in proportion to our level of consciousness, individually and globally. Fortunately, there are intriguing signs of an emerging integration of purpose and perspective in the world, though it remains fragile and as delicate as a newborn. For this integration to mature, we need great patience, and a substantial amount of good luck. Perhaps by being more conscious of the possibilities, we can lessen the need for patience and increase our portion of luck.

Roots of the research
Kennedy, Rabin, Diana,...

There are rare individuals who hold special places in the minds of people around the world. When they speak we pay attention, and when they suffer tragic deaths we feel compassion and shared sadness, even grief. If, like Jack Kennedy and Itzhak Rabin, their deaths are doubly tragic and fearsome because they are victims of assassination, the instantaneous shock and consequent synchronous attention of millions is very powerful. Our profound reactions would be palpable except that such observations are necessarily retrospective because the observer (at least this is my experience) is too deeply engaged to be reflective.

Princess Diana's death is a different kind of tragedy, an accident, but it was a powerful event because she was a much-admired figure. The sudden shock of her death was magnified by her stature as a humanitarian in addition to her presence as a royal, a beautiful princess, and a sometimes-beleaguered public figure.

These events have in common that huge numbers of people come together in a shared focus, and in powerful shared emotions. The emotions are complex but have in all cases a strong component of compassion and a regret for what might have been. For millions of people there is a sense of loss that is in some ways as intense as that for personal friends or family. For the purposes of our interest in a measurement of possible effects of shared consciousness, such events are a model. Of course, we are too late for the assassination of President Kennedy in 1963, but early in the 1990's, I had succeeded in getting a continuous random sequence "monitor" running in the Princeton lab where I worked. So when Israeli Prime Minister Rabin was shot by a crazed young radical, we were able to look at data that were collected during the event. Though the tragedy took place half a world away, geographically, and though I happened to be in Germany, not Princeton, the psychological distance was very small—this was clearly an event with world-shaping consequences. The data sequence generated in Princeton at the time of the murder seems to reflect the intense focus on the tragedy, with a powerful deviation over half an hour peaking just at the time of the assassination. But without a scientific protocol and a formal hypothesis to test, the apparent correlation of the data with an important event in the world could only be taken as encouragement to build a relevant set of scientific tools.

Shaping the experiment

The GCP idea began to gestate three or four years before the birth of the project. A logbook entry from December, 1994, from a meeting at Esalen on intentionality and consciousness describes synchronistic interactions powering delightful insights and intellectual extrapolations. In a premonitory description of the GCP, some of these connections were noted in the logbook.

> *Dec 26 01:30 (1994):* How much web linkage would be required to create an aware consciousness à la Teilhard de Chardin? Like a coherence of quantum optical events, analogous to quantum coherence of other physical/electrical events....
>
> The analogy needs a fundamental unit, perhaps a node which has a self-organizing capacity under the influence of the web field, i.e., the possibility of connectedness.
>
> The conditions need to be tuned to establish a coherent field. If the coherence length is appropriate and the capacity to interact is present, it will stimulate relevant activity and a larger scale coherence will result, leading to an increase in the global coherence until a collapse into consciousness is self-induced.
>
> Fanciful perhaps, but not too far from the practical measures needed to ask a scientific question and eventually to interpret the

resulting data. It isn't much of a stretch to say the image of self-organizing nodes became RNGs and the tuning of coherent fields became the effects of emotional synchronization by great events. In the next few years, events and meetings seemed to coalesce into a path that I was following with a faint but growing sense of it. As I later came to think of it, I was engaged in design by coincidence.

Chapter 4: DEVELOPMENT

There is solid evidence from more than a thousand scientific experiments that there is more than the materialistic model of the universe has [led] us to believe.

—*Charles Tart*[8]

Intimations of a network

The next steps toward the eventual Global Consciousness Project were actual prototypes of the eventual world-spanning, Internet-based EGG network. I didn't have a definite plan at this point, but inspirations and opportunities were flowing together in a series of coincidental connections that were inexorably leading to the GCP. I'll treat these cases in more detail later but it's useful to give an outline here.

While at Esalen, on the California coast, I met people promoting *Gaiamind*, a world-wide, synchronized meditation planned for five minutes on a January day in 1997. At the time I was in a deep personal meditation on implications of the group consciousness studies I had recently been doing, and thinking about Teilhard de Chardin's idea that our purpose was to become a functional layer of coherent intelligence for the earth. I felt called to apply the developing consciousness research technologies on a broader scale, and this chance meeting gave an opportunity to proceed.

I asked all my friends who used random number generators (RNGs or REGs—the same thing, two different names) to take data during the *Gaiamind* meditation. I expected it to bring a substantial number of people around the world to meditate together, focusing on the image of a bright future for the earth—for Gaia. The instruments were various and the data rates differed, but using normalization I could put them all into a common format and average the responses. We had data from 14 RNGs in the US and Europe, and when combined they showed a significant departure from expectation during the period of 5 minutes set for the meditation, from 12:00 noon to 12:05. The comparison was made with theoretical expectation, and also with data collected before and after the meditation period. The outcome in both cases was essentially the same. It was an encouraging result.

A few months later, we looked at another moment defined in a very different way. The news of Princess Diana's death in a tragic crash in Paris went around the world like an electric shock. We could not assess the data from multiple RNGs at the time she died, but I asked my friends and colleagues again to take data during the day of Princess Diana's funeral. We assembled 12 data streams from locations in the US, Europe, and the UK. As described earlier, when the data were combined we found a result that was a striking confirmation of the hypothesis that the "network" of a dozen RNGs would show deviations during the ceremonies. The composite statistic across all 12 devices showed odds against chance of about 100 to one. This means that if this experiment could somehow be done again and again, we would see such an extraordinary result by chance only once in a hundred repetitions.

This was again an encouraging indication that a network of many random number generators might have some potential for capturing effects of mass consciousness. I could see the outlines of a "natural experiment" looking at occasions when large numbers of people were thinking about and doing the same thing, or feeling the same emotions driven by common experiences. It would take a while for the implications to mature into a working plan, but these were the first steps in creating the Global Consciousness Project.

All this had to go somewhere, and the direction was pretty clear. A certain inevitability set in, and I started gathering resources and inviting friends to help create a world-spanning network of random devices to collect continuous data that might be affected by some quality or state of consciousness, as we had seen in the prototype experiments. There was a lot of energy, and it attracted more people to help build the infrastructure and an increasing number who wanted to host a node in the network. We didn't advertise, and yet the project grew rather quickly from a test bed to a pilot experiment to a full-fledged working instrument and a well-defined protocol for the formal experiment. I remain grateful both to the people who jumped in and made it go and to the remarkable serendipities and coincidences that seemed to structure what was happening.

Chapter 5: DESIGN BY COINCIDENCE

The way to do research is to attack the facts at the point of greatest astonishment.

—Celia Green

And, we might add, the way to get on with the research is to listen to the whispers of serendipity. Approach new experiments with a fully open mind and the intention to take hints and surprising suggestions. Coincidence is your friend.

The GCP had its beginnings in a long series of coincidences that seemed to manifest unusual orderliness, almost a design. Quite unlikely meetings and events were instrumental in creating a technical structure with the capacity to register evidence of interactive connections of mind on a world-spanning scale. The purpose was to see if we might detect signs of a coalescing global consciousness. Coincidentally (or perhaps inevitably), this work started at a time in history when it was just barely possible, yet seemed most necessary.

The project emerged out of scientific efforts to study direct effects of consciousness on physical systems. The possibility that mind can be instrumental in the world is an idea with a turbulent history. Once most of us believed that our thoughts had power, and at some level, despite the influence of a modern science that is pretty hostile to the idea of mind affecting the world, most of us still do. We only need to look at the prevalence of prayer, or at our foolish but invincibly persistent willingness to gamble against the odds in casinos or at the lotto vendors. This is literally wishful thinking, and in one form or another, most of us indulge in it purposefully, despite intellectual convictions that mind cannot influence matters in the real world.

The notion of an influential mind was dealt a devastating series of blows by the successes of materialistic science. Descartes said mind was the only directly experienced truth, but that it was, on the other hand, completely and forever isolated, separate from matter. We could imagine another mind, but that mind could never register our imagination, and we saw ourselves as separated except for the various channels of sensation. Communication with each other could never be direct, but would require speech and writing and gesture. We might believe we could share with each other an identical emotion caused by music, but such beliefs about experience could never be tested, measured, quantified, and we "knew" from the teachings of successful scientists that nothing is real that is not objective.

Yet, at some level we are always aware of the deeper meanings and the real importance of personal experiences. We recall our childhood understanding that a stone or a tree or a river could be alive and share our experiences in a richly organic and anthropomorphic world. And we do find ourselves wondering about all the coincidences.

The perspective of science

To take these feelings and intuitions further, there are scientific tools and procedures that sharpen the focus and eventually provide insights we can count on. It is a different form of intellectual adventure, but in important ways, science is just an alternate route to the same destination.

In what was to become the Global Consciousness Project, we set out to capture subtle indications of a converging interconnection among humans across the planet. I found myself thinking of a birthing, the emergence of a new intelligence after a long gestation, and envisioning a possibility that we might look in on a much-needed coalescence of humanity.

An infant global consciousness? What could this possibly mean? For thousands of years, humans contemplating their experience have thought there is a deep interconnection between themselves and the world. They, or we, have constructed religious and philosophical schemes in which the idea of "oneness" is fundamental. Although most of our experience seems as if there is an individual personality or mind located in a vaguely defined space behind the eyes or forehead, we also have bigger experiences. Sometimes the world seems very close and absorbingly beautiful; we forget the individual and melt into our present. Quite reliably, in circumstances such as rituals or ceremonies or in the context of powerful and charismatic theater or music, we give up our separate identity.

We join with other people to generate a group consciousness without realizing it or trying to do so. This is the small-scale beginning of a global consciousness.

These are subtle states, hardly ever recognized, and actually not noticeable while we are participants. The creation and presence of a group consciousness depends upon forgetting the self, and so it can only be recognized faintly in retrospect. Yet we do notice and comment upon very special cases, even on the global scale. Almost everyone in the western world became temporarily absorbed in the emotional ceremonies for Princess Diana's funeral. Even the stalwart "non-watchers" were affected, or converted temporarily to interested observers. When the bombing in Yugoslavia started, the great majority of us came alert and faced common questions and concerns about the possibilities of war. Exactly at midnight for every New Year's, the countdown is a participatory celebration that is perhaps uniquely widespread. Everywhere in the world there is a party with an enormous appeal, perhaps because the group consciousness becomes so strong as to reach out to gather us into its friendly fold.

The subtlety is profound, however, and we have little more than a fleeting perception in memory to note these intriguing instances of group and global consciousness. But quite recently, just in the last decade of the 20th century, some developments in the field of psychic research have opened up the possibility of registering signs of these subtle interconnections.

There is a technology that reliably responds to human intention. A device called an REG[9] or RNG shows deviations from normal behavior when people try to make it do so just by willing or wishing—by "intending" it to happen. The same device, in the context of a group consciousness—a gathering of people thinking and feeling much the same thing—again reliably detects moments of coherence that define a singular consciousness for the group, different from the separated individuals. The measurement shows a clear effect only infrequently; not every time we think the conditions are right, but more often than chance would provide.

Defining the terms of evidence

Designing a rigorous experiment to capture evidence of an influence so slight that we almost never can see it directly is a challenge. There is no meter, no compass needle that deflects in the subtle field of consciousness. Nevertheless, we have a good way to ask the basic question about nonlocal consciousness, the extension of mind into the world: "Is there any there there?" The tool is statistics, the art and science that is designed to detect order in the chaotic presentations of nature. We know what we should see in our data if there is no structure: only randomicity. Against this background, we can recognize changes in the behavior of our detectors, and we can infer effects and influences that are correlated with them. If we are sufficiently clever, we can go one step further to say something about causal connections, but usually we have to be content with evidence for linkage via correlation.

Meaningful meetings

The first prototype of the GCP came about "by chance" when I met Jim Fournier and Juliana Balistreri in the middle of a December night in 1996 at Esalen, just as they were in the midst of promoting a globally organized "Gaiamind" meditation and I was thinking deeply about a network to detect glimmerings of global consciousness. They stopped just for an hour or two in the baths, but this created a moment for our paths to intersect. The coincidental meeting and the matching of their intentions with my vision led me to organize a collaboration to collect "consciousness field" data during the Gaiamind event, and it showed a significant effect.[10] This work was a prelude for our attempt to register effects of the world-wide expression of compassion at Princess Diana's funeral in September of 1997, followed exactly a week later by the ceremonies for Mother Teresa.[11] These were prototypical global events, giving a foretaste of the world-spanning project we would soon undertake.

Shortly thereafter, forces that were to be essential to the development of the Global Consciousness Project gathered in Freiburg, Germany, in late November of 1997, but it was for another purpose, a conference I had begun planning a year earlier on psychophysiology and psi. Dick Bierman was there, and Dean Radin, and Marilyn

Schlitz, all in some way important to the EGG project. The concept was vitalized when Dick and Dean and I were talking during a break about the complexities of physiological measures and the curiosities of nonlocal psi and possible fields of group consciousness. Just weeks earlier, analysis of the data collected from a dozen REGs in Europe and the US during Diana's funeral ceremonies had shown an anomalous effect that could only happen by chance once in 100 repetitions of the remarkable circumstances. Together with the Gaiamind results, this began to look like a global effect of consciousness—like the manifestation of a global mind's inchoate thoughts. Dean whimsically put the odd bits of our conversation together as an image of a world EEG, a fine metaphor, and the EGG was practically hatched. It seemed a natural extrapolation at the time, both creative and very unlikely.

Was this gathering of people and the juncture of topics just a coincidence, or was there perhaps a field, an attractor, drawing together the pieces of a purposeful project?

The weaving of the network web

Certainly, it is hard to credit mere chance with the "coincidence" that Greg Nelson, my son, had the interest and the skills, and—through a most unlikely combination of circumstances—the time to create the exquisitely sophisticated framework of software for the project just when the need arose. I note that EGG is Greg's delightful, richly metaphoric name for the project. It means ElectroGaiaGram, a play on ElectroEncephaloGram, and suggests an analogy to the EEG technology used to record brain waves. Of course, beyond this, the idea of an egg has extraordinarily diverse metaphoric linkages. Our more formal public name, Global Consciousness Project (GCP), came later.

The synchronistic links that ensured I would meet John Walker, the other main protagonist in the development of software for the EGG network and website, are equally remarkable. I had some prior knowledge of the technological potentials Greg could make manifest, but I hadn't the slightest notion of the important connections for the gestating EGG that would be made while I was searching the web in the Spring of 1998 for beautiful pictures of the earth to enhance the GCP website-to-be. There I accidentally met John Walker, the founder of Autodesk,[12] by re-discovering the Retrocognitive Psychokinesis experiment on his richly diverse Fourmilab website.[13] This was another essential link, bringing refinements and new aspects that enabled and enriched the growing EGG, and it is hard for me to think it was just a chance connection.

Converging contexts

Three major threads of context were crucial in shaping the GCP. One is the history of research on consciousness and the development of measures that seem to capture direct effects of intention and group states of mind in an objective, scientific medium. Over the last few decades, technologically and scientifically sophisticated experimental work has produced an impressive body of evidence for effects of consciousness on physical systems, and for anomalous acquisition of information about distant events.[14,15] This research indicates a subtle but pervasive nonlocal interconnection that is manifested by mind and consciousness.[16]

The findings seem consonant with the second thread, namely, ideas like those expressed so beautifully by Teilhard de Chardin on humanity's purpose. He argued that we were to be the source and substance of a noosphere, a layer of intelligence for the earth.[17] Combining these suggestions led naturally to the idea of measuring effects of a possible global consciousness, and motivated me to hypothesize that there might be detectable signs of a consciousness field representing a coalescing interconnection of minds. In a sense, this is an exaggerated but testable form of a question asked by thoughtful people in modern efforts to address consciousness in psychology and philosophy. It is the hard question: is there something beyond the movement of molecules? Are mind and consciousness in a special realm that must be understood from a wider perspective than the physical that we have learned to measure so well?[18]

The third element of contextual shaping for the EGG project is the extremely rapid emergence of our new, but already immensely powerful electronic interconnection via the Internet. Not only is the "web" a lively, growing, practically organic entity in itself—with considerable similarity in many respects to Teilhard's noosphere—it is a vehicle that, by way of some elegant software, enables real-time sampling of a possible consciousness field. The result is a unique opportunity that is only possible now, in the most recent moments of our history, to "measure" the subtle effects of our hypothesized global consciousness. Teilhard warned that we should not be impatient, that his noosphere would develop over perhaps 10,000 years, but remarkably enough, we can ask now whether there might be faint glimmerings of that integrated intelligence already beginning to show. That is the goal of the GCP/EGG project: to try to register the subtle first sparks of consciousness in a possible global mind.

Chapter 6: HATCHING THE EGG

If at first an idea is not absurd, then there is no hope for it.
—Albert Einstein

The extraordinary talents and vision of the group of volunteer professionals who make up the core team of researchers brought the project to life in a remarkably short time. By August 1998 the data began to flow, with one of our detectors, which by now was simply called an "egg," running in Neuchâtel, Switzerland, and two in Princeton, New Jersey. The network grew quickly over the next years, to a relatively steady 60 or 70 devices by 2004.

Experimental measures

Good research over a period of several decades has given a scientific expression to our experience of subtle interconnections, and it clearly shows that the human mind is not isolated within the body. There is solid empirical evidence that we do interact directly with each other and the world in the domain of consciousness, despite physical barriers and separations.[19] Repeated, replicated experiments show an effect on our instruments, not only of individual intentions, but also of group consciousness.[20]

In the laboratory experiments, people sit near a device that produces random numbers, but they have no physical connection to it. They try to "commune" or "resonate" with the machine (for example a random number generator, or RNG) while wishing it to change its behavior to produce higher or lower scores than it should by chance. The accumulated research shows a tiny but highly significant correlation indicating that consciousness can weakly but measurably affect the physical world. What seems to happen is that the "noisiness" of the random sequence is changed very slightly. The amount of information or structure is increased and entropy or disorder is reduced. This seems to happen because the random system is encompassed by our consciousness, which contains and expresses the necessary information and somehow impresses it on the environment. We apparently create a tiny bit of order in the world around us, simply by ourselves embodying structured information.

Enlarging the view

How do we jump from the lab results to "global consciousness"? Why should there be any effect of a world-wide New Year's celebration, or a billion people watching a funeral ceremony, or the beginning of a war, on such RNG/REG devices located around the world? Although it must be recognized as a metaphor, it may be helpful to envision a "consciousness field." Picture a faint radiance of information extending out indefinitely from each mind, with a wavelike interpenetration creating tenuous interference patterns that differ depending on our intentions and our degree of engagement. Again, we are speaking of a metaphor, not an actual physical energy that we can directly measure, but something like a field carrying information that may be responsible for the anomalous effects in group consciousness studies with REGs, field experiments looking for evidence of consciousness fields. These show consistent deviations of the data from randomicity in situations where groups become closely cohesive or focused on a compelling mutual interest. During deeply engaging meetings, concerts, rituals, etc., the data tend to have slightly increased order compared with the expected randomicity, and we are able to predict this deviation, depending on the type of gathering, with significant success. [21]

In the GCP, exactly the same procedure is applied on a broader scale. We predict a detectable ordering in otherwise random data during world-scale events that are likely to engage the attention of large numbers of people around the globe. The prediction is tested by looking for slight anomalous meanshifts in either direction, that is, changes in the variance of the data. The statistics for the continuous data streams registered by the EGG network have well-defined expectations based on theory and calibrations. We compare the empirical data with this background to see whether our hypothesis is supported. Simply put, we predict differences from expectation that are correlated with certain global events. If there is any effect of global consciousness on our detectors, we look for it to be concentrated during those special times when humanity experiences broadly shared interests, feelings, and reactions.

Growing the network

The web of continuously-recording eggs began to grow toward its goal of world-spanning coverage and sufficient numbers to apply sophisticated analyses drawing on the parallel with measures of brain activity. By the end of 1998 we had stations in several European cities and various parts of the US, and well-tested software and technology. Over the next year the EGG network grew to about 30 eggs, with a continuous flow of samples every second transmitted over the Internet from India, New Zealand, South Africa, Brazil, Fiji, Indonesia, and more sites in the US and Europe, and the network continued to grow. All the data were sent to a dedicated server called "noosphere" for archiving and processing.

Friends and colleagues around the world form a network of people with interest in the Global Consciousness Project, willing to set up a computer to host an egg—one of our REG-based detectors. The questions we are asking are far from the mainstream, so our egg-hosts are unusual people, willing to try things off the beaten path. The network of some 60 or 70 eggs runs mostly without intervention, thanks to the sophistication of the "eggsh" or "egg.exe" program at the host sites and the "basket" program that collects and archives all the data at the main server in Princeton, and in recent years in a cloud server at http://global-mind.org.

The sheer size and complexity of the network means that there is almost always something that needs attention. For example, we run special software that reaches out to "timeserver" computers on the Internet to get the correct time and adjust the local computer clocks so that all the data remain synchronized. This generally works, but occasionally an egg will go out of synchrony and will need some correction. When the electricity goes off or the Internet connection is lost for some reason, the data flow may stop for an egg. All the data are stored on the local computer, so nothing is lost, but it does take some attention to restore and maintain the flow. To keep watch on such things, there are a number of automated functions that manage the data, construct daily tables and graphs, and allow monitoring of various activities.

A website on the server provides access to the results and to the story of the project, and access to the raw data as well. This makes the project and the scientific evidence it accumulates for global consciousness completely public and transparent, so that our analyses and interpretations can be checked at any time, by anyone in the world.

The server and website

The main repository for documentation, and the primary communication interface for the project is a deep and comprehensive website at http://noosphere.princeton.edu or http://global-mind.org. It was originally designed by Rick Berger, and several people have contributed updates to accommodate more than 15 years of rapid Internet development. The present version is the work of Marjorie Simmons, who put the site in a 21st-century mode. Its purpose from the beginning has been to provide complete public access to all aspects of the project. The menu links point to the project's background and development, our experimental methods, and the hypothesis registry. The links provide access to the data in various forms, momentary activity reports, and information for people interested in participating in some way. There is a full history of the project, and more than most people will want to know about the technology and the network architecture. This includes a complete description of the experimental design and methodology, and regularly updated displays of the accumulated experimental results. For example, a "Status" table provides current performance indicators and other information for each of the eggs, and an "Eggsummary" page gives access to scores and trends for every day since the beginning of the project, while the main "Results" page provides an up-to-date bottom line for the formal analyses.

In addition to the automatically generated tables and graphs, the website also has some more colorful displays, just enough to see how intriguing it can be to give aesthetic form to presentations of the data. A real-time visual display of momentary egg scores is accompanied by a heartbeat rhythm and gongs to signal large deviations, and we have movies of each day's data as the pattern changes around the world over the course of 24 hours. Some early movies are complete with data-driven music reminiscent of John Cage, courtesy of John Walker. One of the most popular displays is the GCP Dot, which shows the momentary state of network coherence by color coding. It can be added to one's own personal website using a code snippet on the explanatory page.

Chapter 7: ENCOURAGING RESULTS

Humankind has not woven the web of life. We are but one thread within it. Whatever we do to the web, we do to ourselves. All things are bound together. All things connect.

—Chief Seattle, Dkhw'Duw'Absh [22]

The first event for which we made a formal prediction was the bombing of two American embassies in Africa on the 8th of August, 1998. This shocking breach of civilized practice was a focus for concern around the world, and our simple analysis showed a remarkable jump in the absolute scores at the time of the bombing, continuing for a few hours. The network was minimal and fragile at this time, so we were in a pilot or exploratory phase. That given, the analysis was encouraging because this inaugural global event showed a very strong effect, with a probability less than 1 in 1000 that it would happen merely by chance.

We were off and running, but we also very quickly learned how difficult the task would be of understanding the messages presented by the EGG network. A week later, another shocking event struck the world consciousness: the Omagh bombings in Ireland. This time, in a situation that seemed terribly like the embassy event, the data showed not a glimmer of response. We settled in to the development of the growing network and to more thorough testing of our strategies for the assessment of occasional striking moments on the world stage. There were more tragedies, including airplane crashes (Swissair 111, off Nova Scotia about 20 miles from Halifax) and hurricane-induced disasters like the Casitas collapse in Nicaragua, but also some more pleasant moments like McGwire's record-breaking home run (admittedly a US-centered event). We looked at The World Peace Prayer at the UN on the 12th of December, 1998, the US Congress' Clinton impeachment vote, and then Christmas Eve in Europe and the US. Many of these events had strongly suggestive positive data, but some leaned the other way, in the familiar mix of hits and misses characteristic of science at the margins of our understanding.

New Year's Eve, 1998, presented an excellent opportunity to test the essential notion that large numbers of us joining in a mutually engaging event may generate a global consciousness capable of affecting the EGG detectors. Of course, New Year's doesn't happen all at once, but again and again as the earth turns and brings the end of the old and the beginning of the new to each time zone. Our plan was to gather the data surrounding each of the midnights, and to compound all of the time zones into a single dataset that would represent a brief period marking the height of celebration—everywhere. The result was a strong confirmation of the prediction: data from the ten-minute period around midnight differed from expectation with a probability of three parts in 1000 that the deviation was just chance fluctuation. The scores were slightly, but consistently less random than at other times; they were more structured than they were supposed to be.

An especially obvious prediction was that there should be a strong effect of global consciousness at the Y2K New Year's transition. People around the world had been thinking about Y2K in a crescendo of anticipation (some of it fearful) that would culminate in the most extensive celebrations ever. Indeed, the New Year's and the new millennium were greeted effusively, in grand televised spectaculars all around the world, and in quiet observations with family or friends. As a whole, we definitely were paying attention, and surely became more focused and coherent in our thoughts as midnight approached. The main GCP prediction was similar to that for the preceding New Year's, namely that there would be an accumulation of deviant EGG data during a 10-minute period around midnight. The result was again positive.

We will return to "Results" later, with fully detailed examples. First, we need to explain the GCP instrument and how the data are generated and analyzed. In Part Two, we will shift attention to the technology and how the system works.

Part Two: The Instrument

I cannot believe it. Neither the testimony of all the Fellows of the Royal Society, not even the evidence of my own senses would lead me to believe in the transmission of thought from one person to another independently of the recognized channels of sensation. It is clearly impossible.

—Hermann von Helmholz

Progress in modern science has often been driven by advances in instrumentation. Novel instruments inspire creative approaches to experimental study of the universe and its innumerable complexities. Phenomena as diverse as galaxy formation, gene expression, quantum entanglement, terrestrial climatology and human cognition, which have yielded to ever more precise experimental study, would remain beyond our understanding without the aid of new instruments to extend the range of human observation. Notably, all these scientific achievements depend on ignoring or avoiding the observer as an object of experimental study. An indication of real progress is that many disciplines increasingly view this stance as neither necessary nor desirable. In recent decades, a quiet revolution has led scientists across many disciplines to ask how mind can be brought into the purview of experimental science. How can we integrate the insights of physics and neurophysiology with the evident facts of mind and mental experience?

Psi research is especially interesting in this regard because it directly investigates the connection between physical and mental phenomena, while challenging our understanding of each. Psi phenomena can be framed in two ways: as anomalous perception, by which an individual accesses information inaccessible to the ordinary senses, or as anomalous physical behavior, in which measured deviations from expectation in physical systems remain unexplained by physical models.

The latter mode of psi research, which is pertinent here, investigates how mental phenomena may manifest in the physical domain.

One effective experimental approach asks whether the behavior of stable, truly random physical systems can be altered by the directed intention of human agents. In such an experiment, a participant will spend time in the presence of a random number generator (RNG), usually receiving feedback about the device output, while mentally "intending" to alter or bias the output in a prescribed way.

The Princeton Engineering Anomalies Research (PEAR) lab has found correlations between the mean output of RNGs and the directed intention of participants. A 12-year study involving dozens of participants attained a 4-sigma significance relative to the null hypothesis. The correlations varied significantly across people, but were absent in control conditions. The PEAR findings replicate results from other laboratories, and the paradigm continues to be used with varying success in labs around the world. RNG research has been subjected to meta-analyses assessing research dating from the 1960s to the present. While various authors disagree on whether to accept mental interaction as an explanation of the RNG experiments, they concur that a small, unexplained, and statistically robust average effect is evident in the data, and that this effect may be modulated by a number of psychological variables. The Global Consciousness Project technology is an evolutionary development based squarely on laboratory and field research using RNGs. The deviations measured in goal-oriented, intention-based RNG studies can be viewed as correlations that develop when coherent mental states become entangled with the environment. The GCP proposes that these effects (correlations) should similarly be observable in situations involving many people sharing coherent mental states over extended distances.

The GCP thus expands the canonical RNG experiment to its most general realization: Individual participants are replaced by large human populations, the single RNG becomes a synchronous global network, and focused intention is supplanted by clearly defined periods of collective attention in the population.

Chapter 8: INTENTION AFFECTS RNGs

If you can't explain it simply, you don't understand it well enough.
—*Albert Einstein*

In the search for technology to study effects of consciousness, it turns out that randomness is our ally. It seems randomness is a field in which mind and intention, wishes and prayers can play. What that term means technically is that the process is not deterministic, so the future of the system as it passes through time can't be predicted. If we build a good random number generator, it follows the laws of chance almost all the time. But certain states of consciousness and intention appear to change the behavior of such a device, subtly but detectably. The random source is labile, meaning it can move or shift; it can be diverted from its random path. It can actualize a value that is different from what it might have been.

We can think of an RNG as a "sink" for information, a system that is capable of absorbing and integrating structure if it is available and compatible. Our wishes, our intentions and moods, even if transient, are very highly structured. If we hypothesize an aspect or quality of mind that extends into the world, such mental structure becomes a source of potential information (active information, as David Bohm identifies it [23]) which can be actualized where there is a place for it. Because an RNG is labile and capable of change through absorbing and integrating a tiny amount of information or bias, it can become a detector for effects of consciousness. At this point, that statement is merely descriptive, but there is building evidence that it can be developed in a rigorous and formal way.

A scientific challenge

We're broaching difficult questions here. To begin, there is no consensus definition of mind or consciousness, and perhaps as a consequence, these fundamentally important constructs have been given little scientific study until recently. Yes, we know a bit about how neurons work, and we understand on a gross level the physiology of awareness. But we don't know much about the nature or the powers of mind or its range of capabilities. Certainly, the possibility that consciousness might have direct effects in the world isn't typically addressed in psychology textbooks. And yet, common convention in all cultures regards mind as central, the guiding source of planning and decisions, and the record-keeper for life events: "I've made up my mind" or "I'll keep that in mind."

Scientific psychology is making strides toward understanding memory and perception, problem solving and decision making. There is in recent years some attention given to the source of consciousness in physiological mechanisms. But only a small number of researchers are working at the edges of what is known about the capacities of human consciousness, and attempting to capture insights into the subtle functions that seem to most of us to define us as human—our creative and inventive nature, and our conceptions of the spiritual. When it comes to something like the possibility of interconnected consciousness, or changes in the physical world correlated with our thoughts and emotions, the questions look daunting. Our challenge is to devise instruments and technologies that can measure the ineffable. That may sound like an oxymoron, but we'll see that we can make progress by using correlation to gain some leverage on the impossible.

Even a simple tool can help if it is an appropriate one, but we are certainly working in uncharted territory. We're looking for a grasp or a foothold to begin climbing the mountain of difficulties that confront a scientific investigation of mental, spiritual, ephemeral phenomena. To keep it simple, we should start with one person, even though we may be motivated by the intention to study interconnection. And we should start by asking whether the mind can literally create some minimal distinction in the world, like the difference between yes and no, or left and right.

The idea is to accomplish something physical or measurable, not merely to envision or imagine it. Fortunately, there is a background of natural and scientific experiments focused on the possibility that a mind might be able to manifest a distinction, to create a real yes or no in the world. Consider gambling. Though we know rationally that the odds are against us, we still bet on the red or black of a spinning roulette wheel. Is it possible that our intense wishing to win might have some effect? It is hard to discover that in an actual casino, but the question can be handled scientifically in simple experiments, and over the past several decades quite a number of adventurous scientists have taken such matters seriously and brought them into the laboratory to do careful research.

The earliest of these controlled experiments used dice, sometimes with the target of intention being to get more of a particular number—for example, try to get the 6 face to turn up. Or the task might be to get more dice to end up to the left or right of a mid-line on the table, using many dice and a mechanical throwing machine. Such experiments indicated a slight effect of the participants' intentions, but making them 100% clean and controlled was not easy. For example, dice usually have little pits drilled for the spots, making some faces a tiny bit lighter and more likely to turn up; or they have painted spots, with a similar effect. You would most likely expect such biases to be really small, and you would be right. The problem is that the effects of wishing or willing seem to be equally small, so the situation is difficult to manage and the clarity we need for a scientific view is elusive.

A big step in the direction of complete experimental control came with the growing viability of electronics and computer technology during the 20th century. By mid-century, a number of psi researchers had developed serviceable instruments and experiments that were automated and apparently free of mechanical biases. They used a variety of means, but the leading technology was based on random sources that could emulate the 50/50 series of events exemplified by tossing coins. The idea was to provide a natural unbiased series of virtual coin flips that could not be predicted, which would yield an equal number of "heads" and "tails" on average. This kind of experimental random source might use radioactive decay, with a fast-running clock interrupted by a Geiger counter click, or it might use the unpredictable voltage created by electrons tunneling through a diode barrier. These are quantum level effects, which are in principle completely unpredictable and much easier to control for use in an experiment, while retaining the physical quality of "real" objects like dice or coins. Ultimately the random sequences they produce are translated into binary digits, the "bits" that are the language of computers. So, we begin with natural processes and end with random data in the abstract form of unpredictable ones and zeros. We gain also the ability to use precision electronics and computer technologies for recording and processing the data.

The Schmidt RNG experiments

Helmut Schmidt spearheaded the development of experiments using physical random sources in the late 1960's while employed as a research physicist at Boeing Science Research Laboratory.[24] He became curious about random sequences—essentially asking whether they really did behave the way they should according to physical theory. It is an important question, of course, when critical instruments, including some used in airplanes, may depend on the quality of physical devices that depend in turn on random processes. In the course of examining sequences and distributions of nominally random outputs from carefully designed sources, he found aberrations that were mystifying—until he correlated them with states of mind. Simply put, Helmut found that tiny changes in statistical measures like the mean or average output seemed to occur if he "wished" for more 1's or 0's.

The changes were much too small for a confident declaration or easy publication of results in physics journals, but they were tantalizingly persistent, so he began designing serious experiments to find out if the early observations could be replicated in careful, sophisticated research on what came to be called psychokinesis or PK. The early experiments involved machines with one red and one green light, controlled by a radioactive decay random number generator. Subjects would attempt to turn one light on more often than the other—the electronic equivalent of tossing coins and wishing for more heads. Over the next two decades, Helmut created a substantial literature himself, and perhaps more important, laid the groundwork for replications and extensions of the research by dozens of other scientists around the world.[25]

The PEAR Lab

That work was of such quality that it should have been difficult to ignore for scientists with a broad perspective. Of course, it would need to be replicated, and prodded and poked and pulled apart to see what the implications might be for science and engineering. Everybody is busy with their own work, however, and perhaps for that reason, few mainstream researchers took up the challenge, preferring to stay with rather less difficult problems. Yet, a few far-seeing individuals did make space in their research agendas for this question linking consciousness and physical systems, mind and matter. One of the biggest and longest running programs of related research was at PEAR—the Princeton Engineering Anomalies Research laboratory, created by Prof. Robert Jahn while he was Dean of the School of Engineering/Applied Sciences at Princeton University.

He was impelled to do so by seeing results from an independent research project he supervised for a student in electrical engineering and computer science. The student had asked him for help when she found none of her professors would monitor her work attempting to replicate Helmut Schmidt's psychokinesis experiments using an electronic random number generator and experimental protocols she had developed. Bob Jahn had welcomed incoming students saying that if they did well in their courses, they could choose any independent thesis project that would test their abilities. The student could find no sponsor among her faculty, so she came to the Dean to ask him to make good on that promise, and he did. Perhaps he didn't expect to see the striking results she reported, nor the substantial literature she found of reports from other researchers showing apparently excellent evidence for small but consistent effects of human intention on random systems. But he recognized credible indications of phenomena that might be important to science and engineering at the leading edge.[26]

Bob Jahn, besides being one of the top tier officers of a major Ivy League university, was a world class physicist running a NASA-funded plasma propulsion laboratory. But he was a creative and broad-spectrum thinker who somehow escaped the dogmas of "scientific" education far enough to consider with equanimity the mysteries of mind as a part of the physical world. Bob also had a wicked sense of humor, along with an extraordinary memory, which might help explain why he could sing all the lyrics of Gilbert and Sullivan. He combined high seriousness with unfettered creativity, resulting in sometimes whimsical reflections on the conundrums science is designed to untangle. I recall Bob's charming sketch of two ducks, evidently engaged in a difficult scientific discussion. He labeled it simply "Paradox."

He began his own examination of the evidence, and went to meetings of professional parapsychologists to gain perspective. Ultimately, Bob decided the reports and the serious engagement by a small cadre of dedicated researchers justified a substantial high-technology look at the possibility that consciousness might interact directly with physical systems. Was there some fundamental error in what looked like good, though sparsely supported research? Or was there a possibility that the surprising indicators from PK experiments and the remarkable results of remote viewing work might be pointing to fundamental processes and aspects of the world that were not accounted for in standard scientific models? The next step was to find support for a rigorous research program, and Bob turned to friends in the engineering and technology community and in the ranks of Princeton alumni. One of the major sources of support in the early years of the PEAR lab was James S. McDonnell, a fellow Princeton alumnus and the founder of McDonnell Douglas Aircraft. He had both personal and professional interests in the topic and provided funding through the McDonnell Foundation. With such support in hand, Bob proceeded to create what became the PEAR lab.

Sadly, we lost Bob Jahn in 2017, after a long and productive life as a leading thinker, a mentor, and a friend.

Laboratory Manager

A laboratory space was created in the basement of the School of Engineering, and in 1979, the work began, with Brenda Dunne as the laboratory manager. I joined Bob and Brenda a few months later, adding complementary skills and perspectives. The laboratory was unique. Its topic was at the edges of science, certainly not mainstream, but we enjoyed the resources of a great university, with first class facilities and a faculty and staff that could be depended on for expertise to address the thorny questions of forefront research. Bob and Brenda met at a professional meeting where she presented her findings from a series of remote viewing experiments inspired by scientists at Stanford Research Institute. He found in Brenda a kindred spirit, interested in a clear-minded, rigorous effort to learn what was going on in these side-branches of science, and in short order she moved to Princeton to help establish a solid research program.

Brenda first became intrigued with anomalies research when she encountered remote viewing and was struck by claims that people could learn something about remote targets that had *not yet been selected*. She decided to see for herself whether such claims could be validated or, on the other hand, were just nonsense. These experiments were reported by Hal Puthoff and Russell Targ in the mid-1970's in the mainstream journal, *Nature*.[27] Brenda read their claim that people could get information about targets that were miles away and in the future, scenes that had not even been identified yet, and she thought that had to be a mistake. But she was open-minded enough to do her own experiments to see for herself if such a thing could work. She was startled by how good the match was, some of the time, between a percipient's description and the actual scene—once it was chosen hours or days after the percipient report was recorded. She reported on the results at a meeting of the Parapsychological Association, where Bob Jahn was impressed by the quality of the data and her scientific savvy. He asked her to manage a new research program he was starting at Princeton and she said yes.

The next few months were a busy time, designing and building a place where people who would participate in the experiments could feel comfortable. Brenda knew it would be essential for the "operators," as participants would be called, to feel at home and at ease while attempting to do what so many think is impossible, so she created a lab space that was like a comfortable living room.

One of the first projects was to further develop experiments to study the acquisition of information across space and time by remote perception, PEAR's name for the protocol.[28] (Actually we usually called it PRP, for Precognitive Remote Perception, since that was our most used version.) It presents the challenge of attempting to tap into the future, while also creating an extra layer of experimental control. In the experiment we ask a person to envision a randomly chosen location that will be visited by another person in a few hours or perhaps tomorrow or the next day. The task is to perceive something of that situation without any communication or information from normal channels.

Our job as researchers was to create measures that could quantify the percipient reports. We wanted a way to assess individual efforts, so in addition to their descriptions and sketches, we asked people to choose from a list of aspects which ones were present in the scene. These "binary descriptors" could be used to calculate a proper score to be judged against a distribution of chance scores. We sought ultimately to quantify the evidence for or against the hypothesis that human consciousness could reach out spatially and temporally to acquire otherwise inaccessible information.

The results showed remarkable accuracy, almost pictorial descriptions in some cases, and obvious missing in others, but a gradual accumulation, overall, of more information than chance would allow about the distant scenes. More remarkable is the fact that the actual distance between sender and receiver didn't seem to matter, nor did the ability suffer when the receiver was asked to look into the past or the future and describe the scene that had been or was to be visited by the sender.

The bottom line, combining results of several hundred trials, is highly significant, with billions-to-one odds it is due to chance. It's not all hits, but the positive results outweigh the null or negative outcomes by a substantial amount.[29]

Building the Laboratory

The PEAR lab, as it would be called, was carved out of storage space next to the machine shops in the Engineering Quadrangle. But it was furnished with comfortable chairs and couches, and decorated with interesting art and with an ever-growing collection of stuffed animals brought as gifts by visitors. It was a pleasant place to hang out, with coffee and conversation to accompany the focused attention on remote perception or attempts to interact with machines of various kinds. Among the machines was the electronic REG or RNG device that we will consider in more detail later.

We developed a number of others, like Murphy, the Random Mechanical Cascade (RMC), a giant pinball machine whose complexity ensured something would go wrong if it could. You may recognize that as Murphy's law—the source of the machine's familiar name. It also allowed our operators to work their will on a seriously macroscopic device. Murphy was 10 feet tall and 6 feet wide and had 9000 polystyrene balls brought to the top by a conveyor belt, where they dropped from a funnel to begin a cascade through a quincunx (groups of five) array of elastic nylon pins into 19 collecting bins. The balls were counted and the sums for each bin registered in computer files for later analysis, to see if operators trying to shift their paths to right or left were successful. Remarkably, the difference between the two conditions of intention was significant despite the apparent difficulty, and the results added a dimension to the similar findings in the microelectronic RNG experiments.[30]

An additional lesson of some importance in thinking about mind-matter interactions is that careful analysis of the actual paths taken by the RMC balls showed that although the machine was big, the action wasn't macroscopic after all. What was required to achieve the intention was not pushing the balls around, but influencing the decisions they would make when hitting a pin—left or right. High speed motion photography showed many cases where a ball would bounce twice, and a few when it would bounce three times. The choice of left or right was as much informational as physical.

Making Things Work

The new project was created under the auspices of the Dean's office and thus had no departmental oversight, as most university research programs do. So, the University created a special committee to give attention to research protocols, consisting of other high-ranking officers—deans and vice presidents. One of the suggestions they made was to hire a third person with strong credentials in experimental psychology, research design and statistics. Bob's Associate Dean, Jerry Farrington, devised an ad for the *Chronicle of Higher Education* seeking a "cognitive scientist interested in the lesser known aspects of perception." I was a professor of psychology at Johnson State College in Vermont, and saw this ad by chance, adjacent to one a colleague had circled for me. The wording led me to imagine things like the sense of smell, so I was surprised to learn the job would be vastly more interesting—an examination of consciousness at the boundaries of what we know. As soon as I learned this was a project to assess the possibility that human consciousness could interact directly with physical systems, I was intrigued and enchanted by the challenge, and made the decision to leave beautiful Vermont. I arranged a year-long sabbatical from my professorial duties and moved to Princeton in June, 1980, with my wife, Reinhilde (Lefty) and my son Greg, who was 10 and ready to begin middle school.

I joined Bob Jahn and Brenda Dunne to begin a multi-decade odyssey of extraordinary work, coordinating research on subtle questions of mind-to-mind and mind-to-matter communication. The Princeton Engineering Anomalies Research laboratory was designed around the best available technologies and scientific methods, and at the same time gave full respect to the aesthetic dimensions. The intent was to create a marriage of the white lab coat and the white turban, symbolizing the complementary perspectives that are essential for insight into the functioning of mind at its interface with the world.

It seemed that a year should be sufficient time to discover what was going on in these investigations of mind-matter interaction and remote viewing. But after a year it was clear more time would be necessary, so the sabbatical became a leave, and finally a decision to give up my tenured professorship and dive in completely. As it turns out, my work there continued for 22 years, until I retired from the University research staff and PEAR in 2002. This was not, as my wife says, really a retirement, because in 1997 I had started the Global Consciousness Project, which continues to this day and about which there is much more to say. For now, let it suffice that the experience and technologies developed at PEAR were brought to full fruit in this global extension of the research.

Technically Speaking

John Bradish joined the PEAR team in the mid-eighties as our resident electrical engineer and consummate gadgeteer. He was chief in charge of the high quality of our electronic technology, and at the same time was also the final force in designing and building some truly beautiful machines. An example is the Pendulum experiment, which was not only technically sophisticated, but worthy of an art museum. Its bob was a quartz crystal ball suspended by a fused silica rod, chosen because it had a coefficient of thermal expansion near zero, and was a light pipe we could use to give color feedback to the operator trying to influence its motion. We could measure changes in the velocity of the bob with millionth of a second precision. A razor edge attached to the pendulum was designed to cut a photodiode beam and trigger a nanosecond clock. This allowed us to record the damping rate to six decimal points of precision.

John was an old-school gentleman. He was happy to apply his expertise to instrumenting the esoteric questions we asked, even though I guess his interest in those questions was predominately technical. He and I worked well together, making the very sophisticated toys that were the physical form of the arguably metaphysical research program. The benchmark REG, and the awesome Murphy, the Random Mechanical Cascade, were built before John found us, but the list of elegant and highly competent machines that followed all were branded with his electrical engineer's hand and his artist's good taste. I'm not sure John would claim to be an artist, but the devices he built were beautiful.

He's also a sailor, with a shore house (now gone, lost to hurricane Sandy) on the water not far from Point Pleasant. Now and again the PEAR group, which in the best days were a big family, all would trek "down the shore" for a day together at the beach. Good times, and the kind of time that put us on track for the lab's biggest achievements—technically sophisticated, scientifically robust experiments that also had a rich personal quality, built to examine the place of consciousness in the physical world.

A Touch of Physics

As a graduate student in Princeton University's astrophysics program, York Dobyns discovered PEAR and decided to see for himself what was up. He visited, tried his hand as an operator in some of the experiments, then began to engage us in conversations. What did we think this was about in terms of scientific modeling? What is the connective tissue of the psi effects? And soon enough, "How can I help?" Since York is one of the brightest scientific minds around, the question was easy—come join us, and help build the best software, the most creative and sensitive analyses possible. We quickly learned how broad York's interests and expertise were, with an encyclopedic knowledge of seemingly every scholarly and scientific discipline. In fact, he would say, his ability to comment usefully on topics from anthropology to zetetics was simply the result of wide-ranging interests, and a gift for recall (evidently of everything he's ever read or heard.)

York quickly became the go-to person for finely-tuned software to manage experiments, collect and archive data, and for sophisticated statistical analyses. One of his many fortes is scientific or mathematical modeling, useful in astrophysics, but no less so in psi research. To suggest what York could do using these tools, I can think of no better example than his re-examination and modeling of the huge PEAR REG database, which includes both hits and misses, and includes as well some subsets that look to a skeptical eye to be almost too good to be true. (Despite my long tenure in this curious branch of science, I maintain a kind of balance claimed before I joined the work—100% skeptical and 100% open-minded.) York's work helped to settle my personal questions about possible alternative explanations for unusually strong data subsets—could they be a result of selective reporting or related errors? The modeling clearly established that these "extreme" bits of data belong to the proper distribution and were not problematic in any way; they were simply unusually strong.[31]

Managing communications

There is a huge interest in the curious phenomena we were studying at PEAR, and one piece of evidence was the sometimes overwhelming influx of curious people. Some wanted to enlighten us ("I can explain your mysteries."), and some wanted to warn us that we were doing the work of the devil. By far, the majority simply wanted to learn, or to offer help, and many wanted to volunteer as operators in our ongoing experiments. As our program and our fame (or notoriety, according to some) grew, it was clear we needed some specialized hands, and Arnold Lettieri came on board to man the phones and handle the inquiries. Of course, he was, like the rest of us, engaged in the lab work, but he specialized in sorting the wheat from the chaff, and making our communications flow.

There were other staff who were with us for a time, and many visiting volunteers. Sometimes the lab was even a bit crowded, but that didn't slow us down. Good years, and good work. The lab had a strong run of 27 years, and helped establish and strengthen science at the boundaries of what we know of consciousness.

Wishing for good weather

The PEAR lab was a good place to work, for all the reasons you might think, but perhaps most tellingly because there was no limit on creativity. We shared goals, and had many projects that needed all hands on deck, but there was room for lateral thinking and wildly different perspectives. Here is a nice example, in the form of a "natural experiment" that was out of the lab's normal flow, but nevertheless relevant. It was fun to think about, and pretty interesting both in the doing and the outcome.

I arrived in Princeton just in time for a notable annual event called the "P-rade." Each year in May or June, there is a grand reunion of alumni, combined with the ceremonies of commencement. The weather in 1980 was beautiful, perfect for gathering the Princeton University family and friends for picnics, parades, and parties. It was fun, and every year when we could, my wife and I joined in to enjoy the festivities. In the charming way of optimists, I would hear people marveling that the "weather always cooperates" and no rain ever falls on the P-rade or the other outdoor celebrations. Of course, the record wasn't perfect, but there was a striking consensus about the good weather. Since the government keeps useful records on such things, and there had been a weather station in Princeton for many years, I decided to take a scientific look. I got data from Princeton and six other stations in the surrounding area and compared the frequency and amount of rain. For good measure, I also compared the days of outdoor activities to "control" days before and after the reunions. Amazingly enough, there was indeed a significant difference: the weather in Princeton was just a little better than it might have been. I published a report of the natural experiment, ending with the suggestion that when there are large numbers of motivated people hoping and wishing, it seems we might want to rethink the old saying, "Everyone talks about the weather, but nobody does anything about it."[32]

Chapter 9: RANDOM EVENT GENERATOR

Creativity is the ability to introduce order into the randomness of nature.
—*Eric Hoffer*

Let's take a little excursion into the often beautiful equipment built for the PEAR experiments. As the research program grew and the early answers led to a wider range of questions, we built more instruments. An important step in addressing these questions entailed having a second RNG device in addition to the large tabletop "benchmark" machine. I had shepherded this machine through its design and construction by the instrumentation shop of the Mechanical and Aerospace Engineering department of which the PEAR lab was a part. It was a beautiful, functional machine, with lots of controls and options that made it look very business-like. It was built in 1980 and 1981, before the evolution of computer technology from room-filling machines with punch cards and reels of mag-tape to mini-computers and then desktop machines. It was soon to have offspring.

The front panel of the benchmark machine had gauges for temperature and voltage monitoring, knobs to adjust the speed of sampling, the size of the trial, the number of bits that would be collected each second, and a switch to choose between automatic sequencing of trials vs. manual operation for those operators who wanted to focus deeply on each individual trial. This machine was actually version 2, and while its predecessor simply printed the results on paper tape, this one connected to one of the PDP-11 mini-computers upstairs in the Electrical Engineering and Computer Science department. This meant the data recording would be automatic and ready for statistical analysis untouched by human hands, and more important, untouchable by human error. The full-scale use of computers in psi research was just beginning, but its advantages were clear. We could begin to assemble huge databases that embodied the scientific rigor and precision needed to identify tiny effects in a sea of statistical noise. And we could depend on computational accuracy and reliability in the statistical processing. Many potential problems and much time-consuming effort would be managed by computer technology, allowing researchers to work on the most important and difficult aspect of research—asking good questions.

But this machine was hardly portable, and it was time to expand our range of activity to multiple experiments, to replications in other labs, and to ventures out into the world to ask whether group consciousness might affect our random number generators.

The second-generation "PEAR Portable REG" measured about 5 by 6 by 2 inches, and it was designed to be elegant while also technically competent. It used quantum level thermal noise in resistors (Johnson noise) to give good random numbers but left the parsing and calculations to a computer program. It could be paired with a laptop computer and a battery pack in a suitcase to take it into the field, but it was followed in a couple of years by a much smaller device that we could attach to a palmtop computer.

We patented the miniaturized design and arranged to have it manufactured as the MicroREG.[33] The source of randomness was a quantum process called tunneling, which yields truly unpredictable sequences of bits. These smaller versions of the RNG technology allowed us to easily develop new experiments in our lab, and export the tools for replications elsewhere. Most important, the third-generation MicroREG device gave us the freedom to develop an entirely new kind of experiment exploring the real world outside the lab. We'll come to these "Field REG" experiments shortly.

An REG becomes an Egg

Because they are esoteric, it is a little difficult to envision the actual measures and equipment used in the mind-machine interaction experiments, which are also at the core of the EGG project. The basic instrument is a random number or random event generator, and by either name it is an uncommon device. On the other hand, all of us are directly familiar with various random processes in the world, including such things as flipping coins, throwing dice, or watching unpredictable cloud formations. For computer-based data collection, we use RNG devices which are an electronic equivalent of high-speed coin-flippers.[34] They use "white noise" like the random static between radio stations. The voltage level of this noise, which ranges unpredictably above and below an average level, is turned into 1's and 0's that we can count as if they were heads and tails. Such electronic random sources produce a steady stream of unpredictable binary events, or bits. The rate depends on design, and may range from 1000 to 10000 or more bits per second.

These are what are called "true random number generators" to distinguish them from pseudo-random data generated by a computer program. The difference is important. True, or physical random sequences are completely unpredictable, no matter how much you know about the design and structure of the device. The future of the sequence of bits is not predictable because it does not exist until it happens, and the determination whether the next bit will be a 1 or a 0 is dependent on quantum level physics. In the devices used in the GCP network, the underlying physical process is quantum tunneling by electrons through a barrier. The circuit is designed to push electrons the "wrong" way in the circuit, so they try to penetrate a closed diode or transistor switch. This solid-state junction within the component is designed to allow electrical flow in only one direction, and to prevent it in the other. Our circuit is designed with the current "back volted," meaning we set the voltage pressure against the barrier. The barrier is a region within the solid-state junction in which the electron theoretically cannot exist, but a few surmount the barrier by a quantum process called tunneling. They form a tiny fluctuating voltage on the other side, and we amplify and sample the voltage. If it is higher than average it is converted to a digital one, and if it is lower, it becomes a zero. This all happens at electronic speeds, with random digital bits produced at a rate of thousands per second.

For the GCP data, we record a "trial" from each REG (which we call an Egg) in the network, once every second. The trial consists of 200 bits, and its value is recorded by counting the 1's. We expect this count to be about 100 because there is a 50/50 chance for a bit to be 1 or 0. The figure below shows the noisy trace of a sequence of 1000 actual trials from one REG. The horizontal line at 100 is the expected mean for the 200-bit trials, and the expected standard deviation is 7.071.

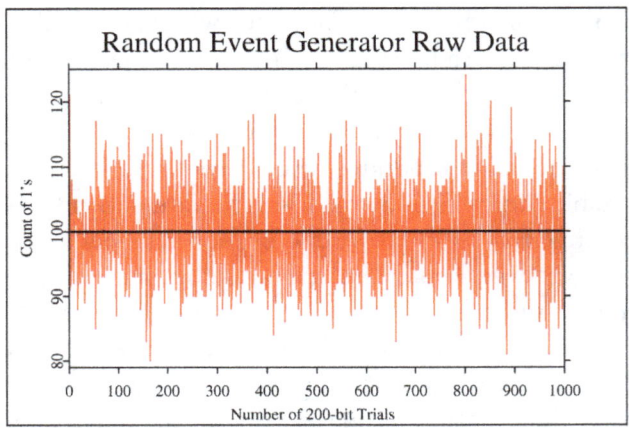

The picture gives an impression of unpredictability, but there is a very well-defined expectation for the distribution of the random data samples. In the second figure, the same data are shown as a frequency distribution overlaid with the theoretical bell curve. The fit is very close, indicating the REG is working as designed.

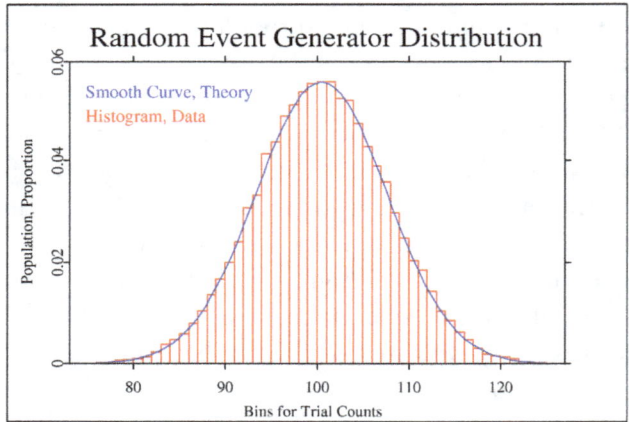

Every RNG/REG device we use is subjected to a rigorous calibration routine. Before being put into service, we collect at least one million trials, or 200 million bits. This huge sample is examined with a custom suite of tests, which compares the actual data against theoretical expectation for distribution parameters including the mean, variance, skew, and kurtosis, and for several other standards, including autocorrelation, run-lengths of consecutive 1's or 0's, fits to the arcsine distribution, and so on. Simply put, we subject the devices to tests that can tell us whether it is performing according to our design, meaning its output is indistinguishable from what theory says it should be. This calibration work underlies our ability to make a specific statistical prediction for the experiment; namely, if we examine data recorded during a special event, we predict that they will diverge from the expectations established for purely random data. The tests we apply to determine whether the prediction is confirmed are specified ahead of time, without any knowledge of actual results, and the whole process is designed to give an accurate picture of what actually happens. We want to know if the mass consciousness engendered by a global event will make a detectable difference in our data.

There are many pitfalls that can confuse and deceive people looking at subtle indicators, and the analytical process needs to be scientific in the best sense: it should produce knowledge. We do not want to waste time with false conclusions, and don't want to "discover" spurious patterns that merely reflect our wishes and desires or some error. This is the place, defining and designing correct analytical procedures, where art and science must balance and enhance each other. The art is asking a creative and valuable question, one that will help us to learn. The science is required to assess the numbers, the correlations, the potential patterns so that the answers we get are nature speaking, and not some fantasy we have generated.

We will see that the ability of statistical processing to reveal patterns and structure goes much further. The data are complex and noisy, but we have developed ways to simplify the data and reduce the noise so any non-random structure that occurs in the data can be seen. One of the best and most readable ways to display the data and see whether changes from expectation have occurred is called the "cumulative deviation" trace. This plots the accumulating sum of the small deviations in each trial, so that the plotted line goes up when the deviation is positive and down when it is negative. A sequence of scores which are mostly larger than the expected mean will show a persistent positive slope, while a sequence with no consistent deviation will wander up and down but show no trend. This figure shows both cases: first a relatively flat trace representing a null deviation, followed by a clearly diverging trace that may suggest effects of consciousness.

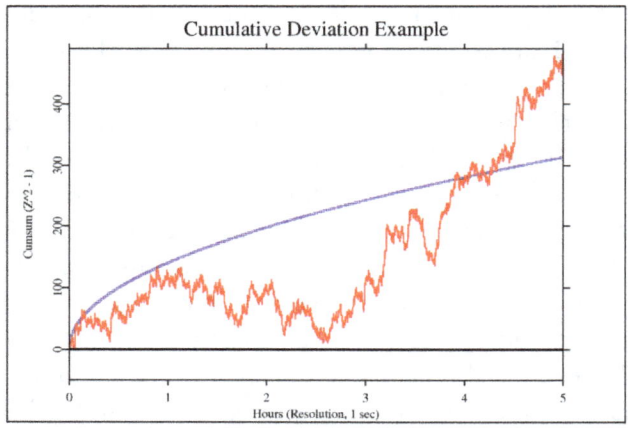

Making an experiment

Physically-based experiments occupied the greater part of our attention in the PEAR lab. We developed a variety of systems and devices, but the point in each case was to ask whether human intention could affect their behavior; that is, change the measured output or performance of a machine from what it is normally expected to do, simply by wishing or willing it to change.

The Random Event Generator or REG experiment was the first and longest-running, and with it we compiled a very large and complex database designed to address several important issues.[35] Some of these were physical (data density, type of random source, generation speed, distance) and some were psychological (flexibility, choice of intention, gender, context). The basis was always the same: a truly random sequence of numbers generated and recorded in computer files. Typically, this was in a rigorously designed experiment, although sometimes data were collected in a "calibration" mode to establish and reconfirm that the machine does produce random numbers according to theory if we leave it alone.

In the experiments, however, when a person tried to change the output of the REG, to get larger or smaller numbers than the expected average just by thinking about it, this actually happened with enough consistency to achieve statistical significance over large databases. Our operators were "unselected," meaning we did not look for or test the abilities of special, gifted individuals. The people producing our data were volunteers who visited the lab and tried the experiments because they had a personal interest. They differed in their achievement, and we tried to learn what mattered from their comments and observations. Analysis showed that about 15% succeeded at the unlikely task, with data that reliably showed structure as opposed to calibration-style randomness.

There was no physical connection, of course, and the machines were designed so that variations in, say, temperature, or ambient electromagnetic fields could not produce such an effect. The experiment was designed so the only condition that could be correlated with apparent changes in the machine's behavior was what the person had in mind, with their intentions recorded beforehand. Such a correlation is referred to as an effect (even though we can't infer causality), and in the case of intention to influence a physical device, the effect is sometimes called "psychokinesis" or "mind over matter." At PEAR we chose a more conservative language and simply called the correlation "anomalous" because it was unexpected and unexplained. Indeed, although one part of the PEAR effort was always directed toward explanation and theory, we had no difficulty admitting that there was much to learn before that effort could bear fruit.

And the results?

The bottom line, over many variations and more than 100 operators during a decade of data collection in the PEAR REG experiment, is a strong demonstration of a weak effect. Depending on what subset of the data we look at, the evidence ranges from ambiguous outcomes to very impressive departures from expectation—as much as 5 or 6 standard deviations (sigma) and odds of many millions to one against chance as the explanation for the deviation. A grand concatenation including all the hits and misses in the REG experiment over a 12-year period, as reported in the *Journal of Scientific Exploration* in 1997, has an overall figure of merit for the primary question of $Z = 3.81$, which has a probability of 0.00007—not very likely to be just chance at work.[36]

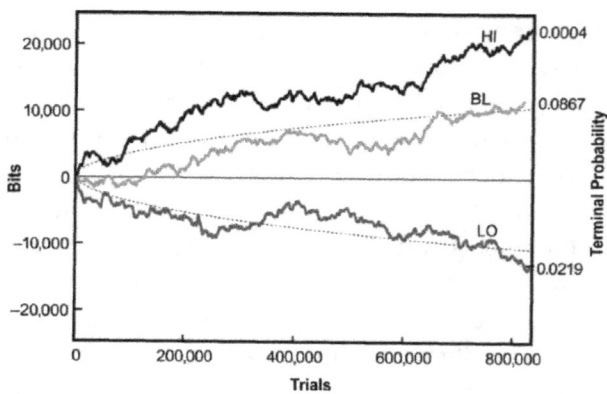

This graph presents the data for the first 91 operators, over 12 years. The three conditions, High, Low, and Baseline, are shown as cumulative deviation traces. Each data line shows the history of deviations as they accumulated over time. Each positive trial score (positive deviation from random expectation) makes an upward step, and negative deviations cause a jog downward. If the overall tendency is positive scores, the line has a positive slope, and vice versa. Although it is highly significant, this is a very tiny effect, compared with the sledgehammer results of experiments in physics and chemistry, and is small relative to many, though not all, experiments in psychology. On the other hand, in medicine and pharmacology we frequently see similarly minuscule outcomes— but we know that these can be very important. Aspirin taken in small doses gives people a slight but clearly established advantage in preventing heart attacks.[37] But the research demonstrating this took years to perform and produced differences very much like those found in mind-machine interaction experiments.

Learning the language of meaningful deviations

The measures we use to evaluate the results are a bit foreign to non-scientists, and quite abstract. The best tools we have show just a faint trace of consciousness making its mark in the statistics of random numbers. From such marks, simpler and cruder by far than prehistoric cave paintings, we begin to read the story of interactions linking mind stuff with physical stuff. We know that consciousness has been there, and had its way with the random device, but we have little more than faded footprints and ruffled blades of grass as our record. We want to know when and how and why, and that's not easy given that simple statistical tools are our only indicators. This is why we need art and poetry and music as a complement to our statistical science. From the poets, and from looking within, it is clear that mind is touching matter and extracting messages, but they are magical messages, and we will only recover their meanings by learning much more.

What we have is just this: Thousands of trials, building to millions gathered over many years in completely controlled experiments, show changes in the behavior of random systems, in protocols that identify *intention* as the link. Nothing else, just the *wish* that the numbers coming out of the random number generator will be high or low according to the experimental instruction.

Just think about it. That is the means available in these mind-machine experiments—just your mind at work, attempting to touch the world. The changes that occur in this situation are hardly earthshaking in themselves since they are tiny. But the implication is huge. Your mind can reach out and make something happen, make changes in the way the world is. The ancients had no doubt about this, but over the last two or three hundred years, a different worldview, that of modern science, has adopted a set of rules and principles that exclude things which can't be measured and counted in a material way. Now it appears that sufficiently subtle science can after all capture indications of mind and consciousness directly engaging the world.

Small yet powerful

To express the size of the effect in the PEAR REG experiments, we can say it is equivalent to changing one bit in a thousand, or perhaps one in 10,000, from what it might have been. This is tiny. One might say the effects are too small to be useful, and it is true that nobody is claiming the slight deviations could be used to mentally control a garage door opener or change TV channels—unless one has an extreme degree of patience waiting for the desired result. But at another level, these tiny effects of consciousness, if real, are profoundly important. They mean that we need to add something to our scientific models to accommodate them. We are not talking about revolutionary changes that destroy the current scientific view, as some skeptics seem to fear, just sharply focused but important extensions.

It is noteworthy that no primary models intended to represent our understanding of the world, either classical or modern, have any representation of consciousness. Of course, our consciousness is a major puzzle. We know without question that mind is real—we experience it directly; but our best models, including quantum mechanics, don't include consciousness in any constructive or explanatory sense. A place is reserved in some interpretations of QM for an "observer effect" that may have a role in collapsing a superposition of possibilities toward a single state, but this is at most an acknowledgment that consciousness may participate in reality. It leaves a vast array of unasked and hence unanswered questions. Research at the edges of what we know about consciousness needs to be done, especially experiments to show its role in the physical world. We really must investigate the dimensions and parameters of that role.

That has been the proposition of parapsychology and programs like PEAR. There are very few scientists who take this road, because it is difficult, and it is not a path that has been particularly rewarding in terms of career or fame and fortune. We can hope this will change, because challenging work at the boundaries tends to be the source of advancements in more general understanding. And the challenges themselves, given a chance, turn out to be extraordinarily stimulating. So as more young (and not so young) scientists become familiar with these hard questions, the field will attract more smart people and better funding and more access to journals and conferences in the mainstream.

Chapter 10: THE FIELDREG EXPERIMENT

Science... means unresting endeavor and continually progressing development toward an end which the poetic intuition may apprehend, but which the intellect can never fully grasp.

—Max Planck

The mind-machine experiments at PEAR were all designed to examine the effect of human intention on sensitive physical systems, and for a few years that was what we did. When I was thinking about the REG experiment while still in Vermont, it seemed that an ideal research program might take advantage of maturing computer technology and record data from the random source continuously, with periods of experiment and non-experiment (controls) registered in an index for later analysis and comparison. It actually took several years, but when York Dobyns joined the PEAR group, he brought much needed technical expertise from his years in Princeton's physics department. York built a number of new programs for the REG research, including one to take data continuously, indexed by time and several other potentially important parameters. At first, it ran in the REG experiment room doing what we thought of as calibrations most of the time, but the program included a facility for marking the time-synchronized index with intentions in 15-minute blocks. This allowed us to identify the "experiment" and "control" periods I had envisioned in my Vermont musings, and also let us begin to explore remote and off-time protocols.

Most significantly, it became possible to ask a new kind of question in a well-defined formal way: what would happen to the continuously running background REG data if someone was performing an intention experiment in the same room? Would the continuous background data show deviations corresponding to the times an operator was trying to get high numbers or low numbers in the REG experiment? In other words, might we see a spreading "field" effect of the conscious intentions to an unintended target? And what would the data show if we had an intense meeting of minds in the room? What about strong emotions during an argument, or a sharing of deeply meaningful ideas? These questions became the target of a kind of natural experiment looking at expressions of interactive group consciousness

Informal observations of circumstances that seemed to affect the results in our REG experiments suggested the value of taking continuous data around groups of people. When we did so, the indications of a group influence were encouraging, and this motivated us to build portable devices which could be taken into the field, to academic meetings, churches, concerts, to rituals and ball games. In this "FieldREG" protocol we were no longer dealing with intentions to change the behavior of the machine, but instead with a possibility that it could act as a monitor responding to some general property of consciousness, almost as if we were measuring something like ambient temperature.

Thus, the continuous data collection from an REG was an important innovation for the experimental program, permitting conceptually new studies. By far the biggest step was not in the lab but into the larger world. We could now record a continuous "history of data" that could be examined to see if there were jogs and wiggles corresponding to things happening in the environment. At first we just looked for changes during special moments—meetings or experiments—in the lab, but as soon as portable computers slimmed down to laptops we paired them with the portable REG to begin collecting data in the field.

The first formal trials in the FieldREG experiment[38] were in 1993 at small meetings of colleagues. Brenda took the equipment to a gathering of fellow researchers called ICRL, and I took it to Esalen for meetings to develop experiments to study mental influence on living systems. Both data sets showed deviations from the random behavior expected from our REGs at times we had identified as notable, and we were off to a new set of challenges. The equipment still needed work if we were to exploit the promise of actual "field" research.

The name of the new experiment was a double entendre, because what we were attempting in these field experiments would lead to learning more directly about one of the contenders for an explanation of the psi effects that had by this time been soundly established in the lab. Could the effects be transferred or imposed by a field? An intuitive picture of the mechanism that comes to most people is something extending outward from the mind to make something happen to the target of intention. But what could that extended influence be? Models of radiant heat and radio waves and electromagnetic (EM) fields come easily to mind, but the laboratory experiments had been designed to exclude EM fields and various ordinary physical influences. On the other hand, our designs could address only the usual kinds of forces and fields that science has come to understand over the last 200 years or so. Maybe there is something else with field-like properties—something which has not yet been clearly envisioned.

The terms used to describe the conditions that most often seem to produce data changes associated with groups are "resonance" and "coherence" of consciousness, referring to the experience people sometimes have when a group really begins to hum with an integrated feeling. We soon found that the conditions that produced interesting results in the FieldREG experiments were mainly in one of two categories: the conducive and the mundane. Small, intimate groups, ritual activities, sacred places, engaging concerts, any situations conducive to resonance tended to show departures from expectation, while mundane business meetings, academic conferences, street corners, and shopping centers produced no change in the random data. The differences that make a difference in this field-oriented research have to do with coherent activities and resonant interactions.

The laboratory research had established the ability of human intentions to induce minute changes and structure in random data streams. Now with the FieldREG experiment, we could increase the reach of this developing science by studying a broader range of questions. The most important difference, and one that is crucial to understanding how mind relates to the world in which it is embedded, is that we can identify linkages and effects that don't depend on conscious intention. Coherent mental activity in the environment appears to be sufficient.

What we are seeing may be effects from unconscious or deeply buried aspects of mind that are typically inaccessible, but the new technology allows us to capture some correlates and indications of what clearly seems to be interconnection—of minds engaged with each other and with the environment.

Leaving the Lab

The earliest field trials used a small, tough suitcase holding a PEAR Portable REG, a (rather heavy) laptop, and a motorcycle battery to provide power for several hours. In one early application, York provided this kit to friends who, as part of their pagan religious practice, did regular rituals in the woods, and they collected data during a dozen occasions. They made notes of special times like the "moons" and pagan holidays, and described the group attitudes and feelings. As in the ICRL and Esalen meetings, these notes identifying *a priori* what we came to see as periods of group coherence or resonance tended to correspond to small, but predictable changes in the data sequence. It was as if the coherence of the group extended to include the REG and its data sequence—it too showed signs of "coherence" in the form of small but detectable shifts away from purely random behavior.

To replace the suitcase FieldREG, John and I began designing a much smaller device, aiming for true portability. The advances in electronics allowed the next version of the REG device to be very small indeed, considerably smaller than the standard cigarette pack. The manufactured version was called the MicroREG, and was about 1 by 3 inches and half an inch thick.

At the same time, laptops were becoming lighter and had increased battery life, and the computer industry was working toward what were called palmtop computers. One of these was the HP1000, which was about 6 inches by 3 inches and one inch thick. It could run MS-DOS programs, and it had some extra memory for storing data. A special edition of the MicroREG was built to connect to the little computer, and York wrote a custom version of the FieldREG program, called PalmREG, which not only collected and stored the data, but had a time-stamped index with provision for marking the beginning and end of special periods. We were set to go with a streamlined series of field experiments, using equipment that could literally fit in a coat pocket or a purse.

Today, with smartphones comprising a powerful computer and many gigabytes of memory, our PalmREG seems primitive, but it gave us access to a new world of consciousness research.

Sacred spaces, meditations and rituals

What defines the extraordinary places and activities where people report experiences of resonance? Does a great cathedral have a special atmosphere enhancing the gatherings for worship? How about the stone circles of the Celts or the temples of ancient Egypt? Did we humans find these special places already imbued with their remarkable character, or did our repeated ceremonial activities and intentions create their sacred quality?

With the continuing miniaturization of electronic technology, we were able to begin testing hypotheses using a MicroREG on a palmtop computer. We could go to concerts and religious ceremonies, sacred sites, sporting events, and meetings and conferences of all kinds. I could carry the "PalmREG" to Egypt in the company of a group interested in the sacred and expecting to do meditations or chanting in the holy of holies in several ancient temples (ruins, but still with presence) and in the chambers of the Great Pyramid.[39]

There was of course a learning process for us as experimenters, because we would inescapably be part of the group consciousness we wanted to monitor. In the field, I had to learn how to make scientific notes and hit the right keys for index marking as a kind of automaton, allowing my "self" to be fully present in the moments where the group melded and became a single entity. At the Metropolitan Opera, Brenda and Bob needed to note the beginning and end of each exquisite operatic aria even as they let go of worldly concerns, allowing themselves to be drawn into the spell of the music.

The series of venues grew to include a variety of concerts and ceremonies, sporting matches and intimate gatherings, and we also took data at academic and business meetings, expecting they might serve as a mundane counterpoint—what we could think of as experimental "controls." Because the effects, like those in the lab, were subtle and very small, we arranged to do repetitions or replications in the same kinds of situations. Thus, even though there might be some hits and some misses, we would eventually have a sufficient database to do reliable statistical calculations. This is an essential aspect of the kind of research we were doing. Nothing can be learned from one probe into such a complicated and difficult area of inquiry. It is like fly-fishing. It takes several casts made with care and thoughtfulness to find out if there might be any trout in the stream, and ever more refined efforts to tempt the fish to strike.

Devils Tower

An example of repeated measures with FieldREG was a trip to Devils Tower in Northeastern Wyoming. A dowser friend, Andrei Apostol, wanted to see if there might be an REG response at points he found "promising" around this awesome natural monument. We gathered a small group there, and we made 10 circuits of the tower, which is the remnant of a volcano, the hardened lava upwelling that still stands after millennia of erosion removed all the overlay. When we did the analysis, we found no large effect to confirm the dowsing hypothesis, even though we did have a decent number of replications.

But we had planned and conducted a second experiment, which focused on the "sacred place" revered by the Native American tribes

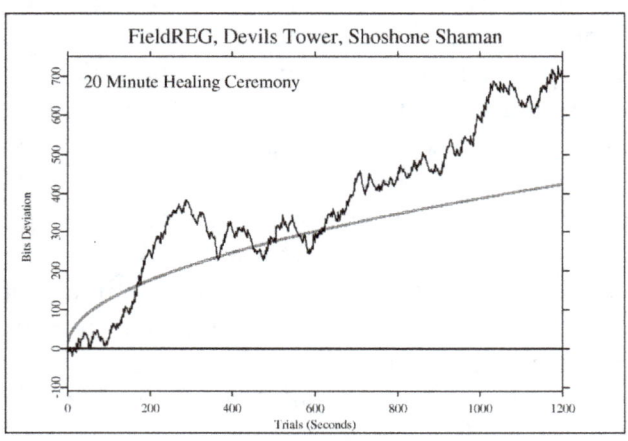

of the area. We had the good fortune to have as part of our group John Tarnese, a Shoshone Shaman whose personal mission is to heal such places from the spiritual harms done by careless people—tourists and others with no connection to the earth's living presence.

John guided us to a power spot for a healing ceremony, during which I was prepared to take data. We also did a control or sham healing at another spot, chosen arbitrarily by one of us. John had nodded indulgently when I tried to explain the FieldREG experiment. Later, when we got back to shelter and I could display the data taken during that ceremony, he said, "Ah, now I see what you mean." The REG data show a strong, highly significant positive deviation during the 20-minute ceremony.[40] One example can't be reliably interpreted, but we found other opportunities to ask the same basic question.

Egypt

In 1996, friends asked me if I would be interested in joining a group traveling to Egypt. The easy answer was an emphatic Yes! The 19 people in the group were nearly all interested in the spiritual aspects of the ancient Egyptian culture, and the plans included visits to as many as possible of the sacred sites, temples, and major pyramids. We expected to join together in meditations in these special places, while also planning visits to the lively bazaars and the streets of Cairo. I planned a series of FieldREG experiments that would allow comparison of the sacred sites and more mundane or chaotic places, and I expected to be able to compare data collected while our group were involved in shared meditations vs. planning meetings, visits to temples vs bazaars. My intention was to collect data more or less continuously, making notes and marking the index to identify locations and activities for later analysis.

The resulting data, taken in a well-defined scientific protocol, shows extraordinary trends, significant deviations with meaning, exactly when we were in the Holy of Holies of a temple, or in the King's Chamber or the Great Hall of Cheops. The results from this Egypt trip were, to put it succinctly, powerful and richly informative. Overall, the data from this excursion are the strongest in the FieldREG database, and they show an orderly matching of effect size with the settings. Group meditations and chanting in the sacred spaces like the Holy of Holies in the temple ruins, or the interior chambers of the Great Pyramid reliably produced strong departures. Effects were on average a little smaller without the "ritual" activity. In contrast, there was little or no evidence for deviations during time spent in the chaos of the streets and markets.[41]

This graph shows the data collected during our visit to the Great Pyramid of Cheops. The first segment shows flat random behavior while we were in the tunnel entering the pyramid. But the next segments have striking trends correlated with the time in several of the awe-inspiring places within the pyramid. They also are correlated with the group chanting and meditating in the Queen's Chamber (segment labeled A) the Grand Gallery (B) and the King's Chamber (C & D). These are big deviations compared with the data trends during periods when we were just casually exploring.

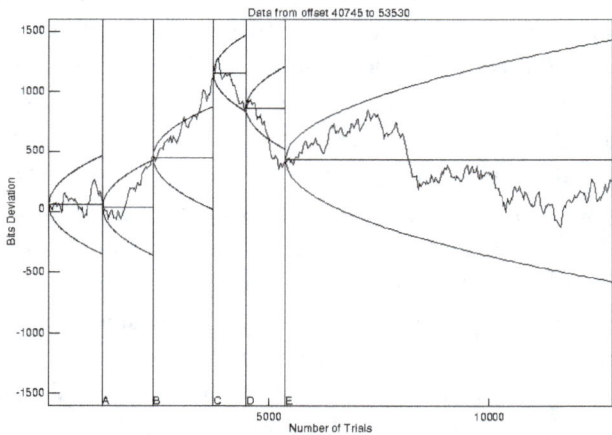

I was also struck by an interesting pattern of results in the ancient temples, or perhaps more precisely, an exception to the pattern. We visited as many as we could, a total of 6, including most of the well-known temple sites. All but one of these ancient sacred sites yielded the predicted positive trend while our group was in the Holy of Holies. The one exception was Philae, the temple dedicated to healing. What was different here? It turns out that this beautiful and impressive ruin was moved from its original site—the location "staked out by the gods" according to the priests of the time. It was to be flooded and destroyed by the new lake created by the Aswan dam, and to rescue this treasure the decision was made to move and rebuild it. The restoration is magnificent, and my guess is that few casual visitors ever sense that it is not the "original" temple. It looks just as before, but it is no longer in the sacred site ordained for the temple of Philae. Of course, as always, this single case can easily be attributed to chance fluctuations in the random data, but the possibility that it reflects some deep wisdom is intriguing. There is little chance of reproducing this particular circumstance to test the question more rigorously, but there are other cases that lend themselves to such repetition.

Replication, the *sine qua non*

Others joined in the search for answers to the group consciousness question, with differences in perspective. Dean Radin asked about the Oscars TV event and the O. J. Simpson trial. Would the huge interest, with millions sharing a moment show up on our coherence detectors?[42] Dick Bierman, in Amsterdam, asked about poltergeists and their intense effect on family groups, and about soccer, the sport that rivets the attention of vast numbers in Europe.[43] In some cases the circumstances or the nature of the event suggested multiple recordings, and we began to coordinate our measurements and share the data, to augment the search for insight on the many intriguing questions. In the PEAR lab also, we continued with many more applications of this interesting approach. We took advantage of meetings and concerts and travel opportunities and collected data in a variety of venues. We knew it would be important to replicate the findings, so many of the applications were in series of similar situations. More than 100 data sets were accumulated in half a dozen different categories, and the results piled up to persuasive significance, with clear differentiation of the "coherent" from the "mundane" venues.[44]

The broad spectrum of replications at PEAR and in other labs led to thinking more broadly. The natural questions raised by such results included the influence of distance—how far might the effect extend? How could we use multiple REGs to good effect, and what analytical statistics might be the best to identify structures and extract patterns from our nominally random data? Would events of positive and negative character differ in their impact? And what about the size of the group? Would 1000 people have a different effect from a group of 10?

These are good questions, for which we have only provisional answers. Based on work of the PEAR lab and other research groups, it appears that the usual measuring standards of distance, time, and number are not directly applicable in the mind/machine studies. What seems more often to be useful are aspects of the subjective mental domain such as engagement, vividness, immediacy, and impressiveness. The REG devices seem to have only one "note" to sing, and they do so when the context is expressive in this more subjective language.

In experiments with two participants trying to change the output of the REG, we find a larger effect size for certain couples, but only if they are really close—what we can call "bonded" pairs.[45] And similarly for groups of 10 or 100 or 1000, but only if they are deeply engaged in a matter of mutually important focus. It turns out not to be solely a function of the numbers of people involved. In the best cases the advantage is only about a factor of 2 or 3, and I think that is a result of the psychological smoothness or the conducive context more than it is an effect of the larger number of potential sources. Ultimately, I think there is only one consciousness in a resonant group, or in the world when we're looking at a global event, and that this "larger" consciousness acts just like that of an individual and has about the same potential for affecting our instruments. We'll see some evidence for this idea later.

These explorations and questions stimulated me to reflect again on the ideas of Teilhard de Chardin, who wrote about evolution and in particular about his expectation that humanity had another stage to enter. He thought our next phase would be to evolve into a sheath of intelligence for the earth—what he called the noosphere. This would be an analog to the atmosphere or biosphere, but composed of mind-stuff, the combined and integrated consciousness of all humankind. These thoughts gradually became working propositions and ultimately the experiment we called the EGG Project or GCP.

Chapter 11: THE EGG NETWORK

We have a habit in writing articles published in scientific journals to make the work as finished as possible, to cover up all the tracks, to not worry about the blind alleys or describe how you had the wrong idea first, and so on. So there isn't any place to publish, in a dignified manner, what you actually did in order to get to do the work.

—Richard Feynman, Nobel Lecture, 1966

Coalescence of ideas

Two months after the emotionally potent event of Diana's funeral ceremonies, the idea of a global network of consciousness resonance detectors came more clearly into focus. As described in the EGG Story chapter, I had organized a meeting designed to integrate the experience of psychophysiologists and psi researchers. Several of my friends and colleagues in the field were there, including Marilyn Schlitz, Dean Radin and Dick Bierman, and in one of those wonderful hallway discussions where the best work gets done, the recent "global" REG experiments and the current discussions of EEG technology overlapped and coalesced into the idea of a "world EEG." The image was immediate, and it neatly captured the implications of growing evidence that mass responses to global events could be registered with our REG technology. Later, my son Greg suggested that we were building an ElectroGaiaGram—an EGG. This delightful acronym stuck as we began work on the "EGG project." The possibilities lit my imagination, and I started organizing the resources and energies for what later came to be called the Global Consciousness Project. The vision resonated with many of my colleagues and friends around the world, and they helped make it not just a cool idea, but a realized instrument.

Our intention was to proceed with work that was clear and scientifically sound, and at the same time interesting and meaningful. From the beginning, the EGG Project sought a balance of science and aesthetics, rigor and adventure. The task we set ourselves was in a sense too grand to complete because of its vast temporal scale, but it was worth investing our time and best energies working toward a well-formed research venture.

Teilhard de Chardin,[46] and before him V. I. Vernadsky,[47] were convinced as scientists that the earth would have eventually a noosphere to complement the atmosphere and biosphere that surround and envelop it. They described the noosphere as a layer of knowing or intelligence, and envisioned it as a natural evolutionary stage for life on the planet. Teilhard wrote of "complexification" and "planetization" as forces that would compress humanity into tighter bonds, and ultimately into a new phase of collective intelligence. By the late 1990's the time was right and the technology was ripe for a scientific effort to look for evidence that this noosphere might already exist in a nascent form.

The Team

The EGG Project was and is a remarkable achievement of volunteers. On the order of 150 people have contributed time and skill to the development of the network, hosting the far-flung EGGs, and analysis of the data. I designed the network with input from several colleagues, notably Dean Radin, Dick Bierman, and Greg Nelson. Greg and John Walker built the robust and powerful data collection and archiving software for Linux, and it was ported to Windows by Paul Bethke. Rick Berger created the original professional website, which was recently modernized by Marjorie Simmons. Many others gave valuable time and energy to the Project, including Dick Shoup, Marilyn Schlitz, Chino Srinivasan, Brad Anderson, Tom Sawyer, Peter Bancel, William Treurniet, Dale, Fernando Lucas Rodriguez, Stephan Schwartz, George deBeaumont, Jaroen Ruuward, Nishith Singh, Taylor Jackson, Kevin Laghleigh, Leanne Roffey, Oliver McDermott, Doug Mast, Mike Meyer, and Hans Wendt (I have surely left out some important people). They contributed ideas, wrote special-purpose scripts and programs, and created a variety of specialized analyses and displays. The necessary expenses have been covered by donations from many individuals, including steady friends like John Walker and Dick and Connie Adams, with non-profit money logistics handled by the Institute of Noetic Science. And then there are the EGG hosts, who are friends I have never met in person, with a few exceptions. Many have been with the GCP/EGG project for its whole history, but we continue to add new people to the team as the Internet penetrates remote parts of the world.

The basic outlines for the GCP have been constant from the beginning. Let's take a look back to the vision for the project in 1998, in a documentation web page written before any REGs were in place. In the spirit of Feynman's observation about raw vs. processed descriptions of science, this is a sample of the raw material:

ORIGINAL PLAN

A General Description and Proposal
Prepared April 30, 1998, last edited July 26, 1998

Introduction
It is one of humanity's most enduring spiritual traditions: the idea that all life or all consciousness is interconnected. Human groups, whether ethnic, religious, or racial; as various as the Iroquois, the Sufis, and Western European Freemasons, all incorporate it into their belief structures. References to it can be found in ancient documents of the classical world, both East and West. It is a very compelling idea, spanning both millennia and the vast complexity of human cultures. Yet, as compelling as the concept is emotionally, only in recent decades has any objective evidence emerged that such a construct might be valid. Even this work, in fields as varied as physics, parapsychology, and biology, has provided only suggestions, largely because the research was not conceived in global terms, but instead focused on more limited vistas. Indeed, much of the relevant research has regarded only individual performances in experiments on anomalies such as telepathy, mind/matter interactions, and distant healing. Somewhat broader vistas are opened in studies of group resonance and morphogenetic fields.

Until very recently, taking the kind of global real-time measurements necessary to evaluate objectively what Jung called the Collective Unconscious, and Teilhard de Chardin described as the Noosphere—a sheath of intelligence for the Earth—was not a real possibility. Two events, however, have changed this picture. The first is the development of a reliable measurement technology using Random Event Generators (REGs) linked to computers, together with soft- and hardware necessary to do very large and complex multivariate analyses on desktop machines. The second is the rise of the Internet, itself a kind of global consciousness network, albeit one linked very much to the physical world of electronics. For the first time, the objective measurement infrastructure necessary to undertake an evaluation of consciousness on a global scale is broadly accessible. This proposal describes such an effort, the Global Consciousness Project (GCP).

A. Background

The impulse for the research proposed here can be traced back over the past 35 years, during which time excellent experiments have demonstrated that human consciousness can interact with delicately balanced physical systems, in particular, REGs. During the past five years, these experiments have been brought out of the laboratory and into "field" situations where the REG devices show characteristic behavior in the presence of people participating in deeply engaging activities. Most recently, the experiments have been extended to gather data during extraordinary global events such as the funeral ceremonies for Princess Diana, with results indicating a measurable effect correlated with the widely shared emotional resonance. It is research which suggests that further explorations might be very productive.

Implementation

The Global Consciousness Project can be conceptualized as an international network designed to record subtle, direct interactions of globally coherent consciousness with a world-spanning array of sensitive detectors. The core of the GCP is a network of REGs placed to record data at sites around the world and report it via the Internet to central computers where the data will be automatically archived, analyzed, and displayed on a dedicated website. To do this experiment, a refined protocol built on the foundation of earlier anomalies research has been developed. The data will be integrated in a variety of standard, well-tested analyses summarizing local and global statistics, with attention to anomalous deviations from chance expectation and unexpected structure in the data arrays, correlated with predictions made prior to data acquisition or analysis. Correlations with major events that engage the world population will be the primary vehicle for tests of coherence and patterns in the globally distributed REG data.

Three Phases

The GCP is designed in three phases, the first of which is focused primarily on building and testing system components in a small network. Phase 1 and part of the subsequent phase will be conducted with considerable attention to confidentiality to allow the acquisition of as large a database as possible prior to broader public engagement. This will allow an assessment of effects of growing public awareness due to publicity that might—if the fundamental EGG hypothesis is correct—create perturbations that can be observed in the data.

During this period, preparations will proceed for Phase 2, intended to have up to 28 sites at opportune university, commercial, and individual sites. Phase 2 will permit the implementation of more complex analysis procedures derived from computational technologies such as quantitative electroencephalography, which require input from a certain minimum of sources.

Assuming the results of the second phase show structure in the REG data warranting deeper exploration, Phase 3 will increase the number of sites to 100 or more and will ask more incisive scientific questions. This phase will address issues based on first principles as well as questions raised by previous results. It will explore effects of simple factors such as the relative density of the network's spatial array, and more complex issues including potential applications. We expect to implement web-based forums to provide public access (qualified by suitable automatic filtering) for people who wish to download data for well-defined analyses.

B. Principles and Policies

This is a voluntary, participatory undertaking. We believe the talents and time needed for all the work will be given freely by people interested in the concepts and willing to help. Because this is a project to assess interactions which, while often defined and debated, are poorly understood, a significant effort has been made to:

- Assure that while all of us have some personal ego needs that will affect our engagement in the GCP, we intend that it should be protected from undue and avoidable influences from this source.
- Assure that the project is protected from destructive influences and individuals whose motivations are inimical to resonant, cooperative interactions.
- Assure that during the planning and development period, there will be no public descriptions of the project. More generally, we will be quiet about grand intentions and expectations, and sensitive to implications.

We do not know whether there is a global consciousness, but we recognize that science is not about what we know will work; rather it illuminates what we believe is worth exploring. We acknowledge that we implicitly assume some form of global consciousness. Therefore, we will be respectful and caring when we describe the project and our expectations. We do know the Earth is beautiful and that nature's systems are elegant, with an inherent integrity. The Global Consciousness Project intends to emulate this character. The project is committed to the highest standards of integrity and scientific excellence. The members of the project are pledged to act with mutual respect, honesty, and dignity, and to work toward public presentations which are elegant and principled.

A dream of lions and advice from the *I Ching*

Working hard to bring all the parts of the project together, I was frustrated at the slow progress. Then I had an amazingly direct dream message about the nature of what we were building:

I received a large package, a giant shipping carton, with instructions for its use. When I pressed the start switch, a long, thin translucent tube unrolled into a receiving basket. I waited and soon felt an internal pushing which seemed in my dream exactly like what a woman giving birth must feel. At last the tube expanded and a small lion's paw and leg squeezed through, to drop wet and stained into the basket. The dream told me that I was attempting to birth a lion, and that this was just a practice run. It told me that I had much to learn, and that the gestation will take its time.

Around this same time, I asked the *I Ching* one of my rare questions—about a meeting I wanted to have. The message was to encourage and allow, and to accept the natural pace of organic growth. This was a moment in my path where it seemed most appropriate to ask the I Ching for its wisdom. The result was a helpful confirmation of the path.

The reading is Ts'ui, hexagram number 45, composed of the lake above and the earth below. Ts'ui is about "Gathering Together" [Massing]. The trigrams relate to the joyous and the receptive, and this hexagram could hardly be more clear as a counsel to trust in the gathering of people in a common interest, and to accept that leadership is required. The Judgment notes that the leader must first of all be collected within himself. On the larger stage, "Only collective moral force can unite the world."

Chapter 12: BRINGING IT ALL TOGETHER

When you put a thing in order, give it a name, and you are all in accord: it becomes.

—From the Navajo[48]

Science on the web

We set out from the beginning to have a balance of science and art in the EGG project, and that intention has helped to make the project more interesting while providing other benefits as well. The aesthetic motive keeps our broader purposes in mind, by posing philosophically intriguing questions that are worth serious effort. The scientific aspect has a special role to play in providing pragmatic, reliable answers. The science has to be exactly right, so we have given lots of attention to certain details that are in the background but are essential if we are to learn something and avoid fooling ourselves. As George deBeaumont, who did many of the early formal analyses, puts it, "It is a subtle beast we are chasing." We know, for example, that the appearance of an effect is partly determined by how we look for it, so that the exact specification of the method has to be established prior to its application and before we have any knowledge of the results. Among the options, we can look at the raw second-by-second data, or we can block it first into scores for minutes or hours, etc. As it happens, such choices are quite important and can partially determine whether a given event is regarded as significant. After a few months, we settled on the second-by-second data for our standard analysis. Much later we were able to establish that the 1-second data are the most efficient blocking of any we tested.

The GCP "Hypothesis Registry"[49] maintains a detailed description of all formal predictions, including the precise identification of the data segments and the pre-planned analysis. Exploration is also required, of course, to learn how best to formulate our questions, but all exploratory analyses are identified as such and maintained separately from the formal predictions. Their outcomes are not included in the GCP's bottom line. The formal predictions are all explicitly identified and analyzed, and their accumulated outcome provides the statistical evidence needed for a scientific evaluation of the overarching global consciousness hypothesis.

In response to a standing invitation, several independent observers regularly have looked at the GCP's procedures and results. They have offered constructive critical comments and occasionally do independent analyses. Finally, since the original data are always publicly available for download, every analysis can be checked at any time by anybody who wishes to do so.

The EGG project is an application of tools and strategies tested in laboratory and field REG research, but on a larger scale. If we can register the influence of one mind and see effects from a deeply engaged group, might we be able to capture effects on a broader scale? Why not ask if the whole world, at least occasionally, becomes sufficiently "resonant" to affect the technology we use for the group consciousness research?

In addition to the pre-network example of Princess Diana's funeral,[50] we gathered in the early years a variety of cases that show departures from expectation which make sense if there is a burgeoning global consciousness.

- New Year's Eve in 1998, 1999, and 2000: showed deviations
- First hour of NATO bombing in Yugoslavia: striking effect
- August, 1999 earthquake in Turkey: deviations start early
- The Pope in the middle east, March 2000: steady response
- And then the September 11 2001 tragedy linked to many days of convincing, meaningful data deviations

In a formal series of such cases the GCP was set up to ask whether world-scale events that engage global attention are correlated with increased structure in data from our random instruments. It is a noisy system, and our predictions are frequently wrong or the results may be inconclusive. But more often than not, the data conform to our *a priori* prediction, deviating in the direction we predict. The gradually accumulating evidence points to a positive answer. By now, some 17 years later, the strength of the evidence is at the level knowledgeable scientists consider adequate to say yes, there is a real phenomenon that we need to accommodate in our models.

Analytical perspective

And what does the evidence look like? There are several approaches to the analysis of such a richly complex database. The most obvious candidates are those developed in psi research laboratories around the world over the past few decades. In particular, the most common tools of the GCP analysis are adapted from the FieldREG research of the PEAR laboratory.

We predict deviations of the trial scores recorded by the REGs during times when large numbers of people are deeply engaged by events in the world. The idea is that this engagement will produce an unusual degree of coherence or commonality we might envision as a "consciousness field." The tentative picture goes on to suggest that the coherence represented in our common thoughts and emotions can be recorded (perhaps one might say, absorbed) by our REG devices, and produce correlations among them.

Readers will likely recognize that such descriptions are in part metaphoric rather than empirical, but they help create a picture leading to precise and effective questions about what is going on in the data. History shows that metaphor has a valued role in science. We learn from Keukle that his conception of the carbon ring structure arose from a dream of a serpent biting its tail. And Einstein claimed his understanding of light came because he could envision riding a starbeam. In any case, the approach here is to describe what we do in the project and what we think is going on, using ordinary language including metaphor if that seems helpful.

Testing the hypothesis

The question we pose in our hypothesis testing, on the other hand, needs to be clear and unambiguous. In the most general form it says that we will see deviations from expectation in the GCP data corresponding to major events in the world. This is too vague to be tested as is, so the general hypothesis must be recast as a specific hypothesis for each event, with a precise *a priori* definition of the event, specifying the beginning and end times and the exact statistical analysis that will be used. Thus, we identify a data segment, usually a few hours long, that represents the event including time for the news to spread and people to respond. Secondly, we specify a particular statistical process to apply to each event. The details are registered prior to the extraction of data from the archive. This protocol allows rigorous testing in a replication series of specific hypotheses, leading cumulatively to a fully competent test of the overarching global hypothesis.

Selecting "global events"

To set up a formal test, we first identify an engaging event. The criteria for event selection are that the event provides a focus of collective attention or emotion, and that it engages people across the world. We primarily select events of global character, but allow for variation in their type, duration, intensity and emotional tone. In practice, events are chosen because they capture news headlines, involve or engage large numbers of people, or represent emotionally potent categories (e.g., great tragedies and great celebrations).

Once an event is identified, the simple hypothesis test is constructed by fixing the start and end times for the event and specifying a statistical analysis to be performed on the corresponding data. The statistic used for most events is a measure of network variance; that is, the momentary variance of the whole network, which also embodies correlation among the REGs. It is calculated as the squared Stouffer's Z (normalized average Z-score) across RNGs per second, summed across all seconds in the event. These details are entered into a formal registry before the data are extracted from the archive[51] We select and analyze an average of 2 or 3 events per month. The selection procedure allows exploration, while the replication design provides rigorous hypothesis specification for each event.

Because the project is unique, with no precedents to provide information on relevant parameters, we started with guesses and intuitions about what might characterize suitable, informative events. Field research on group consciousness suggested that synchronization or coherence of thought and emotion should be important factors, so we began by selecting major tragedies and traditional celebratory events that were expected to bring large numbers of people together in a common focus and shared emotions.

While many observers assume we can and should follow a fixed prescription to identify "global events," this is not straightforward. To give specific examples, we could select a disaster if it results in, say, more than 500 fatalities. But this would exclude slow moving but powerfully engaging events such as volcanic eruptions or major hurricanes, and it would fail to identify emotionally powerful incidents like the enormously disruptive attack that destroyed the Golden Dome Mosque in Iraq in February 2006 but killed relatively few people. What we do is identify, with the help of correspondents around the world, events that typically bring large numbers of people to a shared cognitive or emotional state. The following is an illustrative list of criteria we use for event selection, with examples:

- Outrage and surprise. Terror attacks, especially when they galvanize attention globally.
- Compassion and distress. Large natural disasters, typhoons, tsunamis, earthquakes.
- Love and sharing. Celebrations and ceremonies like New Year's, religious gatherings.
- Powerful interest. Political and social events like elections, protests, demonstrations.
- Deliberate focus. Organized meetings and meditations like Earth Day, World Peace Day.

Experience has led to considerable standardization, and for some kinds of events pre-defined parameters can be applied. For example, events that repeat, such as New Year's, Kumbh Mela, or Earth Day, are registered with the same specifications in each instance. About half the events in the formal series are identifiable before the fact. Accidents, disasters, terror attacks, and other unpredictable events can only be identified after they occur. For unexpected events, the protocol typically specifies a period beginning at or shortly before the moment of occurrence, followed by time (usually 6 hours) for the spreading of news reports. The times are typically set on the hour or half hour.

To eliminate a frequent misconception, we do not look for "spikes" in the data and then try to find what caused them. Such a procedure, because it would have unconstrained degrees of freedom, is not statistically viable. We do no "data snooping" and there is no *post hoc* inclusion or exclusion of events. All events are entered into the formal experiment registry before the corresponding data are extracted from the archive. For details, see http://noosphere.princeton.edu/pred_formal.html.

The analysis for an event then proceeds according to the registry specifications. All registered events are analyzed and the results are all reported, whatever the outcome.

Chapter 13: SUITABLE MEASURES

The Tao that can be told is not the eternal Tao. The name that can be named is not the eternal Name.

—*Tao Te Ching*

In the face of what seems irrefutable ancient wisdom about the difficulty of pinning things down in the subtle realms of consciousness research, we do the best we can.

The earliest descriptions of methodology in 1998 are still basically valid, though the procedures have been refined in the meantime. Here is an excerpt that describes the standard analysis we call network variance, which formally represents anomalous deviation and correlation of the eggs.

METHODOLOGY
The scientific aspects of this project will develop over time, as experience is gained. This page discusses our present understanding of the methods and constraints we believe will yield clear, interpretable results with regard to our basic prediction of a correlation of RNG behavior with identifiable states of collective consciousness. The discussion is ongoing, and some alternative proposals are under consideration as complements to the currently planned approach. The ability to gather and interpret scientific evidence depends on a clear statement of the hypothesis or the question that is being asked. We use operational definitions to ensure that we can extract quantitative conclusions from data, with specific relevance to our questions.

Primary Hypothesis:
The composite variation of the distribution means of data sequences recorded from multiple RNGs during broadly engaging global events will deviate from expectation.

Definition:
The standard measure is called Network Variance. It is the squared composite mean of the normalized deviations across Eggs.

Formal Statistics:
The primary focus of GCP analysis is anomalous shifts in network statistics during periods of time specified in formal predictions. The standard test of such departures from expectation compares the Chisquare of the composite deviation across all eggs during a specified event against theoretical expectation.

The standard analysis is based on the squared composite meanshift across eggs (the Stouffer Z), which properly represents an underlying hypothesis that the behavior of the eggs will tend to be correlated if there is a "global consciousness" effect. The Stouffer Z is defined as $Z_s = \Sigma Z_i / \sqrt{i}$.

The standard analysis in detail:
1. The REG or RNG units produce random bits at high speed, on a computer serial port
2. Each Egg-site records data as "trials" at one per second, summing 200 bits for one trial
3. The 200-bit trial sums have expected mean = 100 and standard deviation = 7.071
4. The deviation of a trial, or of the mean of a specified set of trials, is normalized as a Z-score: (X-100)/7.071
5. A composite (Stouffer) Z-score across Eggs is computed for each second (see the equation above)
6. Squaring it gives a Chisquare-distributed quantity with one degree of freedom
7. Since Chisquares are additive, we may sum across seconds. The sum has N-seconds degrees of freedom
8. The total Chisquare represents the deviation for the predicted period of time
9. This is compared with the appropriate Chisquare distribution to yield a chance probability.

Control Data:
Control data are needed to establish the validity of the statistical results. When the same analysis is applied, control data are expected to produce chance results in contrast with anomalous deviations in experimental data. A control distribution is produced by resampling the non-event data. In addition, a "clone" database of algorithmic pseudo-random data is automatically generated. The active event data can be evaluated against chance expectation as well as appropriate control and calibration data.

The measurement context

The RNG devices in the EGG network are physical, using quantum-level unpredictable events (electron tunneling) to produce a sequence of bits whose future is not determined. These instruments are labile—their outputs can change—and the experiment is designed to capitalize on that possibility. As described earlier, friends and colleagues around the world, many of whom I've never met, volunteer to host one of our devices, and they become the Egg hosts[52] on whose good will the project depends. The Internet had to be ready for us, and it was, just about the time we were ready to go. Each Egg sends its data to the server in Princeton, where a program called basket (what else?) archives the data for later access and analysis.

The basic expectation for a network of random number generators is that the data from all devices will be independent. They are not only separated by hundreds or thousands of kilometers, but are carefully designed and built to produce independent random data, and they do. Both in individual testing and in the assessment of large amounts of data from the running network, we find no significant differences of the mean scores from theoretical expectations. (There are small deviations of the variance from expectation for some devices, detectable with very large samples. Although the effect on overall statistics is extremely small, orders of magnitude smaller than the mean effect size, final rigorous analysis uses the empirical instead of theoretical variance.)

Only in the data corresponding to great events important to humans do we regularly find deviations. But what sort of deviations are we talking about? My early intuitions about the sources of possible effects were drawn from experience in the lab and field experiments. I thought we should look for two things: excess deviation and excess correlation. Indeed, we might find both, in the form of correlated deviations across the network. The measure we developed is responsive to both. Later, we will look more deeply at the mathematics and implications. It turns out that most of the weight and power of this "network variance" measure comes from the inter-Egg correlations, and that has important implications for the meaning of the effects in physical terms.

Picturing the data

One of the best ways to visualize possible effects in the data is to graph the deviations of moment-by-moment trial values from what is expected, and to display the accumulating total—the progression of the average deviation over time. This produces a "random walk" like that shown here, which wanders above and below the expected deviation of zero, but shows no persistent trend. The figure plots the accumulation of small deviations of the network variance (netvar) from its expectation. The cumulative deviation from expectation is compared with a smooth curve that shows the 5% significance criterion. The netvar statistic is designed to measure deviant or correlated non-random activity across all the eggs. If the deviations are consistent, indicating an effect, the cumulative deviation trace will have a slope, but if there is no effect, the trace will show ups and downs, but no substantial trend. In the graph,

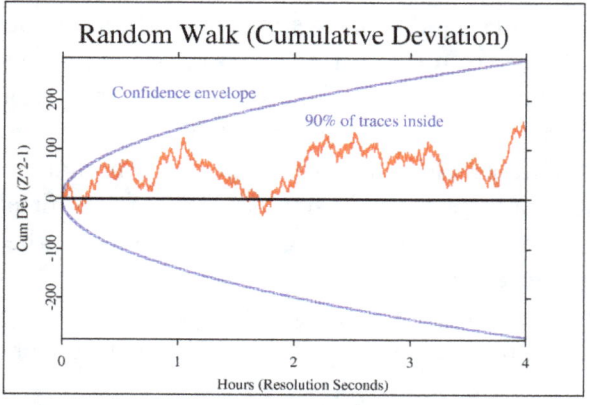

it is easy to see that there is no persistent departure from expectation—this is like a drunkard's walk, movement but no direction.

In such a cumulative deviation graph, consistent departures from the expected mean value are easy to see because the data trace will have a slope superimposed on the random walk. A consistent increase (or decrease) in the squared Z-score will produce many steps in one direction and thus a trend. Even a tiny effect, if it is persistent, will yield a significant departure with a low probability that it is just chance. To see correlations of the data with global events, we look at the scale and the consistency of the deviations.

This figure shows an event that was selected, like others in the formal series, for the likelihood it would bring large numbers of people to a common focus. This is the resignation of Pope Benedict XVI. It was completely unexpected and because of this, a powerfully engaging event for people around the world. The result shown in the graph does not look random; there is a steady trend superimposed on the characteristic random variation of the network variance. The deviation is marginally significant, with odds of about 1 in 12 that it is just chance fluctuation.

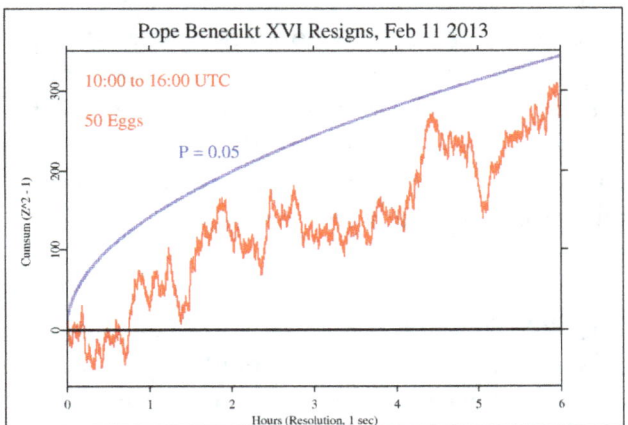

Though it is not statistically significant by the usual standard, the deviation is positive and considerably larger than the average across the database. Because many of the formal events show this pattern—steady, positive deviation—the overall accumulation of evidence adds up to a stronger and stronger indication that there is a small, but real effect.

Such deviations in the data support the hypothesis that human responses to great events will affect the REG network. We take departures from the normal expected behavior as a measure of some manifestation of "consciousness," following principles derived from decades of laboratory research showing that human intentions can affect the randomness of such devices in controlled experiments.

Correlations with meaning

The simplest analyses look for a correlation of the outcome with the prediction specified in the formal hypotheses. The evidence appears as a consistent deviation from expectation in the sequence of data corresponding to the identified global event. The numbers are otherwise demonstrably random with no noteworthy deviations, and the contrast indicates that something has affected the data. Because we select events defined by deep engagement on the part of large numbers of people, the results are suggestive of a globally integrated consciousness. Of course, there are alternative explanations. Maybe it is just chance, but the statistics say that would be a miracle itself. Maybe it is an "experimenter" effect, generated by the few people who know about the eggs and the EGG project, but a detailed examination of the data makes this hypothesis seem unlikely. Perhaps we have made a mistake somewhere, or perhaps we are frauds, but the completely public nature of the project and the direct access to all the data makes checks on these alternatives completely transparent.

Developing the protocols

The GCP experiment required a generally applicable approach to the wide variety of events we expected to examine. There were no precedents for the experiment either in scope or in the definition of its elements. We knew the general direction we wanted to go, but the idea of mass consciousness was even less well defined than consciousness of individuals, and there was (and remains) precious little agreement on even the simpler question. Specifying precise scientific tests in weakly defined areas is a non-trivial challenge. Fortunately, science has developed the concept of "operational definitions" to make clear what is being done in research. This leads to a phenomenological perspective that allows progress, though it remains unsatisfying to some observers. On the other hand, it serves to create an empirical foundation for other questions, and for modeling and theoretical work.

The FieldREG experiment had shown that we should expect a variance measure to be more useful than a directional meanshift measure, and that we needed a precise *a priori* specification of the data sequence to be analyzed. Of course, we were not dealing with one data sequence but several, or many—eventually up to about 70 parallel data streams, one from each Egg. The question was what statistical procedures would best summarize such data during the event. We looked at several possibilities, and discussed them and their implications among the professional research community. I was convinced that we had no choice but to proceed by first identifying an event and then determining whether the data collected during the corresponding time period could be distinguished from normal random data. Others contended we should find unusual data sequences and then look for corresponding events in order to help identify "effective events."

Ultimately, we agreed that this latter idea was unfeasible, or if feasible, terribly inefficient, and settled down to apply the procedure I preferred. In the GCP application the precise form is very particular: we first identify and specify an event that is expected to capture widespread attention, and then apply a standard analysis to the corresponding data. This recipe allows a rigorous and statistically competent series of formal hypothesis tests, and at the same time allows us to examine a variety of different kinds of events.

At the outset, the statistical challenge was to choose a suitable calculation for the "network variance" representing the momentary deviations from expectation across all the eggs. One possibility, which was used by some independent analysts, calculated the variance among the eggs (called the device variance). But the preferred calculation, it seemed to me, had to address all the eggs as a unit, respecting their presence and participation in a network. Thus, the standard formal statistic combined all the eggs into a single score using the squared Stouffer Z-score described earlier.

Interestingly, and happily, this network variance measure is also a measure of inter-node correlation. While it was obviously an appropriate statistic, I didn't at first recognize all the implications of choosing this measure, but it allows the use of the full information content of the database, not just the composite outcome for the event. Specifically, the inter-node correlation measure can assess the second-by-second contributions of individual RNGs, their locations, and the RNG type.

This was not the end of discussion on the complexities, of course. For example, there was criticism of our methodology that focused on the "lack of a clear hypothesis," despite the simple and transparent statement of our basic prediction:

Data recorded during a special event will diverge from expectations established for purely random data.

This was too general for some colleagues,[53] despite the fact that the specific tests of this hypothesis in each individual event were unambiguous and both legitimate and competent so long as all decisions about what data to analyze and what statistics to apply were made before the data were examined.

The general hypothesis was designed to be instantiated repeatedly in completely specified predictions about individual events resulting in a formal series of experiments. All the "replications" were rigorous hypothesis tests, even though they differed in detail (e.g., the duration or the emotive quality) from one event to the next because they were situation dependent. In effect, the experiment was designed to exploit a two-level hypothesis, with an overarching general statement we would assess in multiple fully-specified tests. The critics were looking for something analogous to a simple physics experiment with instrumental measures and precise quantities. Over the years, these issues received a great deal of attention within the psi research community, but less so since our publications in 2008 and 2011 giving full details of the analytical approach.[54]

We ultimately agreed that though it is unconventionally general, the formal experiment tests a valid hypothesis. The hypothesis is so broad that it doesn't tell us much beyond demonstrating that something is going on in the data. But this generality has much to recommend it in our circumstance. Anthony Freeman pointed to the value when dealing with research in a nascent field: "The importance of not overdefining the topic ahead of investigation is routinely stressed by John Searle. He distinguishes between an analytic definition, which is arrived at only at the end of an investigation, and a commonsense definition, which comes at the start and serves to identify the target of the research program."[55]

We chose this two-stage approach to the scientific question, which means that the GCP question is formulated as a complex hypothesis, rather than a simple hypothesis that would have more interpretive power. Its viability is formally tested in the series of specific hypotheses, while its flexibility allows us room for exploration and learning. This was obviously important, indeed necessary and unavoidable, given our ignorance entering unexplored territory.

Chapter 14: THE ART OF SCIENCE

If a man is offered a fact which goes against his instincts, he will scrutinise it closely, and unless the evidence is overwhelming, he will refuse to believe it. If, on the other hand, he is offered something which affords a reason for acting in accordance to his instincts, he will accept it even on the slightest evidence.
– *Bertrand Russell*[56]

As of late 2015, 500 rigorously defined, pre-specified events had been registered in the formal replication series, including tragedies and celebrations, disasters of natural or human origin, and planned or spontaneous gatherings involving great numbers of people. The events generally have durations ranging from a few hours to a full day. The project registers about 30 formal events per year, and the data taken during these events comprise somewhat less than 2% of the 17-year, 30-billion trial database. The cumulative experimental result attains a level of 7.3 sigma (standard deviations) relative to the null hypothesis.[57] The odds against a chance deviation of this magnitude are more than a trillion to one.

The average event Z-score is ~0.33 over 500 events, which may seem unimpressive. But given the huge number of tests, it adds up to a highly significant outcome. These statistics depend on the RNGs producing stable data distributed according to design expectations, and this has been verified across the full database. We don't assume that the RNGs are perfect theoretical devices, and so for detailed analyses we use empirical estimates of the mean and variance for each device based on its entire data history. The analytical procedures are checked for validity by running simulations on pseudo-random data sets, and the formal results are compared not only with theoretical expectation but with control distributions created by bootstrap resampling[58] of the entire database.

Is it probable enough to be possible?
We are far from having devised a mind meter, for the information

signals from mind to machine are faint and not very reliable. This is probably because mind is far more complex than we know how to deal with now. Though we try to ask simple questions in research with our random number generators, we have learned that when dealing with human consciousness, there are infinite degrees of reflection and refraction in the answers. Our best tools are therefore those which summarize and integrate information over many repetitions of the question we wish to ask. We count variations in the random events as they develop, and make averages, and look at distributions, and ask whether there are trends that should not appear in truly random sequences. And as we discover departures from the established expectations, we can ask whether they are merely what we would expect by chance, or if the deviations are substantial and evidently correlated with the questions in which we are interested. Statistics is the science that allows us to find out how probable any such correlation might be. If the trend is real, and not just a chance fluctuation, we take it as evidence that consciousness has touched the physical system and left a mark in the statistics. We begin to take that evidence seriously if it repeats and we see a statistical signature again and again.

Inter-Egg Correlations

It is worthwhile to examine the underlying hypothesis that the behavior of the eggs will tend to be correlated if there is a "global consciousness" effect, as stated in the original methodology description. The reasoning derives from decades of mind-machine experiments, which show that human consciousness can interact with random number generators, and that the effects apparently are not modulated by distance between the RNG and the person. The GCP network comprises many RNG devices and, extrapolating from the laboratory findings, they are in principle all subject to the interaction with consciousness focused by singular events. Logical consideration suggests that all eggs in the network would tend to be similarly affected, and hence that the data from the eggs should be correlated.

Doug Mast, an egg host and early collaborator, looked at inter-egg correlation structure for all of 1999, with results that were positive and modestly significant, with a 1 in 50 chance probability. This confirmed provisionally the observation that the standard analysis outcome measure represents not just a meanshift, but correlations among the widely distributed RNG devices.

Work on this question has been carried further by Peter Bancel. The upshot is that the standard measure we call network variance can be expressed formally as the average pair-wise correlation among the eggs. When we look at the correlation of egg A with B, A with C, A with D, ... and B with C, B with D, ... we compute hundreds or thousands of pair correlations depending on the number of eggs in the network. When these are summed, we find an excess correlation that is equivalent to the excess network variance. Thus, the primary effect of "global events" on the egg network can be understood as unexpected correlations among the RNGs.

For many people, correlation of this sort is a bit abstract, and it may help to imagine buoys floating on the oceans around the world that begin to bob up and down in synchrony despite being separated by global distances. The buoys are not pushed individually enough to notice, but they appear to be riding the same long wave.

In any case, we understand that the primary statistic used for the GCP analyses, the network variance, is approximated by the average of inter-node correlations.[59] Our research-grade random number generators become slightly correlated with each other during major events even though they are separated by global distances. Thus, the GCP effect is not just a shift of the mean output of the devices from expectation. It is more precisely understood as anomalous *correlation* of the RNG means. Rather than changes in their individual behaviors, we see coordinated, shared variation.

As we will describe in detail later, this correlation is just one of several forms of structure in the GCP data. There is a second, orthogonal correlation, an impact of distance separating the eggs, a sensible time course for the effects, and other indications that the nominally random data are changed. The RNGs become slightly correlated during the global events and the correlation strength is modulated by several factors. These elements of structure where there should be none are signs that human consciousness includes subtle aspects that have not been considered up to now by scientists and others attempting to describe the real world.

Merging Science and Art

Before going on to a more detailed examination of the scientific work, the data and analyses, I want to take a moment for a complementary view. Not all deep understanding comes from science, even though it is a wonderful set of tools for examining ourselves and the world we inhabit. Science is not only new—just a recent moment in our history of many thousands of years—it is dominated by a Western view. Given this secular and idiosyncratic quality in the most prominent of our intellectual tools, it is valuable to have another perspective to complement the scientific view. As Albert Einstein famously said, *"Science without religion is blind. Religion without science is lame."*

At some deep level, an aesthetic mode is an essential but often hidden part of the personality of many scientists. Whenever we get beyond their career presence as a neuropsychologist or a nuclear physicist, we're likely to find a musician or an actor. It shouldn't be a surprise, because great science and great art both rest on creativity, and both illuminate the best of human qualities.

Personal experiences and poetry. If these were enough (and they are for many of us) we could stop here and read Shakespeare to find out who we are. But for some purposes it isn't enough, and there are many who need scientific "proof" before deciding what is important, what is real. Science is one of our finest creations, and the art of science is to use it with respectful care—not as a bludgeon, but as a fine-pointed brush to paint a delicate, emerging understanding of the world. Science has been enormously successful directed outward to count and measure the stars, the rocks, and the atoms, but ironically it has been notoriously unsuccessful aimed inward to assess the mind and spirit that created it. Science needs to lean up respectfully against art and music and poetic understanding to reach its full potential. We reap great rewards from a balance of institution and intuition.

So, the GCP makes room adjacent to the strict and rigorous science, for playing with the data, maybe with an expectation that some unexpected insight will arise, but maybe just to make something pretty, or pointlessly interesting.

While I was teaching psychology as a newly minted professor, I also was teaching a course called "conceptual art" and running a seminar for aspiring photographers. My New York City friends from graduate school years came to Vermont to join me and the students and a few adventurous faculty to create multi-media spring spectaculars that brought painters and dancers, musicians and actors, and creative energies of all kinds together. We would take over theaters and courtyards to make programs like "Space Retimed—Time Respaced" and "Seven Minutes of Silence."[60]

The essential lesson of these events, which gave expression to the talents of dozens of people, was that the freedom to create is life-giving. Not to be over-dramatic about it, these cooperative works made everyone, including the audiences, more awake to the beauties of possibility. That, I think, is why it is worthwhile to make "global brain paintings" from the GCP data, and random "tapestries" whose threads are unpredictable sequences with a possibility of patterning. It gives an excuse for making "music" that might be interesting and for some ears quite beautiful, and which just might, because of the deep non-cognitive character of music, also reveal some patterns we couldn't otherwise discern. The ear is justly famous for its ability to wrest patterns and beauty out of the noise that naturally surrounds us, and music focuses that ability in the most remarkable form of human creativity, a manifestation of emotional meaning in a language every culture uses and no-one fully understands.

So, the GCP website has many bits and parts that aren't "scientific" but may contribute something important to the picture.

Daily Movies

These show what's happening across the network as flashing dots of varying size and color on a map of the world. The dots are the eggs, in their earth-spanning locations, and they show the 24-hour day compressed into a few minutes. Each flash is 5 minutes, and the size and the brightness of the color dot represent the average deviation of that egg's scores. The movies were first created by John Walker, and the current movies are the work of Dale, a professional programmer who is also a sage. There's an archive where you can look at special days, like March 11, 2011, when the Japanese Tsunami hit, or the Haiti earthquake, or the day Steve Jobs died. The archive doesn't go all the way back, but momentous dates like September 11, 2001, are there. The subset of the daily movies programmed by John Walker have a musical rendition of the egg deviations. John thought the result sounds like the composer, John Cage, and I agree.

Realtime Display

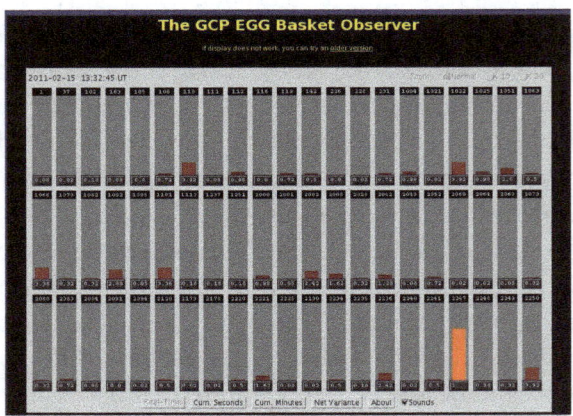

Another special example of the programmer's art is the real time display that shows the second-by-second score deviations of each egg. At this time (early 2017) the display will run only in old browsers because of Java security restrictions. We hope to convert it to HTML5 in the near future. In a rectangular block labeled with the ID number, a color bar rises to a height corresponding to the momentary deviation, and if it reaches a certain minimum, there is a "bing" sound. When the deviation is a bit larger, the bing becomes a more substantial "bong," and if the score is really large, a fairly rare occurrence, the sound is a mighty "gong" of the sort one might hear in a grand ceremony. All this—which is a sparse random composition—is heard against a rhythmic "heartbeat" sound in the background. Designed originally by Dick Bierman and Jaroen Ruuward, it was progressively refined by Nishith Singh, Taylor Jackson, and finally Dale, whose elegant version has been in place for several years. I understand that many people keep this display up on their home computers as a rather unusual background. I like it for a little while, but after a couple of "gongs" I am satisfied to go back to Bach.

The GCP Dot

Another, much quieter real time display (since processing the data takes time, real time means 5 to 10 minutes ago) is the GCP Dot, the aqua-green spot in this illustration. The display was created by Brad Anderson, and it presents the calculated network variance, which is a number representing the "coherence" of the network. The number is translated into a color ranging from blue through green and yellow to red depending on the level of coherence. This "widget" was designed to allow people who like the Dot to download and install it on their computers. Many have done so, and though it can't provide an interpretable measure of coherence (that requires hours of data) it is a captivating live display of the network's state.

The Egghosts Map

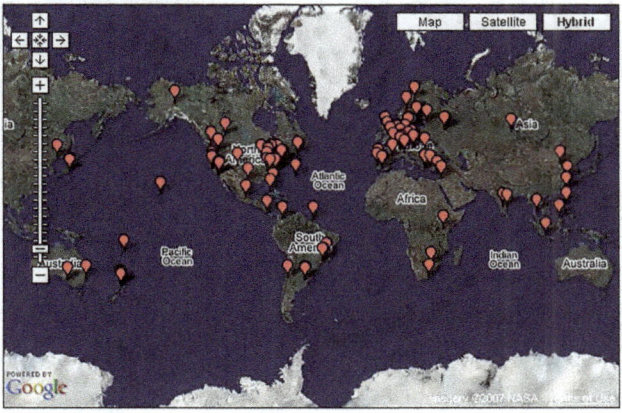

To provide detailed information about the eggs in the GCP network, we have a live Google map with all the eggs that have ever contributed data shown in their locations. There is also a long table accompanying the map, with all the eggs listed, along with

Chapter 14: THE ART OF SCIENCE *123*

the egg host, the location, and some information about the time in service. In a number of cases, the host has changed, but some of the eggs have been running continuously for nearly two decades in their original location. This display is the work of Fernando Lucas Rodriguez, originally, and it was most recently updated by Oliver McDermott. The details of who the hosts are, the exact geographical coordinates, and the date the egg was installed are also available in the Google map mouse-over balloon. The table lists all the pertinent information for people who need it or are simply curious about the eggs and who is hosting them.

Global Brain Painting

Beautiful art created by Bill Scott's "Brainpainting" algorithm shows the GCP data in ethereal displays of color and form. The technology is used by Bill and his colleagues to help identify and treat psychological difficulties by looking at abstract but meaningful patterns created from EEG traces. In the same way, we might be able to grasp something about the structure that occurs in the EGG data. In truth, that is a long shot, but equally valuable at some level is the art itself. Global Brainpaintings are lovely, a felicitous meeting of science and art.

Musical Interlude

One of my aspirations from early in the project was to make music using the random data, especially the segments that were not quite so random. While the full-blown version, with the data processed to specify pitches and rhythms, melody and chords, hasn't matured, several people produced musical vignettes. Leanne Roffey used the data in richly varied short pieces like *Solstice*, shown here, and Jim Burton made a sonic transcription of the long-term data trend. Some samples can be heard at http://global-mind.org/music.html.

I like to imagine that with a thoughtful and imaginative composition, the random numbers would sound like a rich deep chord that is slightly dissonant, with the possibility occasionally to merge into the harmonious song of the universe.

Poetic history

The most obvious aesthetic contributions to learning what the GCP data may be touching upon come from our most intellectual art, the expression of ideas and emotions in language. Especially poetry and the lyrics of song, which are capable of evoking the deeper layers of consciousness. We are moved by music and painting, but language can add understanding to the movement and elicit a more complete recognition of our humanity. The "poetic history" page of the GCP website is a cumulative record of notes and insights that caught my attention as I worked with the often-amazing data over the years. They have a summary quality about them, just as does this beautiful calligraphy by Yifang, which integrates *Focusing, Mind, Nourishing,* and *Qi.*

A scientific aesthetic

Perhaps the value of looking with an artist's eye at the GCP data is to help frame the more difficult questions of meaning and interpretation. Who can say what actually pushes the data away from its normal expectation? It is hard, even for people who know the statistics, to really understand the implications of such departures except in the most mundane way, and even then, with some ambiguity. Is the deviation significant? Well, it depends on your taste in the risks of interpretation. Is it meaningful? What is the criterion by which we judge the importance of tiny differences in numbers that are nominally random—some would say meaningless? What do the statistics really tell us?

For example, most people, including scientists when they are off their guard, don't act as if graphs or Z-scores are mere estimates with a wide range of alternative possibilities. They (we) think that data points are powerful, and that a "significant" score separates winners from losers. But a Z-score has a standard deviation of 1 by definition, and the calculated number represents a range centered on the score and extending both directions. If we have a nominally significant score of 1.645 standard deviations with its corresponding $p = 0.05$, it is our best estimate, but the "real" score might be considerably larger or smaller—there is a 1/20 chance it is actually zero. Of course, it might also be 2.8 or 3 and thus "highly significant," but the point is we do not know, and despite wishing otherwise we must remain humble before the data.

Persuasive conclusions in this statistical realm really depend on repetition, replication of the experiment and a summation across many tests. Each test has the same problem of a low signal-to-noise ratio individually, and real effects are not readily distinguishable from the noise background, but averaging across dozens of instances can raise the signal out of the noise. The noise is random data, while a true effect will have structure, so when we add a dozen datasets together the noise—random positive and negative excursions—will self-cancel, while the structured signal will build up because it comprises relatively consistent deviations. Yet, we often read meaning into singular cases, especially if they match our expectations.

For example

Against this background, I want to show you a picture of data collected when one of our egg hosts died of cancer. Barry Fenn was a friend I never met, though we intended for that to happen. He lived in New Zealand and was an early collaborator, beginning in 1999. The figure shows data from Barry's egg in the upper trace, and data from an egg hosted by a close friend in the lower trace.

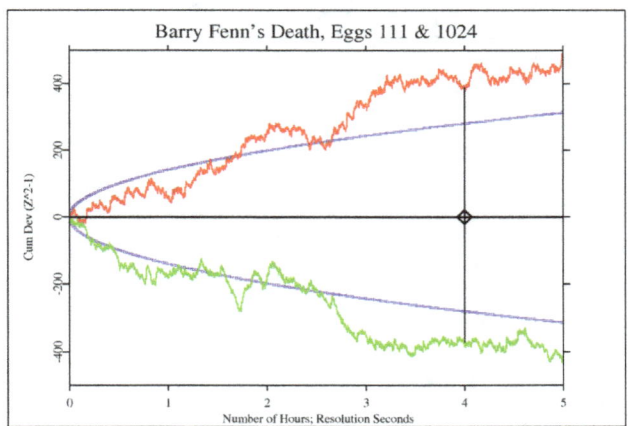

The vertical line shows the moment of his death. We know that the "effects" of consciousness on these devices are so small that individual experiments can't be reliably interpreted—the excursions in a graph like this might be just chance fluctuations. But it is hard to ignore the strength of these deviations, both significant by the usual 5% standard. And it is still more difficult to ignore the symmetry and the timing. I think there is a message here—a vision of love and compassion manifesting in data that should be random, but are not. It obviously is necessary to be careful in such interpretations, but an ancient wisdom has it that a picture is worth a thousand words. When I saw this graph, I felt its emotional power and it brought tears to my eyes. I knew the fragility of the science, but the art went straight to my core.

Part Three: The Results

There is now convincing evidence to challenge the current theory that consciousness can only exist inside the brain.

—Peter Fenwick

Predictions and formal analysis

The Global Consciousness Project maintains a "Hypothesis Registry" in which the details of an event, including the exact times of its beginning and ending and the specifications for the analysis to be used for testing the prediction.[61] This list, which as of late 2015 had 500 events, completely defines the "Formal" database on which we base the statistical analyses that test the GCP hypothesis. The archive of formal event analyses is available on the website in a huge table that contains links to separate webpages for the events. Each event has a narrative description including information from news sources giving times and some indication of its magnitude or importance. There is a summary of the statistical results and one or more graphs showing what the data look like during the event. The results page also includes a table summarizing the current "bottom line" across all events, and two summary graphs, one showing a scatterplot of individual outcomes, and one showing the cumulative deviation over the years. The latter is especially striking because although there are "misses" as well as "hits," the hits clearly dominate, comprising about 2/3 of all the events, and the data curve shows an obvious steady departure from expectation. It is useful to note that the formal series is in fact a meta-analysis of the growing database of replications of a consistent protocol testing the separate and independent event hypotheses. The meta-analysis provides a rigorous test of our general hypothesis.

Analysis strategies

Automated processing assesses the data in a first pass, to ensure all is well. Graphs and tables visualize the data in 15-minute blocks, allowing us to see at a glance that the data meet normal expectations. If an RNG breaks down and produces errant data, scripts using strict criteria flag the errors. We take advantage of modern technology to make sure the data we process in the analysis phase of the experiment are clean.

The hypothesis registry (our list of formal predictions) specifies the timing of events we have selected, and the statistics that will be applied. We look at intercorrelations of the eggs, which can be seen in patterns of mean shifts and variance changes. Graphs are used to visualize departures from expectation, and to summarize results. Secondary analyses look at a variety of independent indicators of non-random behavior, and we will describe these later. First, we'll look at a sampling that gives an idea of the kinds of events we select and a taste of the results. We'll look at positive outcomes, which confirm the hypothesis, and also some "backwards" results, which go against the hypothesis and subtract from the bottom line. We learn a little from each new event, including those which have a null outcome or go the "wrong" way. Among the examples are some that will cause you to scratch your head—how can that be considered a "global" event? The explanation is simple in one sense, though it can get complicated (for example, does strength of coherence compensate for small numbers of people involved?) We want to learn what matters in creating the data correlations, and to do so we need to explore the constraints and the range of situations capable of producing the anomalous effects.

Choices made in selecting an event and the prediction of the exact time period are crucial to the outcome, as it turns out. We have studied the effect of making an event longer or shorter than the original specification, or starting it earlier or later. Such changes can make a large difference in the outcome due to the noisiness of GCP data—the anomalous effect is a small overlay on random variation. Thus, small shifts in the placement of the "event" on the continuous data sequence can produce substantial changes in the statistical outcome simply because the random variation is large compared to the effect size. This means we have to consider the possibility that some part of the apparent effect could be attributable to the experimenter or analyst choosing, albeit without any knowledge of the results, just the right time and exactly the optimal blocking of the data. Of course, the result is still anomalous, but the implications and interpretations must differ.

Chapter 15: EVENT CATEGORIES AND RESULTS

Chance is always powerful. Let your hook be always cast: in the pool where you least expect it, there will be a fish.

—*Ovid*

Great natural tragedies sometimes focus the attention of people all around the world. But which ones? Do we look only at those in which a criterion number of people die or those which are truly surprising, such as earthquakes? Is it still a global event if we are able to forecast and prepare for it, like a hurricane? We should also look at major accidents, like plane crashes that focus global attention, but these share with floods and tornadoes an inevitability, and though we feel sadness or compassion, we accept these as the way the world is. On the other hand, disasters created by human acts are more terrible because we see them as preventable or unnecessary, and therefore as doubly tragic. Sometimes we say and half believe that it is "human nature" to make war or to go on a murderous rampage, but there are real differences from nature's acts. A volcanic eruption and a terrorist attack may both kill, but there is nobody to fear or blame for the natural event, and our compassionate energies can be focused on recovery, undiluted by anger and fear. We don't really know enough to answer such questions *a priori*, so we sample widely, hoping to make some progress toward understanding the subtleties.

We look for positive moments that bring large numbers together as well. Opportunities for conscious cooperation are enhanced in today's communication environment, and the idea of doing something about peace and the creation of a positive future has become the focus of an increasing number of organized "global" meditations or calls to prayer. In a similar mode, major political events such as presidential elections attract and gather attention. World-spanning interest in sports such as World Cup Soccer synchronize the thoughts and emotions of many millions. The variety of possible venues and activities we might select is practically unlimited, but our aim is to accumulate a number of repetitions of similar events in a few categories.

Let us go to some examples for a more concrete picture of the process. These are drawn from the formal results table, and include the event number, its name, and a date written in the form Year Month Day. Thus, for the African Embassy bombings which happened on August 7, 1998, the date is written as 1998 08 07. I will group the events in seven categories that we have regularly observed, rather than in a chronological order. The categories we will sample are:

1. Terror attacks and war

2. Natural disasters

3. Celebration and sharing

4. Compassion and empathy

5. Cosmic and social abstractions

6. Powerful interest

7. Deliberate focus

The examples in this section are presented in some detail, but for complete information about these and all other events in the formal series, please go to http://global-mind.org/results.html. This page includes the description and the outcome for the 500 formal tests along with a link to the formal hypothesis register. It also has a link to the series of exploratory analyses, which are just that—explorations of occasions or events that are not included in the primary experiment. They are excursions attempting to expand the range of questions to see what matters, and were quite often just playful probes to satisfy curiosity.

I've chosen to use as examples major events that most people will recall, though the years have dimmed our memories. The descriptions are what was written at the time, and most of them do convey something of the feelings created by the events. The majority of the selected examples have the predicted positive outcome, but a few cases showing opposite trends are included. Of course, there are the null outcomes—harder to represent usefully—which, depending on the criterion used, comprise a large portion, nearly half of all events. To have a comprehensive impression it is necessary to scan through the long list of results on our website, but this sampling is a good start, selected to give a fair impression of the range and character of the GCP events.

15.1 Terror attacks and war

Terror attacks, especially when they galvanize attention globally, are an obvious subset of major events we should consider. Unfortunately, recent history has provided many examples. The GCP criteria provide that we choose the most surprising and terrible cases. In this category we have also included the beginning moments of wars, attempting to capture the surge of emotional interest that occurs when the world-scape changes.

Embassy Bombings, 1998 08 07 (event 1)
The first actual data were taken in the working network on the 5th of August, 1998, with three eggs running, two in Princeton and one in Neuchâtel, Switzerland. The first event for which we made a prediction was just three days later: the bombing of two American embassies in Africa on the 8th of August. This shocking breach of civilized practice was a focus for concern around the world, and seemed a perfect example of the general idea we were pursuing. The news reports reached me while I was at a conference in Halifax, NS, Canada, and very much out of the normal communication loops. It obviously focused attention from all around the world. There were several colleagues interested in the EGG project who were also at the conference and we took advantage of the opportunity to discuss strategies and tactics for what would be a very long-running experiment.

The embassy bombings provided a real-world example of the kind of event we wanted to study and it shifted our focus from the theoretical to the practical. Of course. we had no background of experience to shape the formal predictions, so this first event required us to take a chance, to make guesses about what data segments we should specify as the "global consciousness event." While all the care and rigor of a formal experiment were applied, this was properly a pilot study to test our planned experimental approach. As we would see, the first simple analyses showed a remarkable jump in the absolute scores at the time of the bombing, continuing for a few hours. In statistical terms, this inaugural "global event" showed one of the strongest effects we have seen, with a probability less than 1 in 1000 that it would happen merely by chance. Here is the event description as written in 1998:

> The first formal prediction for the EGG project was made by RDN, in 1998-08-08, while traveling in Halifax. It concerned the Embassy bombings in Nairobi and Tanzania, on 1998-08-07 at 07:35 UTC.
>
> Upon my return home, prior to examining data, I made the specific predictions described below. These terrorist attacks exemplify a tearing of the social fabric that would shock a global consciousness temporarily. For this particular event, we had only the general outline for predictions: a period of time, say 10 minutes, surrounding the point event, and a period, say a few hours, following the event during which the world becomes conscious of what has happened.
>
> Analysis looked at the event-period from 07:15 to 07:45, and a three-hour consciousness-spreading period from 07:15 to 10:00. The associated probabilities indicate significant deviations for both (overlapping) time-periods.

With more sophisticated analytical tools available, it was possible later to examine the data for this event in more detail. The network was still small and fragile, and there are periods where the eggs were not all running, so the block Z-scores were based on contributions during some intervals from only one or two of the eggs. Because the network was in a testing phase, we consider this and other early events to be pilot work and it isn't included in rigorous assessments of the database. These early pilot trials are, however, retained in the results table for completeness. In any case, the original calculations were confirmed using more robust procedures, showing a significant accumulation of positive deviations across the three-hour period following the bombing.

NATO Bombs Yugoslavia, 1999 03 24 (event 23)

An opportunity to determine whether acts of war or big changes in the course of war might register came on the 24th of March 1999. At 1900 hours UTC, NATO began bombing in Yugoslavia, with the mission to stop the ethnic cleansing in Kosovo fostered by the Serbian regime of Slobodan Milosevic. Although warnings and threats of such an action had been increasing in seriousness, this was shocking and frightening to the world. The prediction was made that the first hour of the bombing would correspond to a significant deviation in GCP data, and a hand calculation using 15-minute Z-scores indicated a thought-provoking outcome with a low probability that it was just chance fluctuation. The 12 eggs running at the time showed a marginally significant deviation, with a chance probability of p = 0.045 during the hour starting when the first bombs fell.

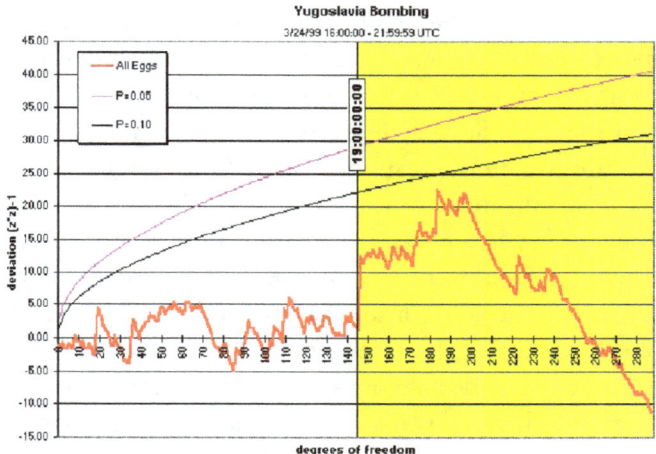

This figure, created by George deBeaumont using the second-by-second data, shows that moment and the surrounding period of 6 hours.

It is tempting to look at the fine details of graphs like these as meaningful, but the formal test of the hypothesis is just the final value of the deviation across the period defined as the event.

Although we know from first principles, as well as from assessment of the small signal-to-noise ratio in the GCP data, that we can't reliably interpret individual events, they often seem meaningful. The graphic display of data taken around the beginning of the bombing actually looks like an appropriate reflection of the dismay and concern generated by this major outbreak of war activity in the world. As George observed, "The emotional analogy is striking (3 hours of calm, 1 hour of shock, followed by 2 hours of despair)." We are, of course, aware of the pitfalls of interpretation in this area, but speaking for myself as a person for whom both objective and subjective aspects are important, I see the correspondence of data with world events linked in this way as a meaningful story.

9/11 Terrorist Disaster, 2001 09 11 (event 80)

One event stands out prominently in the history of the project: the terrorist attacks we refer to as 9/11. The following material shows the behavior of the GCP's network of 37 RNG devices placed around the world as they responded during that day. We'll look at the period of time specified in the formal prediction, and also at explorations to learn more about the context and the broader effects on the eggs. Several analysts worked separately but cooperatively to illuminate the response of the GCP network.

A formal summary of the work was published in the journal *Foundations of Physics Letters*.[62] This was not an easy thing. Four of us polished the paper to make it viable for a mainstream journal by excising all references to consciousness research and scientific parapsychology (except in the references). The result was a canonical objective report, but despite our efforts, the content was so unusual and foreign that it was given to no less than seven reviewers to read. We believe it finally was accepted because the editor saw merit in the paper and very much wanted to make it available to physicists and other experts for study. In contrast, the editor for another major journal, *Nature*, said, "This material would not be of interest to our readers." Science is a great tool, but scientists and science editors can be quite stodgy.

The analyses and descriptions for this event were originally written in 2001, and in the meantime we have learned more. It is clear that the formal prediction for deviation during a period of a little more than four hours covered only part of the action—the deviation that begins during this period evidently continues for more than two days. The informally defined variance assessment, which aroused lots of excitement in 2001, can be much refined now, and we can say that even with a highly conservative assessment it remains statistically significant. Yet, although 9/11 was an exceptionally powerful event, it can't be taken by itself as proof of a global consciousness effect. As we have noted repeatedly, that requires the patient accumulation of replications. Thankfully they do not have to be devastating terror attacks.

For a poignant and meaningful rendition of this event, arguably the most potent we have recorded in the history of the GCP, it is worth reading the description as it was written in the immediate and still overwhelming presence of the event:

9/11—as it was happening

On September 11, 2001, beginning at about 8:45 in the morning, a series of terrorist attacks destroyed the twin towers of the World Trade Center and severely damaged the Pentagon. The disaster is so great that in New York we have as yet, two days later, only guesses about how many thousands of people perished when the WTC towers collapsed. Commercial airliners were hijacked and flown directly into the three buildings. The first crashed into the North tower at 8:45, and about 18 minutes later the second airliner hit the South tower. At about 9:40, a third airliner crashed into the Pentagon. At 9:58, the South tower collapsed, followed by the North tower at 10:28.

The behavior of the Global Consciousness Project's network of 37 RNG devices called "eggs" placed around the world as they responded during various periods of time surrounding September 11 was remarkable. The eggs generate random data continuously and send it for archiving and analysis to a dedicated server in Princeton, New Jersey, USA. We analyze the data to determine whether the normally random array of values shows structure correlated with global events. The underlying motivation for this work is to discover whether there is evidence for an anomalous interaction driving the eggs to non-random behavior. In a metaphoric sense, we are looking for evidence of a developing global consciousness that might perceive and react to events with deep meaning.

The whole world reeled in disbelief and horror as the news of the terrorist attack and the unspeakable tragedy unfolded. The EGG network registered an unmistakable and profound response.

I want to acknowledge that I like the idea of "Global Consciousness," but that this idea is really an aesthetic speculation. I don't think we should claim that the statistics and graphs representing the data prove the existence of a global consciousness. But we do have strong evidence of anomalous structure in what should be random data, and clear correlations of these unexplained departures from expectation with well-defined events that are of special importance to people. The events share a common feature, namely, that they engage our attention, and draw us in large numbers into a common focus.

What we see in the data recorded on September 11, 2001 and the surrounding period is more distinct than usual—the deviations are larger and more persistent than for most events. The statistics we picture are the best description we can give of measurements and effects that are essentially mysterious. We do not know how the correlations that arise between electronic random event generators and human concerns come to be, and yet the results of our analyses are unequivocal. We cannot explain the presence of stark patterns in data that should be random, nor do we have any way of divining their ultimate meaning, but there is an important and uniquely powerful message here. When we ask why the disaster in New York and Washington and Pennsylvania should appear to be responsible for a strong signal in our world-wide network of instruments designed to generate random noise, there is no obvious answer. When we look carefully and discover that the eggs might reflect our shock and dismay even before our minds and hearts express it, we confront a still deeper mystery.

This network, which we designed as a metaphoric EEG for the planet, responded as if it were measuring brain waves on a planetary scale. We do not know if there is such a thing as a global consciousness, but if there is, it was moved by the events of September 11, 2001. We do not know how, but it appears that the coherence and intensity of our common reaction created a sustained pulse of order in the random flow of numbers from our instruments. These patterns where there should be none look like reflections of our concentrated focus, as the riveting events drew us from our individual concerns and melded us into an extraordinary coherence. Maybe we became, briefly, a global consciousness.

Deviation of Network Variance
The formal prediction for September 11 was essentially the same as that made for the terrorist bombing of American Embassies in Africa in August 1998. That specified a period beginning a few minutes before the bombing and included an aftermath period of three hours. Following that model, I specified a period beginning 10 minutes before the first plane crashed into the WTC tower, and ending four hours after, thus defining a similar aftermath period.

The graph of data from the formal prediction for September 11 shows a fluctuating deviation throughout the moments of the five major events, during which ever-increasing numbers of people around the world were hearing the news and watching in stunned disbelief. The formally specified hypothesis test began at 08:35 Eastern time and ended at 12:45. Times of the major events are marked by boxes on the line of zero deviation. The uncertain fluctuation continues for half an hour after the fall of the second WTC tower. Then, at about 11:00, the cumulative deviation takes on a trend that continues through the aftermath period and ultimately exceeds the significance criterion. There were 37 eggs reporting on September 11, and over the 4 hours and 10 minutes of the prediction period, their accumulated Chisquare was 15332 on 15000 degrees of freedom. The final probability for the formal hypothesis test was 0.028, which is equivalent to an odds ratio of 35 to one against chance.

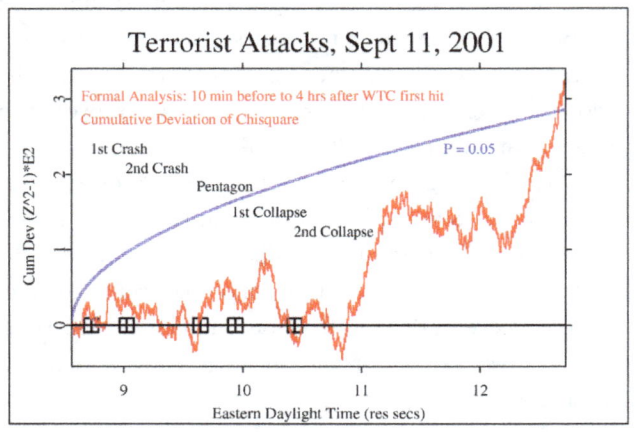

Extensions and Explorations

What we could not know at the time we were trying to deal with the enormity of this event, was that it would have far-reaching consequences, not just in the world, but evidently also in our data. As time allowed, we did a great deal of exploratory work on the data to see whether there might be other indications of structure. Among the analyses was a simple temporal extension to look at four days of data on either side of September 11 in the same format as the formal analysis (Sept 7 to 15). What becomes apparent is that the data from several days before the attacks are a pretty normal random walk, but the data during and afterward are distinctly anomalous. Because any structure there might be in the data is superimposed on random noise, we can't identify changes with great precision, but there is a period on the order of three days during which the data deviations are consistently positive, resulting in a steady slope. Interpretation is limited by the fact this is a *post hoc* analysis, but we know that the database of nearly three years up to that time had no similarly persistent deviation over so long a time.

The figure shows nine days centered on the attack, which is marked with a black square. The smooth curve beginning at the time of the attacks is a 5% probability envelope that provides a

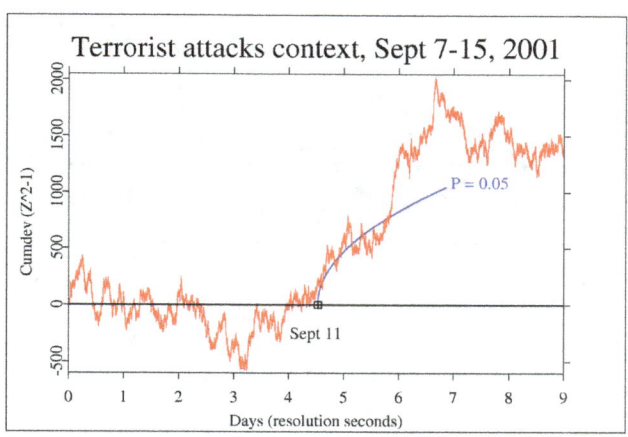

scale for the extraordinary non-random deviation. The slope of the graph beginning when the first WTC tower was hit and continuing for nearly three days, to the end of the 13th, is extreme. An informal estimate for the probability can be made, and lies between 0.003 and 0.0003 (this means an odds ratio on the order of 1 in 1000). If we extrapolate the anomalous trend, it appears to begin well before the terrorist attack. Because the data are noisy this is difficult to confirm, but we will return to the question later when we look at a different measure where it is easier to pinpoint changes.

Dean Radin's analysis of the same data using a different perspective and analytical approach shows an even more stark shift of the data from what's expected. He writes:

"This graph shows results for a 6-hour sliding window, in terms of z scores, from Sept 6–13. In this graph, positive z's mean the RNGs became 'more ordered' than expected by chance. Negative z's mean the RNGs became 'more random' than expected by chance. The peak value in this graph is at 9:10 AM, Sept 11. Between the beginning of the tragedy and 7 hours later this data shows a drop of 6.5 sigma (odds against chance of 29 billion to 1). Such large changes will eventually occur by chance, of course, but this particular change happened during an unprecedented event, suggesting that this 'spike' and 'rebound' were not coincidental."

Dean also looked at the data expressed in terms of their odds against chance, and the result makes clear that the network had

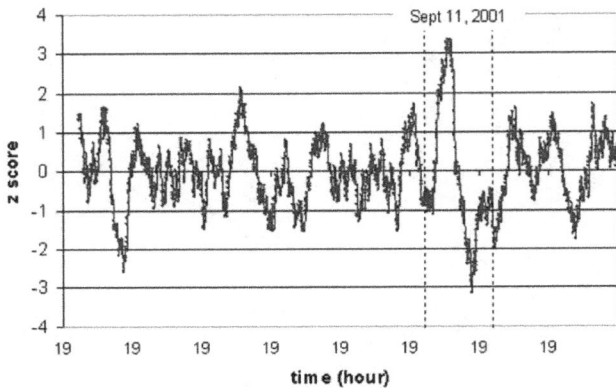

registered something extraordinary. Over the three years of the project, we had never before seen such an extreme divergence from normal expectations for random data. The GCP instrument captured the moment and established its power in the objective language of statistics.

Odds ratios

Another perspective on 9/11 looks at the odds against chance for the second-by-second deviations on September 11. The maximum odds ratio during the day is equivalent to a Z-score of 4.81, and occurs at 10:12:47, EDT, during the heroic struggle aboard the fourth hi-jacked plane, which crashed in Pennsylvania. Such a large Z-score would appear by chance only once in about a million seconds (roughly two weeks). The figure shows this extraordinary spike (the straight line near the middle), along with a trace of smoothed data showing the relative intensity of that moment compared with smaller spikes during the day. The large deviation dominates the graph, obscuring other details, and to display them we use smoothing to reduce the effect of extreme values. Smoothing means the raw data are averaged within a "window" of a specified length, for example, an hour, and then the window is shifted to the next data point. This is repeated across the period of interest, and the moving average is then plotted. The straight verticals show the large odds ratios in the raw data, while the jagged trace shows the smoothed data, which have a different scale. The largest spike in the smoothed data has a chance odds ratio of about 1 in 1000. The smoothing allows us to see the range and the timing of relatively large deviations.

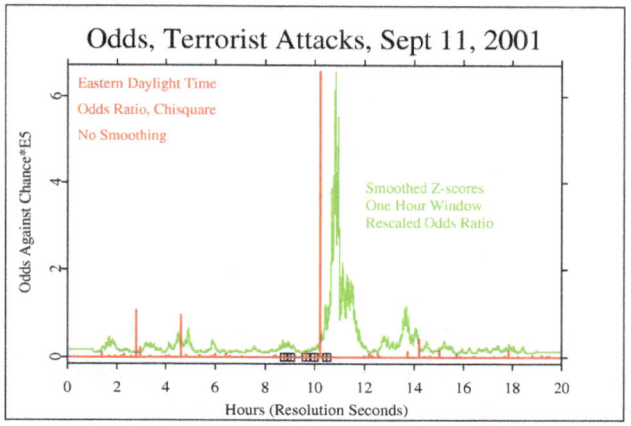

A measure of variance on 9/11

There was a second pre-planned and statistically independent analysis of data on 9/11, although the statistical procedure was not specified with sufficient clarity to be included in the formal replication series. We examined the data using a measure of the variability of scores among the individual eggs. This figure shows the result as a cumulative deviation of device variance across the 37 eggs on September 11. It was generated as a test of Dean Radin's prediction that the variance would show strong fluctuations: "I'd predict something like ripples of high and low variance, as the emotional shocks continue to reverberate for days and weeks." Although this was only a partial specification, it is effectively a hypothesis stating that the variance around the time of the disaster should deviate from expectation.

This device variance measure shows a normal fluctuation around the horizontal line of expectation until about four or five hours before the attack, and then a steep and persistent rise indicating a great excess of variance, continuing until about 11:00. Shortly thereafter a long period begins during which the data show an equally precipitous decrease of variance. For comparison, the figure also shows pseudo-random control data (light blue) treated with the same analysis.

It is difficult to make a direct calculation of probability for this figure, but the extreme excursion in Dean's similar approach

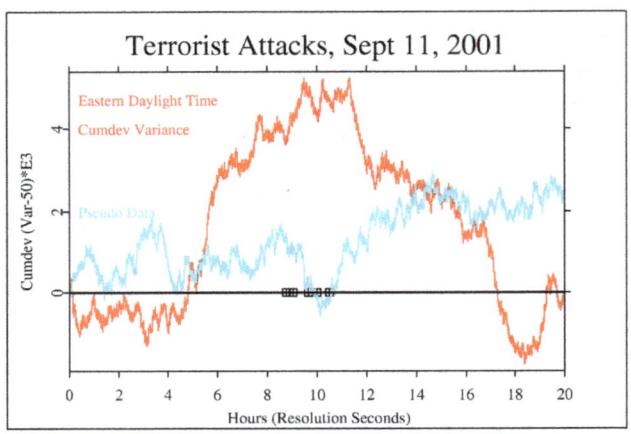

indicates a deviation of more than three sigma after correction for multiple analysis, and that corresponds to odds of less than 1 in 1000. A permutation analysis to determine how often such an extreme excursion occurs in randomly ordered sequences gives a background against which the original temporal sequence can be compared. The result is p = 0.0048, based on 10,000 iterations. A more recent computation using empirical rather than theoretical expectation yields p = 0.0009. These estimates are all in the same ballpark, and they indicate that a chance explanation is very unlikely to account for the variance data.

We don't have explanations for these striking indications, but they point to more questions that deserve attention. One of those is the suggestion that we are looking at experimenter effects, rather than an effect of what we're calling global consciousness. That idea might work for simple, immediate correlations with the intention in an experiment. But it would require a truly remarkable stretch of logic to apply such an explanation to a spreading effect over a range of time around the data like that shown for 9/11. We are in an unusual position because we have complete and continuous data that allows us to look at contextual surroundings, both in space and time, so there is some promise of achieving a better understanding.

When we examine the pseudo-random control data generated for September 11, 2001, we see no sustained periods of strong deviation in any of the measures we use. In other words, the algorithmically-generated data provide another comparison standard against which the 9/11 data stand out.

Autocorrelation

For me, one of the most persuasive displays of the data from 9/11 in statistical terms is one looking at autocorrelation, as shown here. Randomness is defined in part by the independence of the elements in a sequence. Truly random data don't correlate from one moment to the next; each trial or bit in a sequence is a new sample with no relationship to what has gone before. The so-called "gambler's fallacy" is to believe that if a coin has fallen heads several times in a row, the next toss must be tails. That is not true—a fair coin will continue to have a 50/50 chance for heads no matter how many prior tosses were all heads. A random sequence does not exhibit autocorrelation.

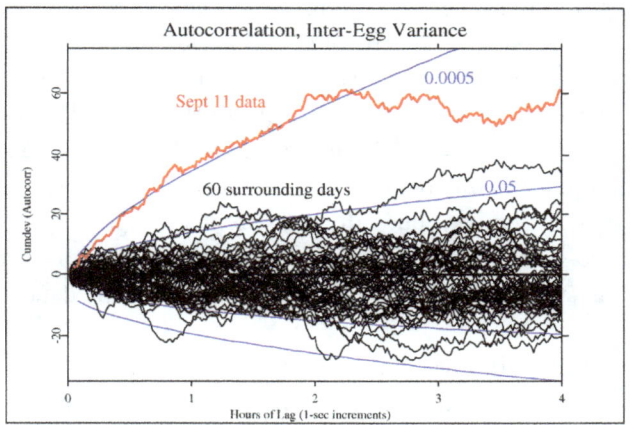

The GCP's variance measure on 9/11 should follow this rule, of course, assuming there is no effect. But it shows strong autocorrelation. The data sequence becomes predictable to a significant degree over periods (lags) up to about two hours. In the figure, which shows the cumulative deviation of the autocorrelation as the lag period increases, it is easy to see that the September 11 data don't belong to the distribution of autocorrelation functions created by looking at days surrounding 9/11, from a month before to a month after that day. This is such a stark difference that the likelihood it is just a chance fluctuation is 1 in 2000. The data from 9/11 are not random. (calculation by Bancel)

Another, and very important question to ask is whether there might be correlations of the GCP data deviations with independent, but logically relevant indicators. As part of the 9/11 analysis effort, Dean Radin asked whether there is any correlation of the deviations with news intensity. Here is an excerpt from the Foundations of Physics article:

> We observe by inspection that world events noted in the prediction registry tend to occur on days with significantly higher average pair correlations among the RNGs. To assess this relationship quantitatively, an objective metric was constructed based on an independent daily assessment of newsworthy events by a professional news service not associated with this project.[63] The count of letters used in the daily summaries of news items was taken to represent the news "intensity," Over the one-year period from Dec. 2000 through Nov. 2001, this measure, though diffuse, is correlated with daily mean pair correlations of the RNG data at r = 0 .15, which has p = 0.002 and a Z-score = 2.9.[64] We note that this statistic is independent of the selection of events in the prediction registry, but fully consistent with the results for the pre-specified analyses since it correlates a measure of the importance of world events with deviations in the database.

Using a variety of exploratory methods in addition to the formal analyses to visualize structure in the GCP data, it appears from several perspectives that there is a concentration of strong deviations around the major events of September 11, and that they are associated with the mass attention given to the tragedy.

We have carefully considered the validity and reliability of our analyses, and they are sound. They provide a solid foundation for other interesting analyses. For example, we can ask whether the responses of the GCP network are affected by the distance of eggs from the locus of the attacks or by the distances separating the eggs. It is also important to develop ways to confirm or reject the suggestions of a precursor effect that shows up in the original analyses. It looks increasingly like effects over both distance and time are normal aspects of our data, suggesting that a unified mind gathers across great distances and may also integrate across time.

Finally, although we have to be careful not to over-interpret the data from 9/11 (because the statistical conclusions have big error bars) they seem strong enough to take some risk. We use standard statistical and mathematical tools to identify the structures that appear in the data, and simple graphs to visualize them. But these are transparent images—pictures worth a thousand words—of real data, showing how strikingly different the behavior of the random numbers was in comparison with other days and with theoretical expectations. It is not a big step to attribute meaning to the statistics, and to conclude that the GCP network could detect and respond to our human shock and pain.

15.2 Natural disasters

Large destructive earthquakes, typhoons, tsunamis, especially when they are characterized by many deaths, evoke strong and widespread reactions. Though we know natural disasters will occur, the big ones definitely create synchronized feelings of concerned horror, sadness, and compassion.

Indonesian Earthquake, 2006 05 27 (event 217)
May 27 (Bloomberg) Condolences and aid pledges poured into Indonesia after a magnitude 6.2 earthquake in central Java killed more than 3,000 people and left thousands injured.

The main temblor struck at 5:54 a.m. local time near the city of Yogyakarta. Most damage occurred further south in Bantul, where homes and buildings collapsed, according to John Budd, the United Nations Children's Fund's communications officer. The earthquake struck about 60 kilometers north of Mount Merapi, where authorities evacuated people this month on concern it may erupt. Later reports attempted to reduce those fears. The quake won't make an eruption more likely, AFP said, citing seismologists. No tsunami has been reported. The death toll has been rising steadily through the day. Indonesia's social affairs ministry most recently said 3,068 people were killed, according to Sky News.

The GCP prediction is similar to that for recent quakes, with a pre-quake period of an hour or so, and total duration of 8 hours.

The statistical result is very strong, with a consistent deviation that culminates with a p-value of 0.0041 and Z of 2.645. The graph shows with great clarity how different the data are from random expectation.

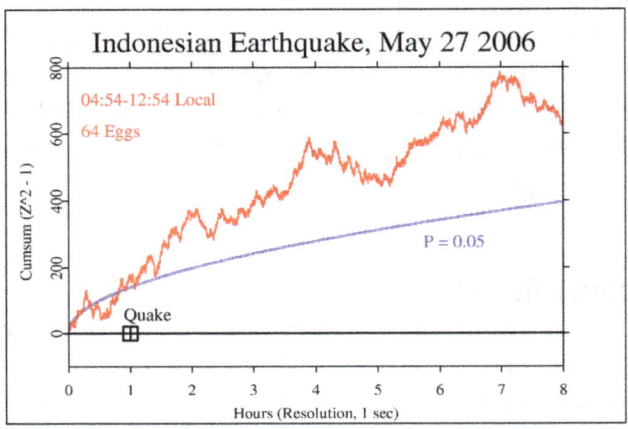

Earthquake Haiti, 2010 01 12 (event 320)

From MSNBC and NBC News:

PORT-AU-PRINCE, Haiti - A powerful earthquake hit the impoverished country of Haiti on Tuesday, collapsing the presidential palace and numerous other critical government buildings and raising fears of substantial casualties in what a witness called "a major, major disaster."

The earthquake had a magnitude of 7.0 and was centered about 10 miles west of the capital, Port-au-Prince, according to the U.S. Geological Survey. It was followed by at least eight powerful aftershocks of magnitude 5.0 or greater, the USGS reported.

"People are out in the streets, crying, screaming, shouting," Karel Zelenka, director of the Catholic Relief Services office in Haiti told The Washington Post. "They see the extent of the damage," he said, but can do little to rescue people.
From The Globe and Mail Wednesday morning:

One of the most powerful earthquakes to ever hit the region slammed impoverished Haiti, leaving the nation in chaos and the global community scrambling to assess the damage and bring aid.

Cinderblock slums collapsed in cascading layers of concrete and dust, government buildings were reduced to rubble and panicked crowds were left trapped in the dark as night fell in areas with few emergency resources.

The 7.0 earthquake hit about 16 kilometres southwest of the densely populated capital Port-au-Prince in the late afternoon. Powerful aftershocks continued into the early hours of Wednesday morning, creating confusion on the ground and internationally as power and communication signals were knocked out across the country.

The International Federation of the Red Cross estimated that up to three million people have been affected by the powerful earthquake.

Spokesman Paul Conneally told The Associated Press on Wednesday that it would take 24-48 hours before a clear picture emerges of the scale of the destruction.

The formal GCP event was set for an 8-hour period beginning at 20:00 UTC, a little less than 2 hours before the 7.0 temblor. The result shows a strong, steady negative trend through the whole time, with $p = 0.980$ and $Z = -2.060$. The odds against chance for this result is on the order of 2 parts in 100.

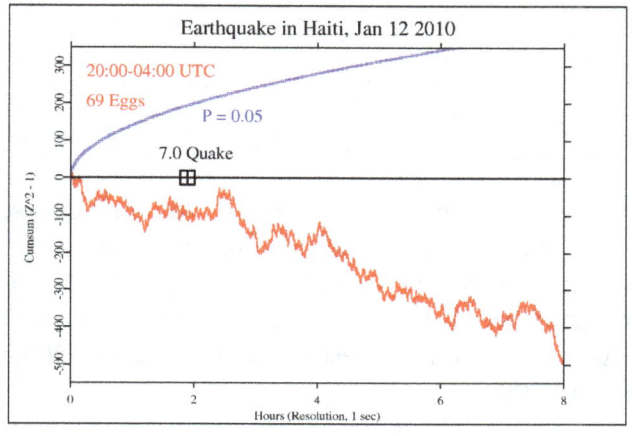

This is an example of what may be a "true negative" effect. Our prediction is for a positive deviation, so this result subtracts from the bottom line that reflects the composite score across all events. Nevertheless, we may be able to learn from it, especially if we discover commonality among events with such strong "backwards" outcomes.

A different statistical view of the data around the quake plots the average deviation of the eggs over time. It is another perspective on a powerful event affecting millions of people in Haiti and evoking compassion and concern from many millions more around the world.

The figure shows this calculation as the smoothed average of the raw data (using a 2-hour window). The data show a large spike exactly at the time of the main temblor. It would have odds of about 100 to 1 if all parameters were prespecified. This exploratory analysis should not over-interpreted, but the spike does have exquisite timing. Towards the end of Jan 13 there is another group of large statistically improbable spikes in the data, perhaps responsive to the horrifying magnitude of the tragedy.

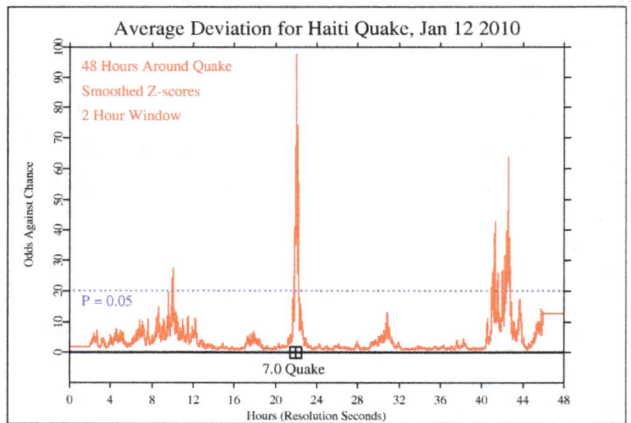

The damage is immense, and there are rough guesses being made about the loss of life, with suggestions of many tens of thousands, possibly more than 100,000 people dead. Ultimately, these estimates were far short of the actual terrible death toll. We know now that the numbers came to at least 250,000, probably more than 300,000.

15.3 Celebration and sharing

Ceremonies and participatory events, like New Year's and various religious gatherings, offer a look at the more positive events that connect us in shared moments. Some of these are sharply focused and geographically localized so the numbers of engaged people can be roughly estimated. Others are more global in nature, with celebrations all around the world, and although there is little information on actual numbers, there is fair certainty that tens or hundreds of millions will be participating.

Y2K New Year's, 1999 12 31 – 2000 01 01 (Event 42)

The transition to the year 2000 was a major event all around the world, and of course a major event for the Global Consciousness Project. Here we present the primary results for the formal predictions along with some of the subsidiary and exploratory analyses which were done to examine the data taken around the time of the New Year's transition.

Based on the results shown during the New Year's transition 1998 to 1999, a similar prediction was made that the Y2K data would show unusual structure around midnight, specifically in the period of midnight ± 5 minutes, across all eggs and all time zones. The hypothesis specified that the raw second-by-second data would be used, and that the measure would be the composite Chisquare representing the total deviation from expectation across all data for the 10-minute period. One of the assumptions made for the sake of hypothesis generation for the GCP is that the effects are spatially non-local, and under this assumption, all the eggs are affected by events, no matter where they take place on the earth. Thus, at midnight in any given time zone, we hypothesize that the effects of the conscious engagement of everyone celebrating at that moment will be felt by all eggs in the GCP network. An hour later, when the celebration reaches the next time zone, there will again be a global effect, impinging on all of the GCP devices.

On Saturday, 1 Jan 2000, George deBeaumont sent the first-cut analyses. He looked at the results for individual eggs, but our planned formal analysis was focused on the network as a whole.

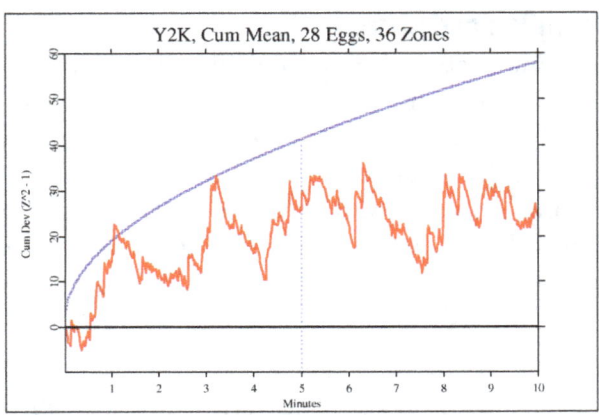

This figure shows the cumulative deviation of Chisquare (Z^2) from theoretical expectation versus the time in seconds (the degrees of freedom for the Chisquare). This is a measure of the degree to which the output of the REG devices departs from the expected mean for the trial values recorded each second. If there is no anomalous change in the mean outcome, the resulting cumulative deviation trace should resemble a random walk around zero deviation. If some persistent anomalous effect is present, the trace will show a consistent trend, which may culminate in a statistically significant departure. The deviation here is clearly positive, though not significant, with a Chisquare of 624.4 on 600 degrees of freedom, and an associated p-value of 0.237.

Independent prediction: Smoothed variance
Dean Radin took a different approach to the data, based on the idea that increased coherence will be present in the data, generated in response to the coherent interactions of large numbers of people celebrating the Y2K transition together. This conception leads to an expectation that the variance of the REG data should be decreased around the moment of greatest engagement. The obvious prediction is for that moment to occur just at midnight, with a buildup before and some lingering period of continuing celebration after. The analysis procedure uses a measure of the variance across all eggs, averaged across time zones, and smoothed with a 5-minute wide sliding window.

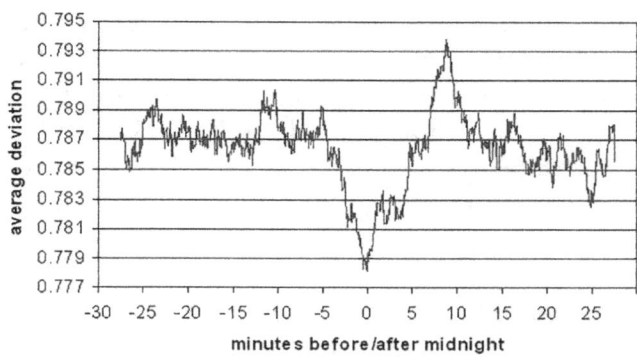

The result is shown in this figure. As explained in the detailed description on the website, this analysis uses a non-standard, exploratory approach, but it has been cross-checked, primarily using a permutation analysis, where the data are scrambled and the same analysis performed repeatedly, in this case 2000 times. This provides a background against which the actual data can be compared, and the Z-score combining the extreme minimum value of the variance with the minimum time separation from midnight is -3.662, a value that corresponds to a probability against chance of 0.0001. Since Dean's analysis procedure was not completely pre-specified, but was developed by trying several approaches, his calculated probability needs to be adjusted to compensate fairly for multiple analyses and the selection of the best of several outcomes. Dean reported that he tried about 10 different analyses and the appropriate Bonferroni correction, multiplying the probability by a factor of 10, still leaves an impressively small probability, on the order of 1 in 1000, for the highly focused minimum at midnight for the Y2K transition.

Ed May and James Spottiswoode have provided independent oversight and cross-checks. Their calculations give similar results, but they do not concur with the interpretations because the strong result is critically dependent on choice of analysis parameters. In addition, whereas Dean originally specified 24 time zones, Ed and James argue that there are large populations in some of the half-hour offset time zones.

The figure suggests that something special did occur in the GCP data around midnight. The variance drops precipitously as midnight approaches, and reaches its extreme minimum at three seconds before midnight, the moment of transition. I explored simpler ways of looking at the measure and found it to be a good indicator of a special time around the New Year's midnight. A rigorously specified version of the analysis has been used for all subsequent New Year's.

What is the source?

These results, and some others in the GCP database, have generated considerable commentary, and among the "alternative" explanations that are offered is the proposition that it may all be an "experimenter effect." This is not meant as a suggestion that there is anything wrong with the behavior of the researchers or the protocols, but as an interpretation that the source of the effect is not global consciousness, but the intentions or the consciousness of the experimenters. I mentioned this concern to a sage I know and she said, "So what? We can all be experimenters."

That made me laugh, for it does so succinctly put the point that a real effect in this stuff is meaningful, even if it doesn't mean what we might have wished, or what we imagined we could show.

Kumbh Mela, India, 2001 01 24 (event 69)

Kumbh Mela is a great pilgrimage of many millions of Hindus to north India where they bathe in the sacred waters of the Ganges to wash away their past sins and cleanse their spiritual bodies. Two correspondents independently suggested it should be a GCP event, Arvind Panchal and Mahadeva Srinivasan. Arvind wrote on January 10th:

> Dear Dr. Roger,
> The results [of the GCP] have been quite encouraging. I would like to attract your attention to one very big event which is going on in INDIA in a few days. It is MAHAKUMBH Bath time, when people take a holy dip in the river Ganges in Allahabad in INDIA. The MAHAKUMBH comes after 12 years and all true Hindus make it a point to visit the place and take the holy dip. As the newspapers reported yesterday as many as 4.2 [million] people took bath. I feel that this is an event which

must show up in GCP. At least in GCP sites in INDIA we must see the change. I would like to know the results due to the MAHAKUMBH event. The local newspaper sites [give] an update on the MAHAKUMBH.

Arvind

Indeed, the event does show up in our data. With the help of Dr. Mahadeva Srinivasan, a colleague from Chennai, India, who is familiar with the Kumbh, the prediction was made for a deviation of the mean across all eggs during the most concentrated time of the Kumbh. On January 24th, 2001, media sources predicted that 30 million people would try to bathe in the Ganges. We decided that the daylight hours should be the focus of the GCP prediction.

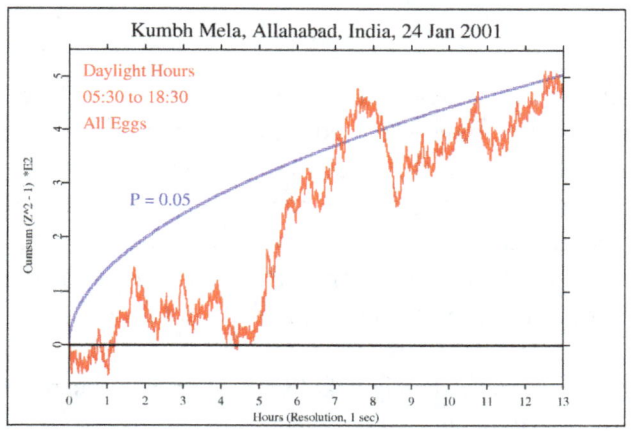

The figure shows the period from early morning to evening, and there is a strong deviation, with a probability of 0.055 (odds of 1 in 20). A control analysis using automatically generated pseudo-random data and the same parameters, has a non-significant p = 0.842. Though the Mahakumbh happens only every 12 years, there are smaller Kumbh Mela events in other years, which still attract millions of pilgrims. We will revisit this huge gathering of humanity with a singular focus in future Kumbh Mela celebrations. It is an opportunity to do relatively strict replications of a natural experiment.

At this writing we have assessed four Kumbh Mela events, and all four have the same signature. Their consistency and the composite result provide good evidence for an effect on the GCP network, with a Z-score of 2.965 corresponding to chance odds of less than 1 in 600.

15.4 Compassion and empathy

Devastating accidents often garner the attention of much of the world population because they are big news events. We also are drawn into a kind of synchronized and sometimes profound social engagement by occasions which demonstrate our essential humanity like the first example below—the remarkable rescue of Chilean miners after weeks underground.

Chilean Miners Alive, 2010 08 22 (event 341)
Over the past few days US media have reported on yet another major mining accident, this time in Chile, where a cave-in trapped some 33 miners. On August 23, our egg host in Chile, Fernando Erbetta Doyharcabal sent an email with the subject line "(Another) miracle in Chile," describing the discovery that all of the miners are alive and the celebration this inspired in Chile.

> Perhaps you have already heard that a miracle occurred yesterday here in Chile.
> 18 days ago, 33 miners got trapped into a copper mine after a landslide literally buried them alive. This happened in Copiapó, in the north of our country.
> Yesterday Sunday 22nd, after 17 days of non-stop work, a probe of only 6 inches in diameter reached the tunnel where the miners supposedly had escaped to (688 meters deep!). And when the technical staff took the probe back to the surface, it had two little pieces of paper attached with messages: "All of us are OK in the shelter". They were alive!
> The news ran in minutes through all our country (and the world) and people celebrated here as if we had won the Soccer

World Cup, children waving Chilean flags, cars honking on the streets, and so on.

All of that happened yesterday mainly since our early morning when we knew that the probe had reached the tunnel (11:00 UTC) until our evening when we had certainty that the miners were alive and OK (23:00 UTC), with one good news following the other. We lived a whole day of real happiness and spiritual communion indeed.

The GCP event was set for 11:00 to 23:00 UTC on that day, as specified by Fernando. The result is quite strong, with $p = 0.016$ and $Z = 2.137$. It looks like compassion in evidence, with odds against chance of about 100 to 1.

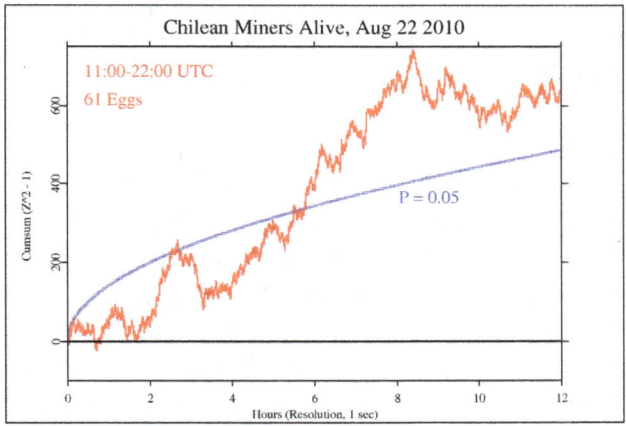

Fernando said that the Chilean egg had been working normally since the last days of July, and thought it might detect the "beautiful emotional atmosphere that we experienced yesterday here in Chile. It would be wonderful to know that. Unfortunately, I am still not able to get the data and process them adequately. So if you or someone in your team could help us, it would be nice. After 18 days underground the first sign came that the 33 miners were alive, and hope for their rescue was reaffirmed."

We did look at the Chilean egg data and found that it also had a strong deviation, mirroring that of the full network.

Nelson Mandela Dies 2013 12 05 (event 472)

Another kind of global event that we examine is based on our admiration for public figures. We definitely pay attention when we hear of the death of a famous person, especially if he or she is honored and loved around the world.

> (CNN) – Nelson Mandela's willingness to forgive and forget helped peacefully end an era of white domination in his native South Africa. But as news of his death spread, mourners there and around the world expressed their feeling that Mandela himself would never be forgotten.
>
> "Mandela's biggest legacy…was his remarkable lack of bitterness and the way he did not only talk about reconciliation, but he made reconciliation happen in South Africa," said F.W. de Klerk, South Africa's last white president before giving way to Mandela, the country's first black leader.

South Africa's current leader announced late Thursday that, after years suffering from health ailments, the man known widely by his clan name of Madiba died at 8:50 p.m. (1:50 p.m. ET) surrounded by family. He was 95. "He is now resting. He is now at peace," President Jacob Zuma said late Thursday. "Our nation has lost its greatest son. Our people have lost a father."

Not surprisingly, many people suggested Mandela's passing should be on our list of global events. I certainly agreed. He was a giant socially and politically, admired and honored by people all

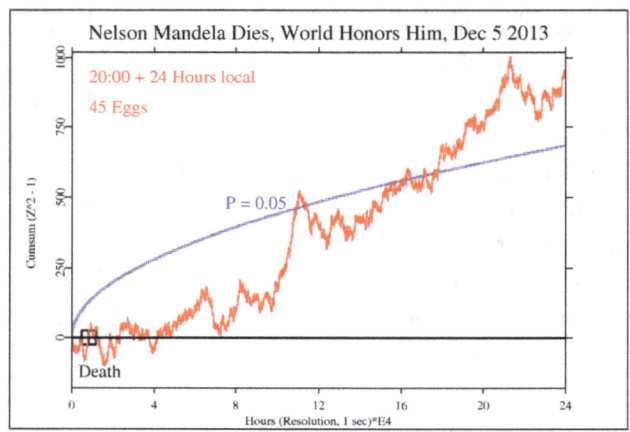

around the world. The GCP event was set for 24 hours, beginning almost an hour before his death, with a time period modeled on the deaths of Ted Kennedy, Michael Jackson, and Pope John. The result has a probability of 0.013 and Z = 2.238. The odds that this is a chance fluctuation are about 1 in 100.

Robert Jahn Dies, 2017 11 15 (Post Formal Series Event)

I continued running the GCP network after the formal series of hypothesis tests ended. My intention was to explore options and to look at important events that might occur for their own sake, not simply to increase the already sufficient database. I want to include this event because it touches on the meaningful, personal character of the work the GCP is designed for, which is of a piece with the work of the PEAR lab. We are ultimately interested in the presence and power of consciousness in the world.

The description here is as I wrote it at the time:

> Dean Robert G. Jahn created the Princeton Engineering Anomalies Research (PEAR) laboratory in 1979. It soon became one of the most productive psi research centers in the history of the field. Together with Brenda Dunne, who managed the lab, and a team of scientists from several fields, Bob broke new ground while also confirming and replicating research from many other sources. The PEAR lab had three major aspects, one assessing mind-machine interaction (MMI), one looking at remote viewing, most notably precognitive remote perception (PRP), and a third aspect focused on theory and modeling.
>
> Bob died on Nov. 15, 2017, early in the morning at his home in Princeton, surrounded by family and loved ones. He had a remarkably influential role in psi research, and the PEAR lab became a home for many and a beacon for far more people looking for inspiration and models that could help understand the extraordinary capacities of human consciousness. He was known around the world as a seminal figure in consciousness research. Among the several independent projects and research programs based on work of the PEAR group is the

Global Consciousness Project. His passing was a profoundly meaningful moment for a great many people.

Given these factors and the interconnections of PEAR and GCP, we decided to look at the data from the GCP network, using the standard analysis procedures applied for other major figures.

Bob died at about 3:00 am on 15 November 2017, which corresponds to 0800 UTC. The GCP event was set for 24 hours beginning at that time. The outcome is a striking trend, shown in the image here, and the analytical result has a probability of 0.001 and $Z = 3.096$.

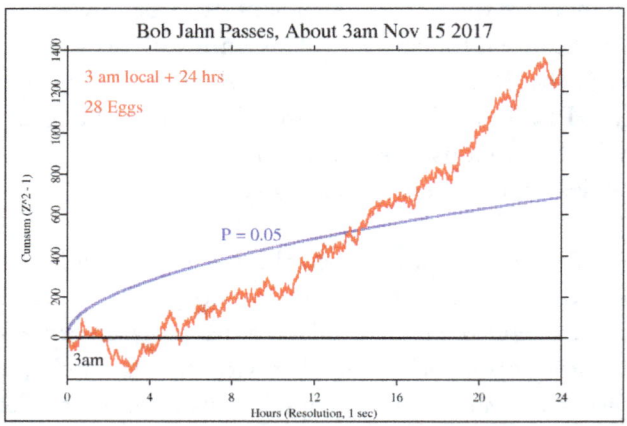

15.5 Cosmic and social abstractions

Humans have probably always sought to chart and understand the great world of nature and the cosmos, and we have created many rituals and celebrations that memorialize our interest in time and the changes of seasons. We learned eons ago to calculate the solstices and predict eclipses, and to generate astrological guides and counsel. We continue most of these traditions even with slight evidence they could matter.

Solar Eclipse, 1999 08 11 (event 33)
A solar eclipse is rare, and for those in its path it definitely demands attention. Does the whole world share the intense focus?

On August 11, 1999, a full Solar eclipse passed over Europe and parts of Asia, in view of large numbers of fascinated people. This figure shows the path of the moon's shadow and the regions where the eclipse could be directly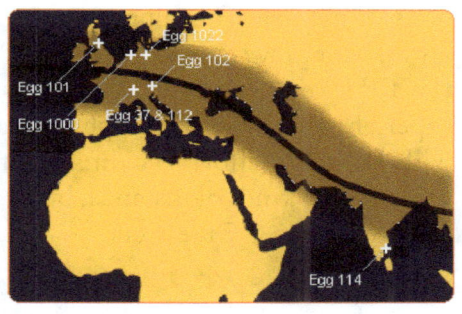
experienced. We predicted the event would generate a widespread coherence of attention and a correlated effect on the GCP eggs. The result was highly instructive. Overall, the deviation was not significant, but George deBeaumont separated out the seven eggs that actually were in the path of the moon's shadow and extracted the corresponding data. For this subset the outcome was highly significant, with a probability of only 3 parts in 10,000.

id	location		peak			period		
			df	chi-sqr	p	df	chi-sqr	p
101	Edinburgh, Scotland	data	5042	5231.3	0.0308	9481	9687.3	0.0678
		control	5042	5023.5	0.5706	9481	9494.7	0.4585
1000	Amsterdam, Netherlands	data	4712	4812.2	0.1511	9421	9549.6	0.1743
		control	4712	4755.0	0.3269	9421	9372.6	0.6362
37	Neuchatel, Switzerland	data	4982	4930.0	0.6970	9961	9957.4	0.5083
		control	4982	4936.6	0.6735	9961	9960.2	0.5004
112	Neuchatel, Switzerland	data	4982	5082.8	0.1563	9961	10041.0	0.2843
		control	4982	4905.6	0.7772	9961	9898.0	0.6710
1022	Braunschweig, Germany	data	4742	4912.2	0.0415	9481	9588.8	0.2163
		control	4742	4529.2	0.9865	9481	9437.3	0.6229
102	Wien, Austria	data	4952	5170.1	0.0151	9901	10136.0	0.0483
		control	4952	5048.2	0.1667	9901	9987.2	0.2691
114	Madras, India	data	2372	2521.1	0.0166	4741	4843.5	0.1464
		control	2372	2379.9	0.4506	4741	4849.3	0.1334
		data	31784	32659.7	0.0003	62947	63803.6	0.0081
		control	31784	31578.0	0.7928	62947	62999.3	0.4407

This is one of the most persuasive results we have seen thus far suggesting that locality is an important factor. But what sort of locality? The people who could enjoy the live eclipse in progress had to be in a certain geographical area, to be sure, but they also were privileged to be in a special psychological domain as well. They were sharing an extremely rare and impressive experience.

I'll show one example of the egg behavior in an area with a long exposure to the full eclipse. This is Vienna, where people experienced 99% totality and 2 hours and 45 minutes sharing this unusual moment. The upper trace shows the Vienna data, and the lower, light gray trace is control data. People elsewhere could watch the TV images and listen to explanations by newscasters, but their experience was both geographically and psychologically remote. It will take more effort to gain insight into the relative importance of these two kinds of distance, but it seems likely that both may be relevant to the GCP effects.

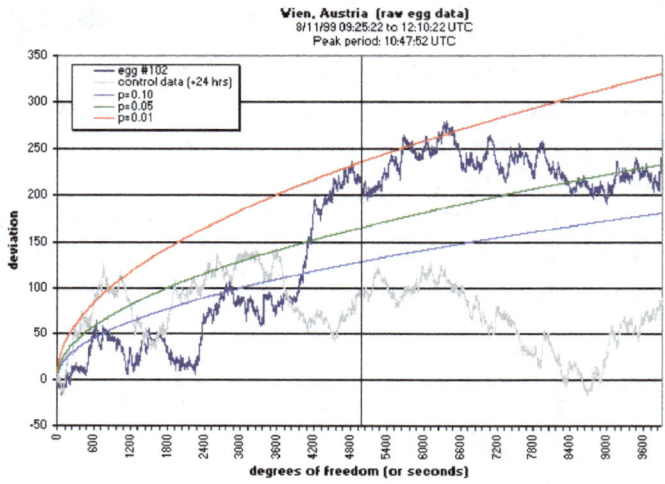

Although some other cases suggest otherwise, the eclipse results indicate that the egg network is sensitive to relatively local influences, apparently contradicting one of our ingoing assumptions, which says that the location of events relative to the eggs should be unimportant. If this indication is confirmed in other cases, it means that although the anomalous interaction of minds and machines that we use for our measure is nonlocal, it isn't unboundedly so. The intensity of regard, or the concentration of attention may have an effect that is stronger on machines least distant from the people who generate the group consciousness. Later we will look at a comprehensive assessment of the distance issue. We have to learn much more before drawing conclusions in this complex area.

Astrological Moments, 2001 12 09-14 (event 96)

This event is treated as a rigorous formal analysis, but it is also a highly speculative exploration of an unlikely source of predictions for global events. I was approached with an unusual proposal by a financial consultant whose clientele are investment firms. He had decided to extend his quantitative modeling to include astrological predictors for real world applications—stock market analysis. The astrological descriptions are one of a hundred indirect indicators for decision making, addressing world conditions and events such as natural disasters, threats of war, attacks, etc. If the predictions are effective in that context, my correspondent argued, they also should point to GCP events and data deviations.

We agreed to test this hypothetical correlation by analyzing a few of the astrological moments identified by his methods for decision analysis. I received a list of five times:

> The broad area of Dec 9–14 is the highest probability window based on a combination of astrology, psychic predictions, and the religious holiday calendar. Within this broad band, a few specific times are isolated using the fast aspects of the moon as a trigger.
>
> Dec 9, 3:15 PM EST. Moon occupies 14.1 Libra, degree of Mercury on 9/11 attack date and Nov 12 American Airlines crash.
>
> Dec 13, 9:06 PM EST. Moon occupies position of Pluto at 12.6 Sag on 9/11 attack date.
>
> Dec 14, 1:35 AM EST. Moon occupies 15.1 Sag (hot spot of Mars during 2001)
>
> Dec 14 2:03 AM EST. Moon conjunct Pluto at 15.4 Sag and activates Saturn-Pluto opposition.
>
> Dec 14 6:10 AM EST. Venus occupies 15.1 Sag (hot spot of Mars during 2001)

...

As the moon is usually very precise, a time window of +/- two hours is appropriate with the morning of the 14th probably lumped into one test.

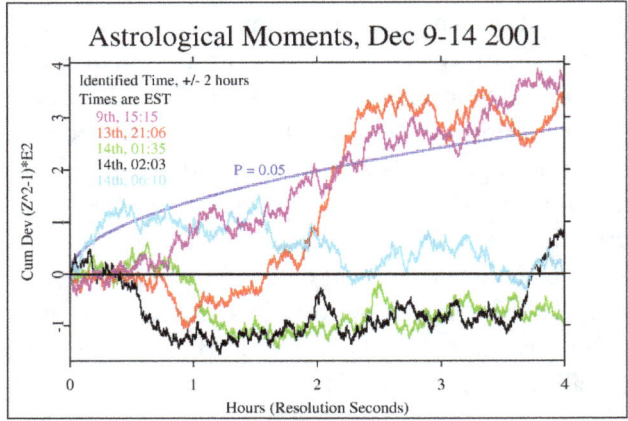

While I did not understand the references or the implications, the specifications were unambiguous. This figure shows the standard analysis of GCP data corresponding to the five identified points centered in the recommended time window of +/- two hours. The composite probability for the formal test based on the four-hour periods is significant with a probability of 0.037. Note that the periods on the 9th and 13th have independent probabilities of 0.018 and 0.022, respectively. It is further worth noting that there was on December 13 an attack on the Indian Parliament by terrorists, leading to a fearful increase in tensions between India and Pakistan affecting more than a billion people.

15.6 Powerful interest

Political and social events like major elections and great sporting events definitely bring lots of people into periods of shared focus and engagement. These occasions are often examples highlighting our competitive nature more than our integrative or compassionate tendencies, but in any case, they are a category we need to examine in the search for scientific insight.

World Cup Soccer, 2002 06 07 (event 109)

A number of people suggested that the great interest in the World Cup Soccer matches in the summer of 2002 would show up in the GCP data. Though my experience in FieldREG experiments suggested that sporting events are not reliable sources of resonance and coherent consciousness, it seemed desirable to test the notion formally. To do this, I asked one of the correspondents, Tobias Bodine, to pick a particularly good sample according to his intuitions, and he suggested the England/Argentina match. Shortly thereafter, I received a note from Pedro P.B. de Oliveira, who hosts an egg in Brazil, suggesting that the great victory of Brazil, becoming the world champions, would be a strong candidate.

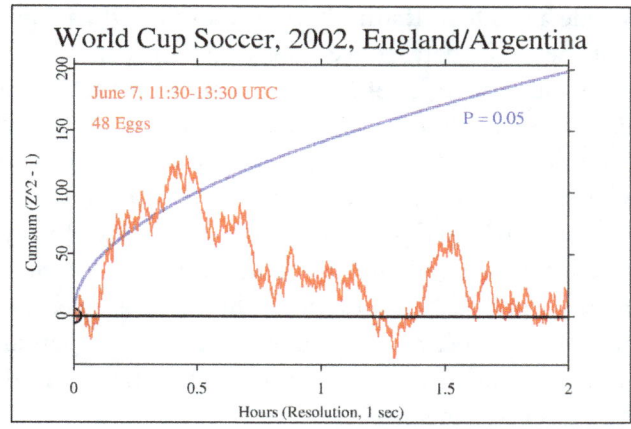

These figures show the actual results for the England/Argentina and Brazil matches, and they clearly do not support the hypothesis at a persuasive level. Of course, two cases shouldn't be taken as evidence that great sporting events have no effect on the egg network. These are sample results that are relevant but not a final answer to the question.

The Argentina/England match had a p-value of 0.477—almost exactly a null outcome—and the Brazil win had p = 0.478. These are remarkably similar outcomes, coincidentally, and awfully close to chance in both cases.

The data in these experiments are noisy, and a small number of tests can't be conclusive. In any case, two people, James

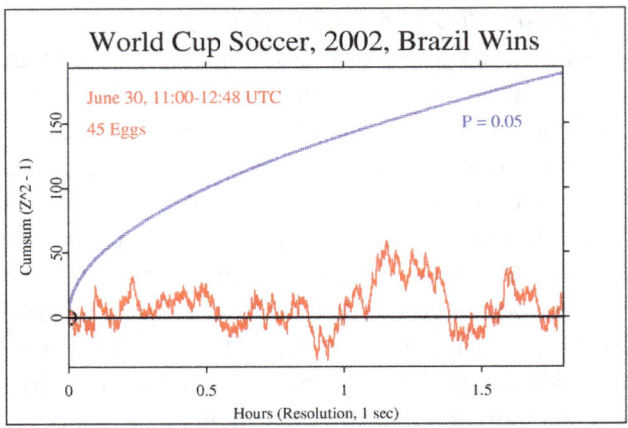

Spottiswoode and Dean Radin, have proposed to do a comprehensive look at the WCS data, so we should stay tuned.

In the meantime, such an assessment actually was done a few years later by Peter Bancel, who looked at the 2002 and 2006 outcomes. The first dataset, in 2002, did show a significant deviation across all matches in the World Cup, making it seem reasonable to say that competitive occasions, if they gather widespread attention and engagement, could also be moments of deep sharing. But the 2006 outcome, though positive, was barely different from chance. So, the question remains open and calls for further efforts to see whether sport can bring us together into coherent consciousness.

US Elections, Obama, 2008 11 04 (event 280)

Barack Obama has been elected as the 44th president of the United States of America.

After nearly two years of intense campaigning in primaries and the general election, voters gave an overwhelming victory to Obama. "Change has come to America," the first African-American leader tells his country.

There was so much excitement and participation in the feelings of celebration around the country and much of the world, that this was a natural event for us to examine. It was the beginning of an extended replication subset based on Barack Obama as the central figure. We will return to that later, but for now look at the news and descriptions of a remarkable time in politics and US culture.

Story by Alex Johnson, Reporter, MSNBC:

> Barack Obama, a 47-year-old first-term senator from Illinois, shattered more than 200 years of history Tuesday night by winning election as the first African-American president of the United States.
>
> A crowd of 125,000 people jammed Grant Park in Chicago, where Obama addressed the nation for the first time as its president-elect at midnight ET. Hundreds of thousands more—Mayor Richard Daley said he would not be surprised if a million Chicagoans jammed the streets—watched on a large television screen outside the park.
>
> "If there is anyone out there who doubts that America is a place where anything is possible, who still wonders if the dream of our founders is alive in our time, who still questions the power of our democracy, tonight is your answer," Obama declared.

The GCP prediction for this momentous event was set for the 24-hour period beginning at 15:00 Eastern time (20:00 UTC) on November 4th. This includes several hours of election day in the US, and enough time for the votes to be counted to determine the winner of the election (assuming the margin would not be razor thin) and continues until most of the world has awakened to begin a day with a new US President-elect. The data show a consistent trend that continues through the declaration that Obama had won at 23:00 Eastern time and his subsequent speech to 125,000 people at Grant Park in Chicago. The formal data depart significantly from expectation, with a chance probability of 0.046, and $Z = 1.686$. This is a large effect size compared with the average $Z = 0.33$ over the full GCP database.

This figure shows the data starting when the outcome became clear, late in the day, with Pennsylvania and Ohio decided for Obama. By this point his win appears to be a fait accompli. At around 9 pm, two hours before the official declaration, the data take on a steady, and very strong positive trend. It continues through the

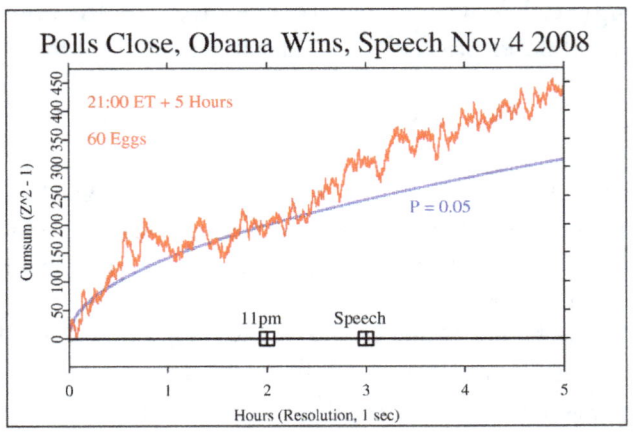

formal announcement and McCain's concession speech at 11:00 pm, and for two hours after Obama's acceptance speech in Grant Park at midnight. This particular figure shows a selected segment of the formal result. The trend is consistent with the formal data, and with our prediction that the widespread and intense emotional response to Obama's election might register on our network.

Shouldn't the effect be bigger?
Given the powerful emotions aroused by Barack Obama's success, and the feeling of wonder and joy generated in huge numbers of people around the world, we might expect a correspondingly powerful effect in the GCP data. The formal outcome is positive and significant at the usual 5% level, but it isn't "off the charts." Quoting one correspondent, "I had hoped to see a bigger response; this only increases my doubts about the consciousness hypothesis."

This offers an opportunity to discuss the statistical nature of the GCP question: "Is there a correlation of structure in our data during widely shared states of consciousness and emotion generated by great events?" The tools we have to answer this kind of question are averages and variance measures and correlations among the scores from all the devices in the network. Such measures have intrinsic variability, which is another way of saying they are "noisy." When we look for structure, we have to expect some difficulty differentiating real patterns from mere noise—both signal and noise are represented by the same simple numbers.

In general, to understand the data we have to examine the distribution of the numbers to see if they are pushed away from the theoretical mean value or spread out unexpectedly. If the distribution is distorted in identifiable ways corresponding to the predictions or hypotheses we have set, then we can say there is evidence for the signal we are looking for. Yet, because of the intrinsic variability, it can happen that the signal is obscured or weakened by an accidental but entirely normal variation in the noisy background. Or, equally problematic, we may see an exciting trend or spike of activity that is actually just normal fluctuation.

In addition to this signal-to-noise issue, we know from categorization studies that celebrations (and the 2008 Election has a great deal of this quality) show relatively small effects in the standard Network Variance statistic, but relatively large effects using one of our alternate measures which looks at second order variance of the inter-node correlations.

15.7 Deliberate focus

We see in recent years an increasing number of very large organized meetings, synchronized prayers, demonstrations, and mass meditations, fostered by new communication technologies. Social media and personal networking via the Internet and, increasingly, via mobile phones and texting, enable a deliberate and organized focus during moments shared by thousands or millions of individuals. Some of these events have become traditions.

Earth Day, 2001 04 22 (event 73)

Earth Day is April 22, and this year it was on a Sunday. Since 1970, Earth Day has been an annual event for people around the world to celebrate the earth and our responsibility toward it. The Earth day network says, "Volunteer. Go to a festival. Install solar panels on your roof. Organize an event where you live. Change a habit. Help launch a community garden. Communicate your priorities to your elected representatives. The possibilities are endless! Do something nice for the earth, have fun, meet new people, and make a difference."

Earth Day 2000—the 30th anniversary—was expected to stir 500 million people on all continents and in more than 160 nations. The expectations in 2001 should be similar. Despite the setback for recognition of global responsibility from the US refusal to accept the Kyoto accords, there is a growing recognition that we must pay attention to the earth's needs.

Given the basic character of the Global Consciousness Project, with purposes that include helping more people recognize that we can have a better future by becoming more conscious of our interdependence, Earth Day seems a natural event to examine. Since the Earth Day observances are very diffuse, with no central, focal moment, we decided that the most sensible prediction would be that the whole day should show the effects of large numbers of celebrations, rituals, meetings, and consciousness-raising events around the world. So the full 24 hours of data for 22 April, 2001, based on UTC time, were extracted and processed. The figure shows the cumulative deviation for the 24-hour period, which has a p-value of 0.037. This is another example of a repeating event like New Year's and the Kumbh Mela. It allows us to examine relatively strict replications of our natural experiment, using the same specifications for the event each year.

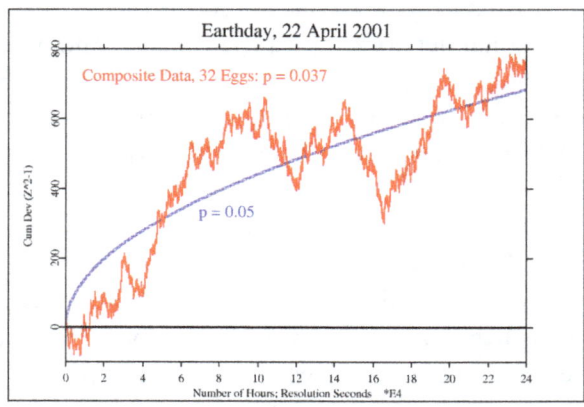

Earth Day is the same day each year, April 22, and it's been a big gathering with international reach for decades. GCP has data for 18 of them; 7 have a null or negative outcome and 11 are positive (matching the prediction). Their average effect size is Z=0.503 to compare with overall average of 0.33. It was interesting to run them off one by one because from 2000 to 2009 the trend was all positive, with a cumulative Z-score of 6 (billion to one odds) by 2009. Then the tendency turned around to create an opposite trend, canceling much of the positive accumulation and bringing the composite Z down to 2.5 (hundred to one odds). I don't know what might explain the turnaround, or whether it might just be chance statistical fluctuation.

Climate & Peace Activism, 2014 09 21 (event 487)
September 21, 2014, was a day for a variety of demonstrations, especially for climate change. It was promoted by organizations such as Avaaz.org, 350.org, worldpeacepoetry.com and many more. For everyone, the focus included world peace and a brighter future in general.

For example, hundreds of thousands of demonstrators marched through Manhattan on Sunday to demand bold action to combat global warming. Sen. Bernie Sanders joined the march that organizers said drew 400,000 people. Bernie and Senator Barbara Boxer are the co-sponsors of the most comprehensive climate change legislation in Congress—a bill that puts a tax on carbon and billions of dollars into energy efficiency and sustainable energy.

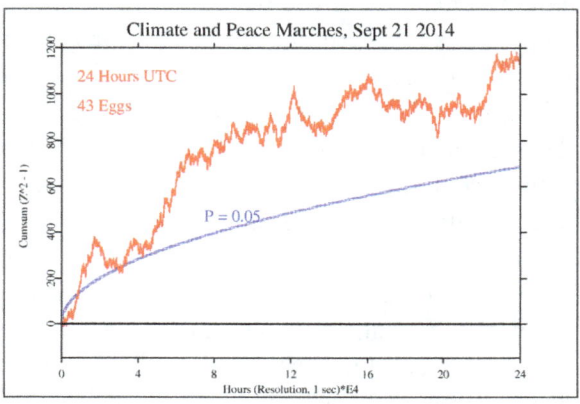

In interviews in New York City, Bernie said that it was an international embarrassment that the Republican Party was blocking almost all efforts to reduce carbon emissions. "You have a major political party that is rejecting science and is impeding us at every step of the way," said Bernie, who serves on the Senate energy and environment committees. "The only way to put pressure on government is to do exactly what we are doing today—taking to the streets."

Sanders praised fellow Vermonter Bill McKibben, who founded the international environmental group 350.org. "Bill and all those who worked with him to organize this extraordinary demonstration know that the only way we defeat the powerful fossil fuel companies, and reduce carbon emissions, is when people around the globe take to the streets and demand action from their governments. Sunday's march was a great step forward in that effort."

Peace and Climate Change, 2015 12 12 (event 500)

I had decided to end the formal series of events when we reached number 500. This turns out to be a fortuitously interesting and complex "event" because two major happenings coincide. One is the culmination of the long and difficult negotiations on Climate Change, and the other is a huge collaboration of many groups organizing mass meditations for peace and a brighter future.

It is somehow fitting that this 500th formal event should be one that demonstrates one of the particular difficulties in testing the GCP hypothesis. We predict data deviations corresponding to events that engage huge numbers of people. But all events are embedded in a complex of happenings and engagements that may include competing focal points. This makes it quite difficult to identify a single source of possible effects with any certainty because there are likely to be all kinds of happenings which could influence what we see—assuming the notion we're testing has merit. Fortunately, though there may be multiple possible events, they won't typically start at the same time, so we can aim carefully for the target of interest. Our methodology relies on precise timing and statistical leverage, and we have succeeded in making a persuasive general case over the years. But despite the general success, interpretation of single events remains out of our reach. In any case, the results for event 500 are very interesting.

COP21 climate change summit deal in Paris

A deal to attempt to limit the rise in global temperatures to less than 2°C has been agreed at the climate change summit in Paris after two weeks of intense negotiations. The pact is the first to commit all countries to cut carbon emissions. The agreement is partly legally binding and partly voluntary. Earlier, key blocs, including the G77 group of developing countries, and nations such as China and India said they supported the proposals.

The President of the UN climate conference of parties (COP), who is French Foreign Minister Laurent Fabius, said: "I now invite the COP to adopt the decision entitled Paris Agreement outlined in the document.

"Looking out to the room I see that the reaction is positive, I see no objections. The Paris agreement is adopted."

And on the same day, we have one of the largest Mass Meditation efforts ever organized. I give one example description to represent the dozens of focused gatherings:

Global Meditation to Raise Vibrations of the Planet

The Master Shift has teamed up with 20 other meditation groups including the Dhammakaya of Thailand to create a shift in the collective consciousness. On 12.12.15 we will meditate together at 9:30 PM JST and again at 9:30 PM EST. The Master Shift will provide a free guided meditation that will be available the day of the event or feel free to create your own meditation event.

The results of the collective meditation experiment will be measured by the global consciousness project (http://www.global-mind.org/) and the global coherence initiative (https://www.heartmath.org/gci/). The results will be featured in a documentary called "Awaken—Time to Evolve" produced by a London based Film Production Company called Broxstar Films. Further details about the event can be found at: awakentimetoevolve.com/global-meditation-day/.

The GCP event was set for the full day of December 12, to include the Climate Agreement reached at some unspecified time, as well as the first day of the World Peace Weekend of mass meditations around the world. The result is Chisquare 86821.188 on 86400 df, for p = 0.155 and Z = 1.013. This outcome is according to the prediction, with a final Z-score that is about 3 times the average over the whole database. I work to ensure that everything about the GCP experiment remains objective, but I must admit I was happy to see a positive result for our last event in the formal series. Not extreme, but definitely in accord with the long-established hypothesis.

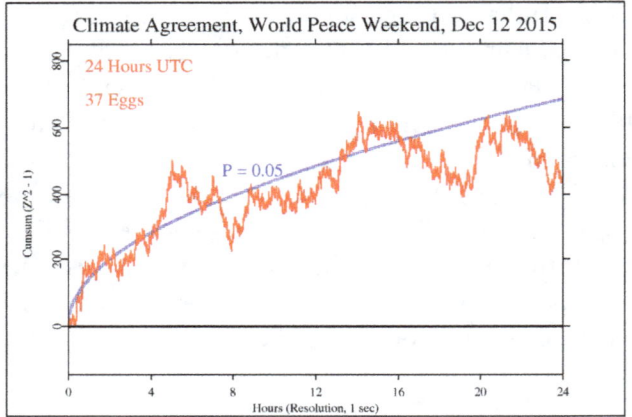

This visual display of the statistical result shows the second-by-second accumulation of small deviations of the data. As in the whole history of the experiment, our prediction is that deviations will tend to be positive. When this is so, the jagged line will be the usual random walk but with a trend—it will tend to go upward. If the endpoint is positive, this is evidence for the general hypothesis and adds to the bottom line.

Once again, for those interested in more detail, or for technical discussion of procedures or interpretations of the results, please go to the GCP website. As always, though this graph looks pretty cool, the caveat about interpreting individual events has to be kept in mind. The signal-to-noise ratio is too small for a confident or reliable reading of the statistical result or the graphic history of the data deviations shown for the individual events.

In the following chapter we'll get to the next level, where in fact it is possible to judge the outcome of this very long series of tests with high confidence. We will look at the bottom line which forms the basis for deeper analysis and interpretations.

Chapter 16: THE BOTTOM LINE

When we try to pick out anything by itself, we find it hitched to everything else in the universe.

—John Muir

The events described in the previous chapter are examples drawn from the full formal database of 500 events. They were selected as illustrations, and they may give an exaggerated picture because I chose mostly interesting and illustrative cases where the hypothesis was confirmed. In fact, there are many events (roughly one third) where the analysis shows a null or negative outcome. Those are outnumbered, however, by events with a positive outcome, and all together the formal series is an accumulation with a strong positive trend. This composite constitutes the basic, solid evidence for a scientific anomaly, which in turn is the foundation for a growing conviction that we may be in the presence of a nascent global consciousness. It is strong evidence for the predictions we have made, and it provides confidence that we can dig deeper and seek answers to the wide variety of questions that arise.

After 17 years, we calculate the likelihood that the accumulated departures from expectation are just random fluctuations is on the order of one in a trillion. The EGG project is much broader and more informative than this "bottom line" indicator alone can convey, but it acts as an anchor to assure us that we are in fertile waters where we can throw more audacious nets. I will have more to say about instructive explorations later, and about alternative views, after we take a thorough look at the bottom line and some immediate extrapolations.

Over the years, the small deviations, which match our prediction more often than not, have accumulated to a composite Z-score of more than 7 standard deviations. The common term for such a departure from chance expectation is a "7 sigma" effect, and in most fields this is more than enough to take it seriously. For scientists familiar with the work, this bottom line provides high confidence in the reality of the anomalous deviation. It is a small effect, but it has an importance out of proportion to its magnitude. The well-established result implies a need for efforts to integrate mind and consciousness into our scientific models, a task that has proven dauntingly difficult.

Picturing the small effect

Let's look carefully at the accumulated database using different ways to plot the results. The first figure displays all the event Z-scores in a conventional scatterplot that shows the individual scores as they spread across the range from positive to negative and along the (evenly spaced) time axis. The solid line is the grand mean of the 500 Z-scores, and the dashed line shows the null expectation. It is apparent that there are no outlier scores, and that the distribution is fairly smooth over the range of Z-scores. When we test the parameters of the score distribution, we find that it is not distinguishable from the expected theoretical distribution, except that the mean is shifted. At the same time, looking at the difference between the grand mean of the scores and the line showing expectation, it is clear that the effect is quite small. The difference is about 1/3 of a standard deviation, but the large N results in a 7-sigma total effect.

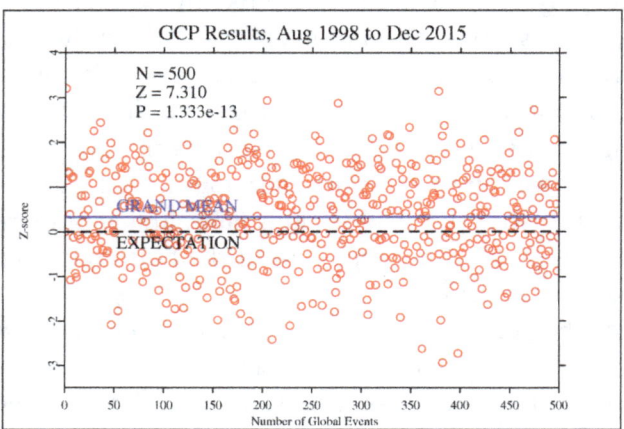

When we plot the same data as a cumulative deviation as we've done for most of the examples of individual events in the preceding chapter, the picture becomes more striking. The deviation of each event Z-score from expectation becomes one point in the series, and is added algebraically to the sum of the preceding scores. That is, we plot the accumulating difference from zero as more tests are done over the months and years.

The jagged line in the following figure shows the history of accumulating departures from expectation for the 500 formal events, which can be compared to dotted smooth curves showing the 5%, 0.1% and 0.0001% significance criteria. The bottom line is that we have a highly significant cumulative deviation of 7.3 sigma, with chance odds of less than one in a trillion. The trend of the growing total deviation for all formal predictions as of late 2015 has a fairly steady slope, although it continues to show the ragged ups and downs of noisy data.

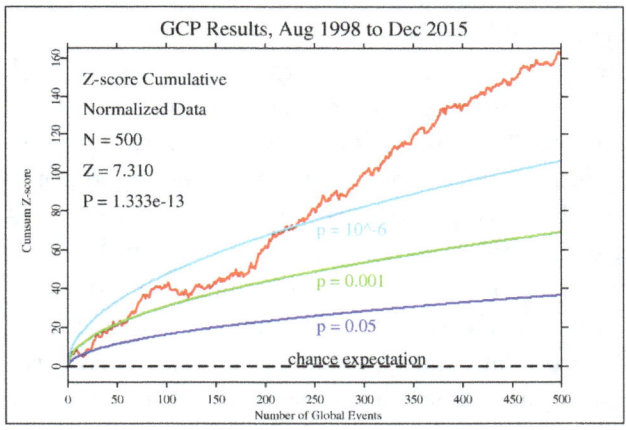

The figure offers an informative perspective on the variations over time because it averages the scores over the sequence of events and years, and it reveals some aspects of the database that are not visible in the scatterplot. For example, there is a period from about event 100 to 200 with more than usual negative or null scores, which reduce the slope to near expectation. It also appears that although the grand mean has been fairly steady, there are some suggestions of decline in the last third of the database.

As discussed elsewhere, the design and conduct of the experiment allow us to be confident that the 7-sigma bottom line is no mistake, but represents a real effect. The next questions we will explore ask what else the data can tell us, and how we should interpret and apply these findings.

Control Data

Before going on to deeper analysis, we should consider the question of controls. Most experiments that depend on statistical comparisons have a "control" condition in which no effects should be found, in contrast to the active experimental condition. There are several possible ways to provide this in the GCP experiment. For example, we can examine arbitrary or randomly selected data segments where we've identified no "global event." Or we can sample pseudo-random data extracted from a pool using the same parameters (event duration, number of eggs). We do in fact create such a pseudo-random database in parallel with the RNG database, and it is always available for use.

But there is a still better way to create a control background, namely by "resampling" the actual data outside of the formal events, repeatedly sampling it using the same parameters as in the formal series, but with random offsets or incursion points for the start times. This is repeated many times to produce a well-characterized distribution of sequences just like those in the formal experiment, but taken from the 98% of data not in those formal events. That is, we effectively repeat the experiment using randomly selected control data multiple times, and create a background control distribution against which the real experimental data can be

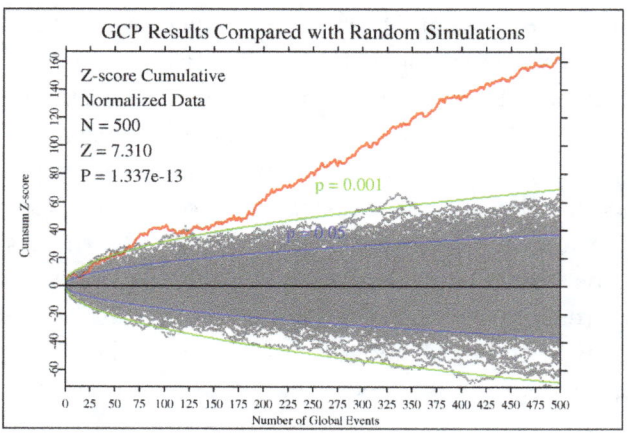

judged. A similar procedure uses mathematical simulation based on random draws from the appropriate theoretical distribution to create a comparison standard. The figure shows the real data (the upper jagged line, which we saw in the previous figure) in the context of such a control distribution. It is quite easy to see they differ. The actual GCP data, generated during the times we have identified as global events, are clearly not from the same distribution as the control data.

One more observation on the bottom line as displayed here. Given that a "decline effect" is often seen in both psi experiments and mainstream research, the average effect size in this experiment has been surprisingly constant (which means the slope of the cumulative deviation curve is steady, albeit with fluctuations). We can see a suggestive small decline in slope of the cumulative deviation, but it is not significant even though the database is very large. The effect size on average is just 1/3 of a standard deviation, but because there are so many replications, this small effect becomes highly significant. The GCP composite Z-score is greater than 7 sigma, very much in the range considered persuasive by scientists in most fields, including physics and cosmology. We will turn to questions about interpretation and implications in the next chapters.

Chapter 17: DEEPER ANALYSIS

The human eye sees the physical form, but the inner eye penetrates more profoundly, even to the universal pattern of which each man is an integral and individual part.

—Sri Yukteswar

The Question

Is there an earth consciousness, a Gaiamind? Can we better understand our own place in the world? Can we create new meaning and give shape to our future on the earth? Can we record and play back the subtle beauty of the conscious world? These are questions we wish to ask, and it appears that the answer to most or all of them probably is yes. To address these questions, however, we must accept that although there may be a deep simplicity, maybe even a grand unity in the world, the manifestations we are able to examine seem to be very complex. Our deeper examination of the GCP data shows that the answers certainly are not simple, but they are very interesting.

The most basic function of the EGG project is to record random data 24/7 from a world-spanning network of research-grade physical random number generators. Day after day and month after month, at each node custom software collects one 200-bit trial per second and sends the data to Princeton for archiving and eventual analysis. The result is a 17-year database of synchronized parallel sequences from independent, widely separated RNGs. It is like a broad virtual tapestry of randomly colored threads unrolling through time.

It takes a special attitude (and great patience) to regard this swath of unpredictable numbers as interesting, but by pursuing a simple question about possible correlations between consciousness and random physical systems, we have discovered remarkable facts. The random behavior is modulated sometimes, and shows faint correlations or structure. This is an undisputed fact, discoverable by anyone who takes the time to examine the publicly available data, and it poses serious questions for physics and for psychology. Assuming that the unexpected data deviations are not due to some unknown error or an unremarked electromagnetic influence, they require accommodation in physical models that have no obvious place or explanation for such correlations. And because the anomalous effects are correlated with consciousness via the experimental design, they need to be accommodated in psychological theory.

Addressing the latter issues first, let's consider the design. The network was built to extend laboratory and field RNG experiments, which have shown effects of individual and group consciousness, respectively, to a global scale. We designed a protocol that could ask whether RNGs respond to mass consciousness: If millions of people think and feel the same thing, driven by an identifiable shared experience, will there be a shift in the random network data corresponding to that special state of congruent consciousness?

The short answer is yes. Terrible tragedies and great celebrations can be linked to small but ultimately significant changes in the network output. We find structure where there shouldn't be any, in the form of correlations between the widely separated, truly random sources. Over the years we have repeatedly asked whether the data show anomalous deviations during events like terrorist attacks, natural disasters, religious pilgrimages, political moments, and web-organized meditations. The defining quality of all these examples is that they are situations that create or are defined by collective human consciousness and emotion.

Replication, Replication, Replication

Thus, the GCP is a natural experiment with replications defined by selected moments in the ongoing history of the world. We study the data generated during those moments, and we've collected a database of 500 experiments in a conceptual replication series testing the hypothesis that data recorded during deeply engaging events will diverge from random expectation. Each test we conduct addresses this same proposition, but in widely varying contexts—we lump together 9/11, the Japanese tsunami, New Year's, and the election of Barack Obama. Each test is rigorous, but the variety is not something seen in ordinary experiments, and this prompts some critics to claim the GCP hypothesis is vague. Let's consider what happens when we sharpen it.

A number of types of GCP events lend themselves to quite exact replication, at least as natural experiments go. We can look at the composite results of these data subsets, which, although they don't comprise repeatedly dropping the same ball and feather, are at least all apples (or all oranges). I believe these replication clusters help illuminate the GCP work, and touch on broader questions about the role of consciousness in the world.

In addition to general categories (positive vs negative, large vs small, external vs internal source or stimulus) we can extract and analyze several sharply defined replication subsets. We have 15 tests of the "Obama effect" most of which show positive results (except for the two inaugurations!) We have half a dozen cases looking at the "Pacquiao Effect" combining aspects of sports and politics in boxing matches of Manny Pacquiao, the hugely popular Philippino politician. There are over 100 assessments of prayer and meditation events in service of peace and a brighter future. My colleague Bryan Williams refers to their commonality as Global Harmony, and he recently reexamined that ethereal category, showing it replicates well, with composite odds against chance of 2000 to 1. We'll look at these in more detail later.

The formal series itself is a large set of replications, which may be regarded as conceptual rather than strict replications because there is so much variety in the types of events as well as flexibility in the *a priori* parameter choices and analytical strategies. In the subsets, there is little of this variety, and we may speak of exact replication—again within the limits of a natural experiment. The long-term project has provided many lessons and insights, but we can't avoid the proverbial observation that "more work is called for." An independent replication of the GCP experiment would strengthen the evidence and answer new questions raised by the original. We know some important upgrades, such as improving the time synchronization of the network nodes, and recording vastly more data including multiple trials at each node, would produce an enhanced replication of the whole experiment. An important improvement, which is now possible with the immense capacity of cloud storage, is to record and archive many concurrent variables, such as social media indicators and geophysical/cosmological measures, which might serve as modulating variables.

As I write, there is a well-developed team effort headed by Adam Curry to create a mobile app that can emulate and enhance the GCP experiment called "The Consciousness App."[65] I hope this and similar ventures prosper because they could help answer good questions. But that is for the future. Let's return to the material in hand. It is deeply interesting.

New Year's, again and again

One of the first events I decided we should examine was New Year's. Even in parts of the world that celebrate a separate cultural new year, large numbers join the multitudes waiting for midnight on the last day of December. It is a time when we can reliably expect a significant part of humanity to have a shared focus. In other respects, New Year's is completely different from most of our events. It is just a moment in time—the transition from one year to the next—and it is entirely abstract, something we invent without any natural stimulus. There is no emergency or disaster to focus our attention, just a traditional sharing of the moment, perhaps with a hug or a glass raised to toast the new year. The emotions aren't strong, but they are very widely shared: a generous attitude toward fellow celebrants, some hopeful thoughts about the future, perhaps just the simple enjoyment of being together and sharing an easy, human custom. And it has an added feature appropriate for replications—it repeats!

We make two predictions for each New Year's event. One is the GCP standard measure applied to a 10-minute segment of time centered on midnight in each hour as the moment passes from one time zone to the next. We average across all these epochs; that is, across all the time zones. There are some countries that have half-hour offsets relative to the GMT standard, so the result is 37 epochs rather than 24. Some exploratory work has indicated that the effects are larger if we look only at time zones with large populations, but the standard protocol is to use all 37. The composite result for this measure is positive but not significant, although a variant calculation (using concatenation instead of epoch analysis) by my colleague Peter Bancel shows a much stronger 3-sigma deviation, with roughly 1 in 100 odds it is chance fluctuation.

The second of the formal predictions for New Year's looks at the variance across devices rather than the network variance during the 10-minute segments. This is a direct measure of the variation of their behavior (rather than their correlation). The development of this analysis for the Y2K transition was described earlier. By 2001-2002 the protocol was stable and sharply focused on the prediction of reduced variance near midnight. Each year we test this hypothesis with the same procedure: the variance across eggs is normalized as a sequence of Z-scores for each second, then plotted with smoothing to remove high frequency statistical noise using a moving average in a window of 240 points (4 minutes). In most years, the prediction is borne out, but there are exceptions. We have seen a couple of New Year's where the variance sharply increased around midnight, and it is rare for the curve to minimize right at the transition moment. But the prediction is nicely confirmed in most years, and the composite across years is statistically significant.

The same process of epoch averaging used for each New Year's dataset can also be applied to the sequence of years. Just as we "stack up" the data from all time zones and average across them, we can make a composite across years. The results show that although there is considerable variation, there is enough similarity in the structure from year to year that the general pattern maintains when we average across the years. For a composite of all the hits and misses, we can again use the permutation-based probability calculation we apply in individual years. For the data shown in the next figure, which includes all the hits and misses over the first 10 years of the project, the permutation-based probability is 0.027, meaning the combination of magnitude of the variance reduction and proximity to midnight of the maximum deviation has chance odds of about 35 to one.

The figure shows the results combined across many years of New Year's. Even though there are backwards and null cases, the composite appears to confirm the prediction that the variance among the eggs will diminish by a small amount around midnight—they show slightly more similar behavior than expected. It is tempting to imagine this is a reflection of a merged

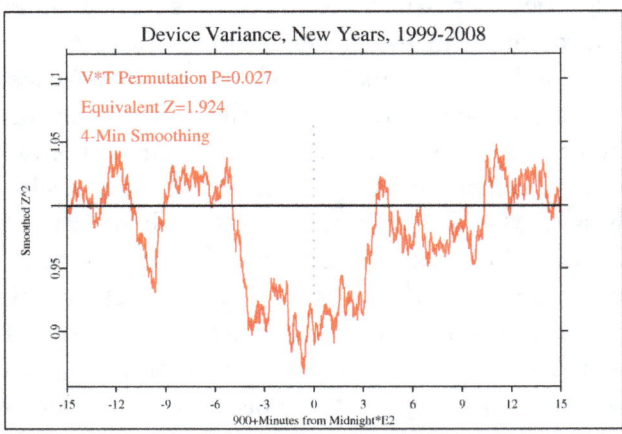

sensibility and a coherent attitude we share during this moment. It is abstract, to be sure, but we don't treat New Year's that way. We take it as an important occasion, one to celebrate in large and small gatherings.

Earthquakes, land and sea

One of the values of a continuous data archive is the possibility that new analyses can be done on events that occurred in the past. We have focused on several examples of earthquakes that were severely destructive and deadly. But there are many more quakes, and they can be sorted by magnitude. Several years ago, Peter Bancel examined all quakes with Richter magnitude 6 or greater, those which cause major damage.[66] He found 600 of these in the records, about 100 of which were on land where buildings may be destroyed and people may be killed. While there were no signs of structure at all in the 500 quakes in the oceans where they had no effect on humans, the land quakes showed considerable structure in one of the statistical measures called covar. This was particularly notable in two major subsets (Americas and Eurasia) in which the data showed a striking downturn beginning about 7 or 8 hours before the main temblor, reversing at that time to create a V-shaped picture. In other words, the pattern seemed to show a precursor effect beginning several hours before the main temblor.

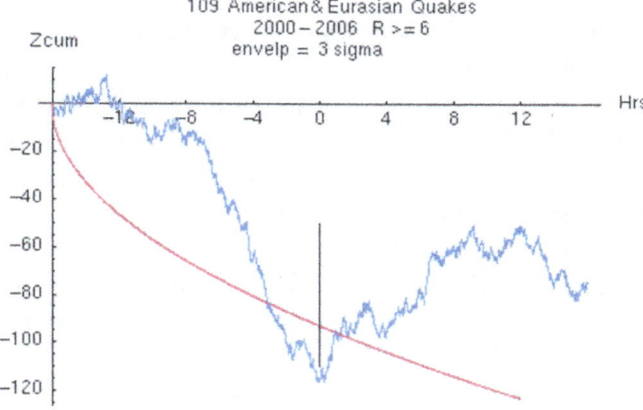

This pattern also showed striking similarity in the traces for the two independent clusters of data. Even so, Peter now disregards this work as exploratory. His caution is understandable if the explorations are data mining. The caution is also justified because another subset of quakes in the Japanese Pacific rim group did not show the same pattern. Thus, despite the intriguing signs that there may be informative structure in the data for these powerful, land-based earthquakes, we have to accept that the indications are ambiguous.

Charismatic figures

An unusually high level of attention and excitement developed during the Democratic primary campaign in 2008 when two strong candidates were vying for the Democratic nomination. Hillary Clinton was well known as the former First Lady and a powerful Senator from New York. Should she be elected, she would be the first woman to become President of the United States. Her strongest rival was Senator Barack Obama from Chicago, who brought both intelligence and charisma to the fight. If he were to succeed, he would become the first black President.

The US Presidency is of great interest not only in the United States, but around the world because of the enormous power and influence of the office. In addition, the political "horse race" as it is often called, is a prime subject of media interest not only in the US, but in other countries. In June 2008, the battle for the Democratic candidacy was over and we saw headlines like, "World Welcomes Obama Win." One AP article said, "Excitement about Barack Obama emerged as a global phenomenon Wednesday as commentators and citizens around the world welcomed the news that he had sealed the Democratic presidential nomination."

So, we set this as a global event, the first of a series with Barack Obama as the central figure. It was followed by the election and inauguration and a number of important moments or actions during Obama's Presidency. Putting these together we could ask whether there might be an "Obama Effect" capable of producing consistent deviations. The answer seems to be yes.

Early in the campaign for the Democratic nomination there was high interest, and as the campaign gathered momentum it garnered more attention from around the globe, due in part to Obama's gifts as a speaker, but especially to the possibility people could see for a new development in the US national character: There was a powerful focus on a black man with a real chance to become the President of the United States, the first in our history.

Over the years since that possibility actualized, we assembled a compelling aggregation of GCP network responses during especially notable events with Barack Obama as the central figure. As of June 2012, we had specified formal hypothesis tests for eleven events, beginning with the nomination in June of 2008.

- Obama wins the Democratic Party Nomination
- Acceptance Speech, Democratic Party Convention
- Barack Obama is elected the 44th President of the USA
- The Inauguration of President Barack Obama
- Obama wins the Nobel Peace Prize
- Obama gives his first State of the Union Address
- Obama signs the Health Care Reform Act
- President Obama declares the long Iraq war is over
- President Obama speaks at the Tucson memorial service
- Obama gives his 2011 State of the Union Address
- Obamacare survives Supreme Court test

These *a priori* formal hypothesis tests provide reliable statistics that can be safely, if cautiously, interpreted. In keeping with the understanding that we learn most by compiling replications of similar events, we can put together what turns out to be a compelling aggregation of GCP network responses during events with Barack Obama as the central figure. In the 2012 summary analysis we found that of the 11 formally specified events we examined, 9 yielded a positive result in accord with our expectation, and four of these met the 5% standard of statistical significance individually. We combined the results for the 11 formal tests using a Stouffer's calculation of the average Z-score across the tests. This procedure gave an unweighted (composite) Z-score of 3.284, which has an associated probability of 0.0005, or an odds ratio of about 2000 to 1. Although this is a US-centric collection, Obama has such a large presence on the world stage that it's fair to say that the "Obama effect" is global.

In subsequent years we added four more events in this series, and only one of the four is in the "right" direction. Perhaps Obama's luster is diminishing, but it is also possible this is random fluctuation. In any case the accumulation with the additional events is still significant, with odds against chance of 200 to 1.

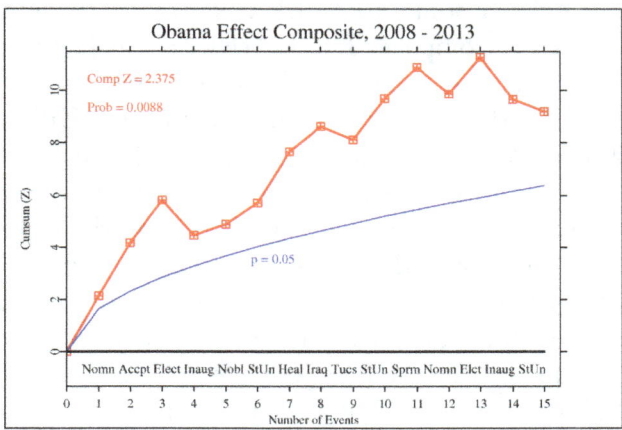

This graph displays the sequence of 15 scores as a cumulative deviation trace. The expectation is a level series of random steps varying around the horizontal line at zero. The actual data are shown as the jagged line with an obvious upward trend. Each point in the trace represents the accumulated deviation up to that time. The last value is the final composite value, which is the test statistic for the hypothesis that there will be a positive deviation when President Obama is central to an event. While the accumulation of events in the category of "Barack Obama as a central figure" is too small for strong interpretation, it is well along. The results certainly are thought provoking, particularly for questions about what drives the correlations in the GCP network. We think a likely factor is a kind of coherence of emotions shared by large numbers of people, and perhaps that is reflected in the Obama data. He has shown himself to be a charismatic figure on the world stage.

Peace, Prayer, Meditation

Another category that deeply interests large numbers of people is organized efforts to affect the social climate in the world. These are most clearly represented in organized "peace" prayers or meditations such the International Peace Day that occurs on September 21 each year. There are many more events of this sort, defined by a common thread that runs through widely promoted gatherings intended to achieve something that most of us desire but feel we are powerless to accomplish. They all share an ancient notion that what we wish and pray for is more likely to happen.

Our scientific assessment of effects on GCP data isn't designed to test that notion specifically, though it may ultimately be a resource in that context. What we are asking is whether there is an effect on the GCP network, and by implication some actual effect in the world, whether or not the prayers and meditations achieve their stated goals. The data suggest there is a real effect correlated with these gatherings of intention and emotion, a correlated shift in the random data we collect. The GCP effects are tiny and subtle, to be sure, but I would like to believe they reflect vastly more important changes in the world of human perceptions and actions.

My colleague Bryan Williams wrote to say he had recently refreshed his comprehensive assessment of this general category of GCP events:

I've recently been invited to give a general talk on parapsychology to a spiritual group. Because this group promotes the message of peace and harmony for humanity and the Earth, I was reminded of the exploratory analysis I did several years back as a follow-up to the one you did in early 2001 on the GCP events related to "global harmony" (where mass gatherings of people are organized in order to pray or meditate for the well-being of humanity), and I thought that was something that the group might relate to as a possible example....

I went back through the accumulated formal database of GCP events from 1998 to 2012 to identify the individual events that seem to be in line with the concept of global harmony, on the basis of two criteria:

1) The event listing made reference to prayer, meditation, ceremony, ritual, healing, humanity, Earth/nature, and any other synonyms of a similar context.

2) The description of the event [indicated that] the intended theme, focus, or goal of the event was in line with the concept of global harmony (i.e., it had to have a positive message for the future of humanity, promote peace or healing to the Earth/nature or some aspect of human society), and that it encouraged the shared participation of a large group of people.

> For this analysis, I extended the event inclusion criteria a bit to include a small number of mass social activation events (e.g., public demonstrations for peace, anti-war rallies, etc.) because although these events tend to be quite different in activity from organized meditation and prayer events, both seem to have the same goal of promoting global harmony in mind.
>
> I identified 110 events in total. Collectively, these 110 events have a Stouffer's Z = 3.283 (p = .00051), with an associated odds ratio of about 1,960 to 1. The mean Z was 0.313, which is comparable to the mean Z for the formal GCP database. Variability is considerable for these 110 events, as well (Chi-square = 157.62, 110 df, p = .0016). The following graph shows the results in terms of a cumulative summation of Z-scores, akin to the overall GCP events graph.

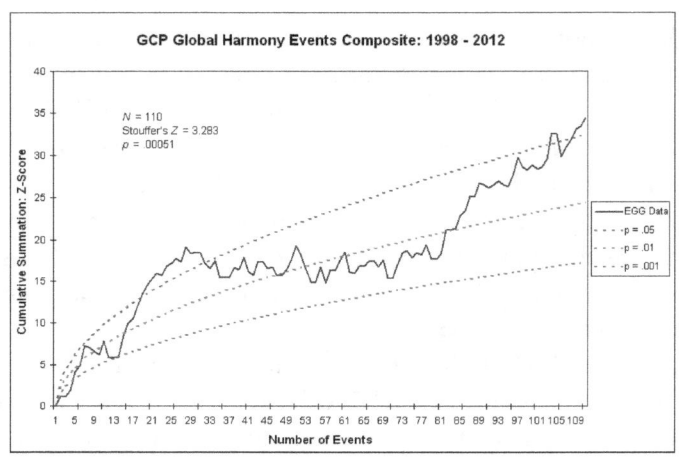

I enormously appreciated Bryan's aggregation of this category of events, partly for its analytical value but also because it is important to have independent perspectives on the GCP data. I also had some comments and questions for him, about such things as what factors or subsets of the 110 events contributed to the large variance. Are some event types reliably associated with negative deviations while others tend to yield positive outcomes? And what about that long stretch in the middle of the figure where the trend is flat? We haven't yet pulled the data apart to search for answers to these specific questions, but this is a great example of the progressive accumulation of scientific understanding. New questions inevitably accompany research at the edges of what we know. And each new answer generally points to another good question to ask. Bryan's report on this work is available on the GCP website.[67]

Patience and the power of replication

Probably one of the most important elements of good science is the recognition that our experimental findings need replication. This is especially true for work that depends on statistical measures because they always come with "error bars." Every data point is an estimate, and it represents a distribution of possible outcomes, not an established fact about the world. A deviation that is said to be significant because it is 2 standard deviations out has a certain likelihood of being just 1 sigma away from expectation—or it may be 3 sigma. Two thirds of a normal distribution lies within +/- 1 sigma of the mean value. The same is true, of course, for the distribution around the experimental outcome value. Until the statistic gets quite large, 3 or 4 sigma, we need to be cautious in our interpretation; even in our conclusion that something noteworthy has happened.

This might be discouraging for anyone doing work in an area with small effects, but I've been talking about a powerful tool that can make a big difference. It is replication. Simple repetition of an experiment using the same design and analytical tools can improve the power of the research. Done wisely, we learn far more from a series of replication attempts than from the best or biggest individual experiments. It is possible the first results were a fluke, and if several replication attempts indicate they can't be reproduced even though all the important qualities of the original experiment are in place, we have to accept that there may have been no effect after all. In an area such as psi research, those "important qualities" are very difficult to identify and reproduce, however, so it is easy to be misled by "failed" replications.

In fact, it appears that in addition to replication, there is another essential tool that must be applied in difficult research areas, namely, patience. It won't do to try one replication because the same considerations about point estimates apply to every statistical evaluation. Even when power estimates (to determine how big the replication has to be to have a good chance of identifying effects) are used, the new experiment is still capable only of producing that fragile and fuzzy point estimate. It is easy in principle to understand this, but it is frequently forgotten. In my experience, non-scientists generally take a "significant" result as definitive, rather than as an estimate. Unfortunately, this is common among trained scientists as well. We want the world to be neat and focused, and we don't like ambiguity.

An example may help make this issue clear. After the Princeton group had published the compounded results of many years of RNG research, a big, three-laboratory replication attempt was designed. Each lab did a large number of trials using equipment and software similar to what had produced the PEAR database. Power calculations were applied, and after many months of data accumulation, the planned number of trials were in hand, and analysis could proceed. The result was that, although the Z-scores were all positive, ranging from 0.2 to 0.6, none of the three labs produced a significant bottom line. Many observers, especially those who are skeptical, concluded that this apparently failed attempt to replicate meant that PEAR's RNG results could be cast aside, ignored. They blithely, but incautiously, concluded that there is no effect of intentions on physical systems.

It is actually easy to see the asymmetry of this interpretation— one experiment, albeit a large one in terms of the number of trials, does not have the weight of a patiently assembled collection of many, many replications. Add to this the question whether the "important conditions" are replicated, and it is obvious that drawing conclusions on the reality of intention effects is premature. There is a literature on what is called meta-analysis that is relevant, and it is worth looking up.[68] Meta-analysis is a particular form of quantitative review applied to an experimental literature. It can be usefully described as a larger scale experiment, where the data points of interest are the outcome statistics for each of a collection of individual experiments. For many kinds of research, it is an essential tool; for the GCP, it is a good description of our experimental design.

More examples of replication: The Kumbh Mela

We have seen four Kumbh Mela events, two of which were the exceptionally large Mahakumbh Mela gatherings that happen every

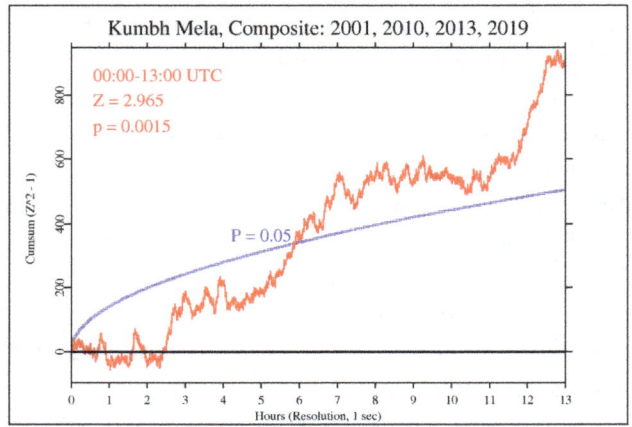

12 years. All four have a generally positive deviation trend, and a picture superimposing them suggests that they may be driven by a common source. It is too small a group to draw strong conclusions, but the four have a composite Z-score of 2.965, which translates to less than 1 in 600 odds that this consistency is a fluke of chance.

School shootings and lone berserkers

We are shocked and saddened to an unusually strong degree by an occasional berserker invading a school or a workplace and murdering as many people as he can (until now only men, as far as I know, seem to be captured by this demon) before his assault rifle jams or his handguns are out of ammunition. We've looked at 17 of these, the majority of which happened in the US. They aren't therefore major global events, but the pain and unsettling character makes them seem more universal than perhaps they are. In any case, the composite outcome is not much different from null, with a Z of 0.357. About half of the cases show a negative trend, and some of those are quite strong, but there also enough positive deviations (conforming to the GCP prediction), to keep the composite out of the negative territory.

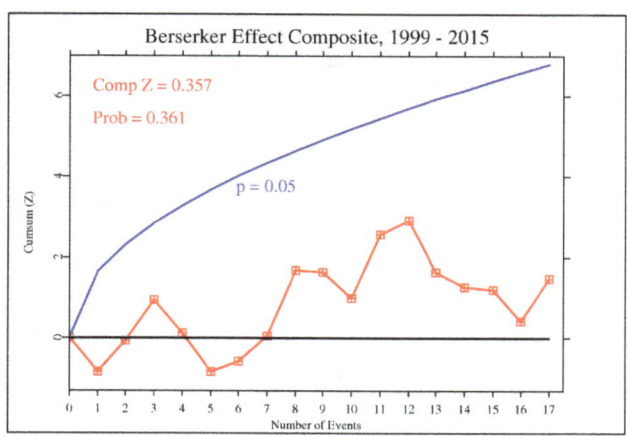

It is a collection of events that seems important and meaningful in terms of the GCP concept, but it isn't interpretable in any simple way. At this point we don't know whether the backwards-going tendency and the weak overall outcome means this kind of event doesn't affect the network because of its nature, or because the events aren't actually global, or because the low signal-to-noise ratio has buried anomalous effects. It is important to recognize that even when we do gather a decent number of replications, our assessment may still leave us only an ambiguous conclusion. There is probably some useful information which could be extracted—when and if we proceed with the oft cited "further work."

Chapter 18: INDEPENDENT SUBSETS

The great tragedy of science—the slaying of a beautiful hypothesis by an ugly fact.

—*Thomas Huxley*

As their last word in a paper entitled, "The Global Consciousness Project, Identifying the Source of the Psi: A Response to Nelson and Bancel," published in the *Journal of Scientific Exploration*, 2011,[69] May and Spottiswoode write:

> There is, however, one simple thing that can be done from this point forward that would go a long way to answer the questions raised in our debate. Rather than posting the GCP data for every second, post only, say, the even-numbered seconds. Then data snoopers and data-mining programs can be unleashed with impunity to isolate events that show significant correlations....
>
> When the data mining produces a significant effect on the even-numbered seconds, it must also be seen nearly exactly on the odd-numbered seconds which now act as a formal "within session" control. Any causal or correlational effects should replicate on a second-by-second basis.

This proposition is easy to understand, and has the further merit that in principle it is easy to check out. As always, however, there are devilish details, which in this case amount to disregarding the signal-to-noise ratio, which we know from years of work with this database (indeed any REG or RNG-based psi research) is very small. The evidence clearly indicates effects that are much too small to support the M&S prediction that a significant effect on the even-numbered seconds must also be seen nearly exactly on the odd-numbered seconds. In any case, the future experiment they suggest as a test has already been implemented using the present data. Here we take a look at that work.

We know that the average effect size per event is about a third of a standard deviation, which directly implies that we must look at dozens of events—on the order of 50 to 100 total hours of data, to get reliable statistics. It makes sense that a subset of events with unusually strong effects might improve the situation, but it remains dubious to postulate that subtle correlational effects should replicate on a second-by-second basis. That is a proposal based on experience only with simple classical physics.

Nevertheless, it is worthwhile to take a look at a comparison of odd and even seconds in the data for a particularly strong case, using unpublished analyses done several years ago by Peter Bancel. His work revealed a small but meaningful positive correlation of the alternate seconds during one of the GCP's most powerful events. In some respects, the terror attacks on September 11, 2001, are almost uniquely suited to serve as a sample. There is good evidence for a true effect, not just random fluctuation, which remains after a dedicated search for flaws and alternative explanations.

If we examine the data from odd vs even seconds for a long period of consistent deviation, beginning a few hours before the first plane hit the WTC and continuing for 48 hours, we find a significant correlation. The t-test for the correlation is 2.603, which corresponds to a p-value of 0.0092, or chance odds of less than 1 in 100. In other words, the split data show the same structure, confirming that the data do "replicate on a second-by-second basis" in this case despite the generally low signal to noise ratio.

For a graphical exploration of the odd vs even data we look at a span of five days centered on 9/11. The graph shows the cumulative

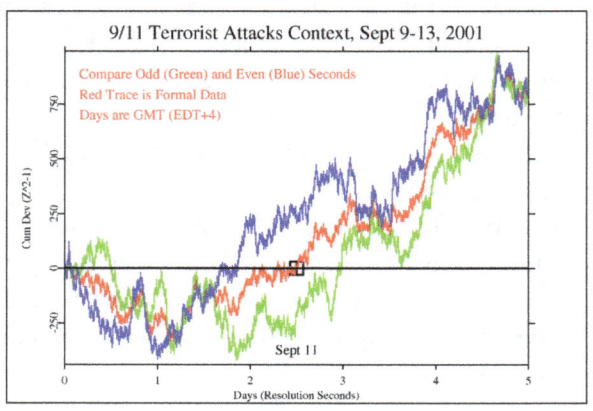

sum of deviations of the network variance, and two subsets created by splitting the data into alternate seconds as proposed by May and Spottiswoode. It is easy to see that the odd-second and even-second traces track each other well, and that they add up to the original trace with both subsets contributing similar amounts to its slope. Because such a cumulative deviation graph is autocorrelated, a general correspondence is not conclusive, though it is consistent with the statistical finding.

A related analysis of the device variance measure was done by my late friend and colleague, Dick Shoup, one of the four co-authors on the 9/11 paper published in *Foundations of Physics Letters*. He separated the data from the whole network into subsets in various ways, and plotted the smoothed cumulative deviation of variance for each. It is visually obvious that all the subsets produce much the same general picture: a sharp rise early on Sept. 11, a peak a few hours later, and then a decline back to the expected level over the next several hours. (The times shown on the axis are UTC). Thus, we see that whether we look at the network variance for alternate seconds, or the device variance for arbitrary or random subsets of the eggs, the data show similar patterns. This is what is expected if there is a real and persisting influence on the GCP network.

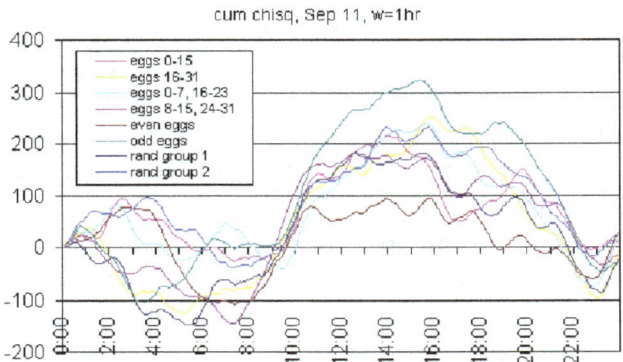

Informal explorations where we're dependent on visual comparisons for assessment of similarities may be suggestive, but we have no simple way to estimate the likelihood of the correspondence shown in these graphs, or the significance of visible trends. On the other hand, they add a dimension to the more formal analytical picture. And as we will see, there are indirect ways to judge the reality of apparent trends.

Long-term trends

Almost all of our analyses are focused on the sequence of defined formal events. But it is possible to apply the same techniques we use for the formal series to larger amounts and other parts of the data. Indeed, it is possible to cast a statistical net over the full database of many years of data. This allows asking a different kind of question; namely, whether there might be any trends over time without regard to the history of events in the world. Maybe the "global consciousness" not only changes quickly in response to focal events, but also in slow-moving shifts that may be reflected in GCP data correlations.

One application for such analysis would be to determine whether a baseline correction might be required for rigorous analysis of the individual events. If there is a background trend, it needs to be accommodated. A more difficult but very interesting question is whether we might identify a "reason" for any long-lasting, consistent deviations in our standard measure. Perhaps there are influences that parallel human-scale alterations of mood and perspective that are the contextual background in which we see momentary events.

It turns out that it is possible not only to see trends in the long-term data, but to test them for statistical significance. Finding explanations for them is a nontrivial matter, however, since we have to undertake the search without a pre-specified hypothesis. Obviously, if there were no substantial or statistically impressive deviations, there would be no need to scratch our heads seeking their meaning. On the other hand, if the evidence for long-term trends is clear, they become interesting and justify some effort to understand what they might mean.

This figure shows the period from January 1, 2000, to August 8, 2012, almost 13 years of data processed in the same way we analyze the individual formal events. The latter are typically a few hours long (6 hours is the most frequent specification). Here we are looking at almost 2 orders of magnitude—nearly 100 times—more

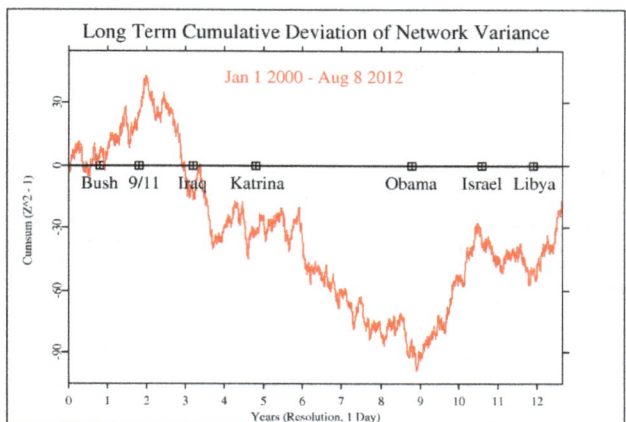

data. This trace doesn't represent particular moments, but is literally a graphical look at the long history of all data collected by the GCP. The calculation is the squared Stouffer's Z-score across all eggs each second—the same statistic used to evaluate the formal series of global events—which we refer to as the network variance. The plotted line is the cumulative sum of this measure, and its expectation is a horizontal random walk.

The data definitely show long trends of consistent deviation. The trace spikes after 9/11 and then starting at the end of 2001, the network variance tends to be low (the graph has a downward slope) until near the end of 2008. This persistent trend looks impressive, and an analysis by Peter Bancel showed that it is statistically significant.

A 6-year sample, from Oct 1, 1998, to Sept. 8, 2004, was separated as previously described into rigorously independent subsets by odd and even seconds. If there is non-random, long-timescale structure in the cumulative deviation, it should be present in both datasets. If correlations are found between the odd and even subsets, this constitutes good evidence for an anomalous effect. We can plot the two subsets separately to see if they vary together as would be expected if there is a common source driving the deviations. The next figure shows this. Visually, the two lower traces (odd and even seconds) generally track each other reasonably well, especially after the 9/11 event marked by the vertical line.

As previously noted, it is difficult to test directly for correlation in the structure, but an effective indirect approach is to create

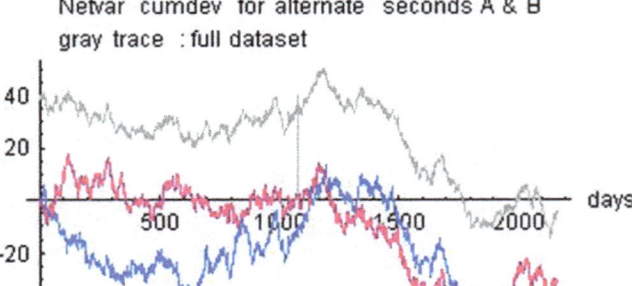

a mathematical fit to the cumulative deviation curves for the odd and even datasets, and test for correlations between the two sets of fitting parameters. The results are highly informative. When the parameters are set to accommodate trends over months or years, we see a clear correlation that is statistically significant, with a calculated probability of 0.001 (Z-score = 3.0). Thus, at the 3-sigma level we see that the GCP data contain non-random structure on long timescales. A detailed explanation (documentation by Peter Bancel) of this analytical work can be found on the GCP site, global-mind.org. Search for "longtrend."

Back to the long-term trend: it reverses in late 2008 and shows an even more extreme slope upward for the next couple of years, then it returns to what looks like the expected random variation for such data. What might explain the structure in this figure? As noted, there is no straightforward way to answer this question. There is, however, a striking parallel that can be drawn. The two long persistent trends in this 13-year figure correspond largely to the tenures of US Presidents George W. Bush and Barack Obama.

Looking for sociological variables that might correlate with GCP data, a useful source is polling data. Many polling organizations in the US and Europe repeatedly ask certain kinds of questions. Tapping into this resource, Peter gathered data on US presidential approval ratings over the years and found some 500 data points on this specific question from 2001 to 2009. Exploratory analysis discovered a substantial correspondence between the trends of the ratings and the GCP data. Literally, after a peak in the ratings for George Bush following the attacks of 9/11, the polling showed a persistent decline until the end of his Presidency. Obama started with high popularity ratings, and though his numbers have fluctuated, his popularity in the later years has been unusually high. We should not conclude there is a causal relationship, but the correspondence is thought provoking. If the GCP data are responsive to a widely shared mood or emotional tendency, we should expect trends that picture our global state of mind.

But the story is in fact much more complicated, and it's useful to give another example to reinforce the understanding that we are looking at correlation, not causation. I had a note from someone interested in stock market trends, recounting his effort to figure out why the GCP long term data curve looked familiar. He eventually realized it looked like the DOL index, a measure of the US dollar against other currencies. When he compared the curves, he found a strong resemblance—the two data sequences track each other closely. When the GCP data shows generally positive deviations, the DOL tends to be high, and vice versa. Thus, we have a second apparent correlation but no indication of cause: we should not conclude that our shared perceptions of US Presidents or our responses to the US dollar market necessarily affect the GCP data.

While we can't identify with certainty any simple source for it, the appearance of long, statistically significant trends in the GCP correlation measure seems important, and it is worth looking for some meaning. It may be that these slow-moving changes in our data reflect or symbolize a worldwide perspective on how things are going in global affairs. Might they represent widely shared concern over years about society's direction or, on the other hand, persistent global optimism? At this point we are clearly just guessing, but such speculative notions may stimulate more research and better questions.

On the simpler technical question about the background trend affecting the calculations in our event analysis, the answer is that it does have a small effect. Subtracting the background would make our data slightly stronger. But the difference is small, so we continue to use the simpler (and more conservative) original analysis.

Chapter 19: Characterizing Event Categories

Eventually everything connects—people, ideas, objects. The quality of the connections is the key to quality per se.

—*Charles Eames*

Natural tragedies focus attention from around the world on the locale. At the site of a disaster there is tremendous pain and fear and grief, but the news spreads, and these events also arouse widespread compassion and hold the attention of the world for long periods. An early GCP event was the terrible earthquake in Turkey, August 17, 1999. The EGG data appeared to "see" the quake, showing a 1 in 100 deviation in the half hour exactly centered on the main temblor. A big part of this deviation actually preceded the moment of the first big temblor, suggesting that the EGG network might be sensitive to precursors or tensions that signal such an event.

Even more potent and long lasting in the consciousness of the world were the 9/11 terrorist attacks. It could be said that we still are feeling the effects, though they have morphed and changed in many ways. On 9/11 too, the effects in our data seemed to begin early and they definitely continued for much longer than the period of time we identified for our formal testing. Certainly, those attacks had a powerful effect on subsequent history, and on very large numbers of humans. It seems justified to expect the same potency of influence on a nascent global consciousness. We were changed individually and internationally by forces set in motion on September 11, 2001. The world of human activity has been shaped and reshaped by hot active wars, and by simmering international strife, fomented and urged by reactions to the terrorist attacks. As a result, expectations that I think many people shared for an increasing cooperation in the world have been dimmed. The hostilities among and within nations seem to have grown more virulent instead of less, and much of the reason for that can be traced back to the anger and fears so bitterly symbolized by 9/11 and our responses to it.

But it isn't only tragedies that capture and hold our attention. Over the years we have been collecting data and selecting events, we have seen an increasing number of web-organized gatherings of people who want to cooperate and synchronize their intentions and wishes for a better world. These take many forms, but all have the common thread of conviction that mental and emotional acts such as prayer and wishing for peace are worthwhile. In an early example, the Yugoslavia war engendered a month-long "Prayer for Peace," with a specified time for people around the world to join for a few minutes in willing the war to end. A corresponding GCP prediction was made, and the data showed a positive, though not significant trend. A little later, in October 1999, a "Billion Person Meditation" for peace was organized, and the analysis showed a 1 in 100 probability for the deviations in the corresponding EGG data. These are early examples of a new social perspective that has grown stronger as the Internet and social media have become more important. As detailed in the comprehensive analysis by Bryan Williams described earlier, these mass social gatherings add up. As a group they show a reliable, significant effect in GCP data.

We can pursue the question of what kinds of events matter by categorizing the entire database into sensible subsets. What specific categories to choose is in practical terms a matter of taste, and deciding where each individual event belongs is often a subjective issue on which people might differ. Even with these caveats, it is nevertheless worthwhile and certainly is interesting.

A question many will ask is what sorts of events produce the largest effects? Taking a very general perspective, we can segregate the long list of events into a few types based on similarity. Deciding whether a given event belongs in a particular category is straightforward for most events, though some are debatable. This figure shows the average effect size for events in seven categories. The categories have "error bars" that depend on the number of events in each group. A long error bar means we have fewer such events, so our estimate of the effect size is relatively poor. While the differences among these categories are not big enough to be definitive, the order is interesting. It suggests that extreme or violent events are not necessarily the ones that produce the largest effects in our data. Celebrations and events with a religious or spiritual flavor seem to be those where our human interconnections are most evident.

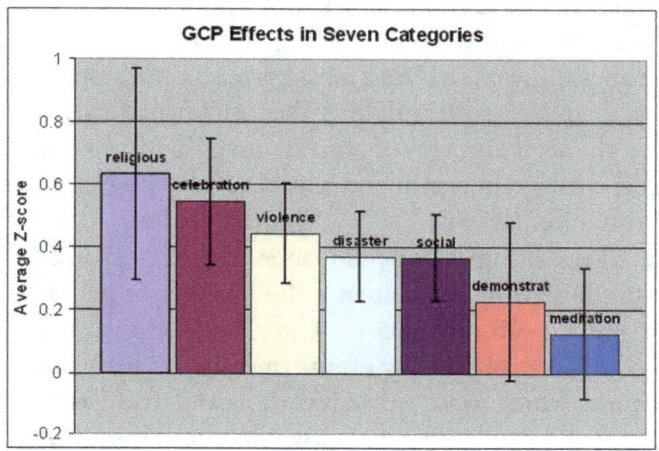

Some categories are relatively objective, for example the size the event or the number of people engaged. Of course, we have to keep in mind that even when we can objectively count cases there may be confounding because of conceptual overlap, so our category statistics may not be independent. Perhaps large numbers pay attention because the event is important—unusually numinous or compelling in its own right.

We can readily agree on the valence of most events, identifying some as positive and others as negative in their emotional quality. We also can say in most cases whether particular emotions are strongly represented. For example, we can ask whether an event embodies compassion, or fear, or happiness. Answering yes or no will be a subjective judgment, but when we ask two people or a group to make such assignments, there is a high level of agreement. In principle it is possible to make useful, even if imperfect assignments enabling us to find out what kinds and what characteristics of events tend to produce larger effect sizes.

The results of pilot studies on categories are interesting and clearly show this is a worthwhile research direction. It is something that can be pursued at any time and by people not originally involved in the GCP, since the event descriptions and the associated scores are publicly available. If multiple independent ratings or assignments correlate well, indicating the ratings are reliable, they become usable parameters for describing and modeling the effects of global consciousness. We have only begun to explore this area, but the tentative results are stimulating. In a nutshell, it appears that what we are calling global consciousness reacts and responds in most cases just as an individual might.[70] That isn't necessarily surprising, but given the several stages of abstraction going from human emotions to the data representing a possible global consciousness, it is actually quite remarkable.

Let's look at some particular cases. We see that size or importance as indicated by estimates of the number of people engaged by the event is a substantial contributor to effect size. For example, we can compare scores of big events that engage millions of people against those which draw only a few thousand. It is easy to identify large and small events, but if we ask what determines the size, we quickly see a confound with the "importance" of the events, defined in any of several ways. In any case events judged to be large or medium in size (importance) have a composite effect size approaching 4 sigma, while small events are about 2 sigma.

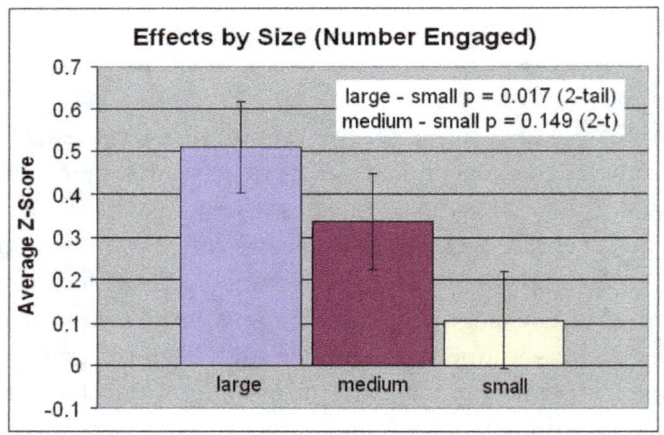

Events with either strong positive or strong negative valence produce significant effects, while neutral events show smaller deviations. Many assume, or would like to believe that one or the other of these types should produce much bigger effects. The analysis says this isn't so. Both positive and negative events produce a composite effect size of roughly 3.5 sigma, while events categorized as emotionally neutral yield an effect of about 2.5 sigma. Emotion is important, but it seems not to matter whether we are frightened and angry, or feeling profound sympathy or deep compassion.

On the other hand, the level or degree of emotion, regardless of valence, is a highly significant predictor ($p < 0.005$). The largest effect sizes in the database are produced by events characterized by high levels of the powerful emotions such as fear (4.5 sigma), or compassion and love (3.6 sigma). Again, we have to recognize that the situation is complicated by questions of which comes after which. Perhaps the high level of emotion is evoked because the event is unusually important, and thus engages huge numbers of people. Or because it is powerfully numinous.

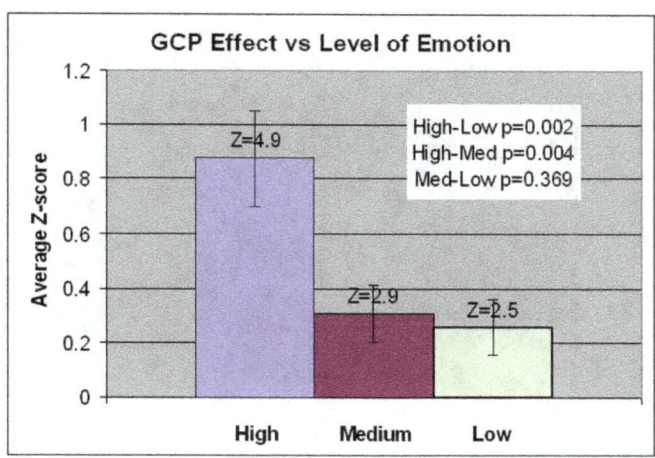

Such questions aside, we have found that several emotions are clearly identifiable at various levels in the global events, and subjective ratings can be made with good reliability. While not all events can be assigned to such categories as, for example, William James' four basic emotions (fear, love, rage, grief) or the modern equivalents, we can assess the presence of some of these emotions in the responses of our operationally defined "global consciousness."

My favorite example is compassion. Events that are judged to evoke or embody great compassion have a much larger effect size than those showing little or none. Finding that compassion produces what appears to be "global consciousness" makes very good sense when we think about its characteristics. The defining quality of compassion (or love) is that it is interpersonal—it is something that two or more people do, so it is a natural foundation for interconnection. It is more than that, of course, as described in our wisdom traditions. The Dalai Lama's position is striking. For years he has promoted one simple virtue as the heart of Buddhist spiritual practice: *"If you want others to be happy, practice compassion. If you want to be happy, practice compassion."*

That simple rule is also a prescription for more connections to our neighbors and even to strangers. It suggests a clear path to a brighter future and healthier human relations.

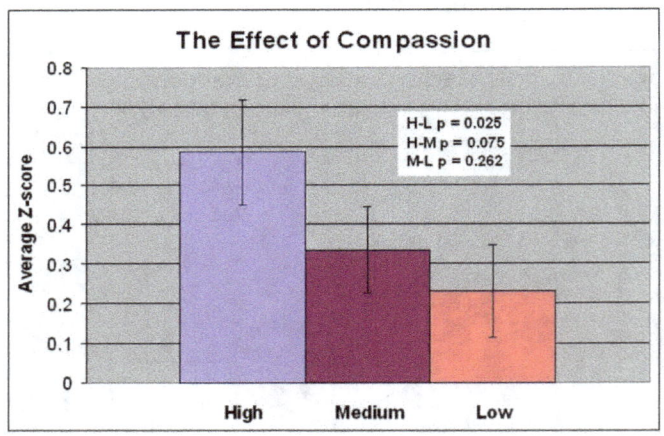

When we consider more comprehensive generalizations across emotional categories, regularities appear. For example, an interesting meta-category separates the source or direction of the stimulus for event-linked emotions and attention into external vs. internal motivation. Terrorist attacks and natural disasters are external sources which impinge upon us, while meditations and celebrations have an internally generated character. When we separate these, we find a characteristic distinction of effect size. Events in the external group tend to produce stronger effects in the primary measure, network variance (netvar), which is essentially measuring interegg correlation. There is a second type of correlation between the eggs (variance of the netvar) and the internal group tends to show stronger effects in this measure, on average. Thus, we see differences in two correlation measures depending on a meta-categorization.

One implication of this analysis is that we must interpret apparent differences across categories carefully. For example, meditation events produce smaller average effects, but this likely is in part because the categorization studies use only the primary GCP measure. A substantial number of meditation events show netvar deviations that are weak or in the direction opposite to prediction, but positive second order (variance of netvar) effects. In addition, these events in most cases involve relatively small numbers of people, adding another confounding influence.

The categorization research also points to details that are implicit in the overall bottom line results, but more easily articulated in this context. First, the subset aggregations confirm that there is some form of interconnection (or common response) of human consciousness at an unconscious level, supporting in turn the notion of a "global consciousness" as we have operationally defined it. Secondly, it appears from various perspectives, but especially from the categorization research, that the possible mass consciousness has characteristics that make sense in human terms. Our global consciousness appears to be emotionally responsive in ways familiar from studies of individuals and groups, giving the construct face validity.[71]

Chapter 20: STRUCTURAL ANALYSIS

Relationship is the fundamental truth of this world of appearance.
—*Rabindranath Tagore*

One of the most difficult problems faced by researchers studying subtle phenomena like those we see in the GCP data is how to deal with small effects in a sea of random noise. We have taken a two-stage approach. The formal replication series sets the stage with a robust aggregate score that allows us to estimate the likelihood of the experimental hypothesis. We know there is a 6 or 7 sigma effect, so we can confidently pursue deeper and more sophisticated analyses. The experiment is ongoing, and it can be likened to a continuing meta-analysis that updates the significance of its measured effect with each new event. If the bottom line is persuasively robust, it means, as Gertrude Stein might have put it, "there is some there there." In other words, we have a real phenomenon and it needs deeper examination.

The confirmation of our basic hypothesis provides the foundation for a broad research program searching for the parametric details we need to construct and test explanatory models. The next step is to create a more detailed picture of the database by going directly to the fundamental trial scores: the second-by-second outputs for each RNG in the network. This differs from the network variance measure that summarizes across the eggs and across time in the events. The summary approach yields a clear formal result expressed in a Z-score for each event, but the details of the second-by-second trials provide a much more complete description of the experiment. We have the trial values with their time-stamps for each device, the geographical position of the RNGs, and the event labels. The trial-level description permits analysis of all aspects of the experiment.

The secondary analysis program is largely the work of Peter Bancel, who has been studying the GCP data since 2002. Some of the basic results are publicly available,[72] but several important findings remain to be published and can be presented only in descriptive form based on personal communications.[73] Peter's work typically uses a reduced dataset excluding trials from the first few months when the network had less than 10 nodes. Events longer than 24 hours, as well as a few events where the original analysis did not use the standard correlation statistic also are excluded. Comparison shows that the reduced dataset yields virtually the same composite statistics as the full database.

Inter-RNG correlation

The trial-based examination confirms our early expectation that effects on the egg network would show up as correlated shifts in the behavior of the RNGs. The primary formal statistic, which we call network variance, can be approximated by the average of inter-node correlations.[74] This means that our high-quality quantum tunneling-based random number generators, which are located all around the world, become slightly correlated with each other during the global events in the formal series.

The network variance statistic can be decomposed to show its relation to synchronized RNG-RNG correlations, and this leads to an understanding that the primary effect can properly be described as pairwise correlation of the RNGs, rather than simple changes in their individual behaviors. This directly confirms early descriptions of the hypothesized effect, while also providing a detailed and mathematically rigorous account. Understanding that the primary effect can be expressed as inter-node correlations has important implications for modeling. This explicitly identifies a physical relationship that is unexpected given the nature of the instruments and their placement in a world-spanning network. In addition, this means that we actually have two levels of correlation: the anomalous inter-node correlations are themselves correlated with events of great importance to humans. We are looking at unexpected and unexplained relationships in both the physical and the psychological domains.

Details of the pairwise correlations

Different kinds of analyses are enabled by using the correlation pair-products of second-by-second trial values. If we call the correlation between RNG pairs C1, it can be represented as C1 = $z_i z_j$, where z_i is the (normalized) trial value of the ith RNG for one second, and similarly for z_j. The elements of C1 include all possible combinations of RNG pairs with identical time-stamps.[75] That is, C1 is the average of the correlations of all possible pairs: RNG 1 with 2, 1 with 3, 1 with 4, etc., and 2 with 3, 2 with 4, and so on. With 65 RNGs there are more than 2000 distinct pairs, so the average correlation can be estimated with good precision. Under the null hypothesis, the expected average value of C1 is zero, and a deviation from this expectation has the same meaning as a deviation of the event Z-score. In the formal event data, the pair-product mean-shift is positive at about 7 sigma, the same level as the original network variance measure we call netvar.

That measure confirms the formal prediction and successfully identifies an effect. The pair-product measure, C1, independently confirms the effect while also providing more detailed information. Specifically, C1 shows that the effect can be understood as synchronized correlations of RNGs in the network, and that gives physical insight into how the effect arises. In addition, because C1 uses the individual device data, it allows a more detailed look at what happens during the events.

In addition to the trial-based correlation, further analysis looks for other independent effects and correlations. Such additional measures have a special status because they represent structure that was not predicted by anyone involved in the experiment, including the main experimenter, prior to about 2005, some 7 years into the project. This is interesting for a number of reasons. Newly discovered structure that is independent from the original GCP measure points toward models that describe the anomalous effects as physical; that is, real changes in the data. The new findings specify more dimensions of the problem and help identify multiple characteristics of the effects, and allow us to focus useful models.

One of the most important new findings is that in addition to the C1 correlation, there is a second, independent correlation in the network data. The C1 statistic suggests a class of correlation pair-products, $z_i^n z_j^m$. Using algebraic analysis, Peter Bancel was able to show that only the simplest variant, $z_i^2 z_j^2$, is independent of C1.[76] This means we can calculate a second correlation statistic that provides a different, independent dimension that contributes to a richer description of the anomalous effects. This second correlation, which we can refer to as C2, is particularly interesting because it has the same structural form as C1, but represents an orthogonal correlation channel that is not addressed in the formal experiment. To place these correlation measures in the context of more familiar statistics, C1 can be regarded as a correlation of means, while C2 represents a correlation of variances. In parallel with the correspondence of C1 and netvar, the C2 correlation is referred to as covar. A simple but formal description of the two measures and their values estimated from the data was given by Peter Bancel in 2007,[77] summarizing the recent developments in structural analysis.

The estimated values of C1 and C2 have changed as the database has grown, with C1 increasing to the current value of about 7 sigma, while the C2 value has decreased to about 1.4 sigma from the earlier estimate of 3.3 sigma. Peter therefore does not consider C2 to be an established characteristic of the data since the correlation is not strong. Of course, that is correct, but we need to keep in mind that we are dealing with noisy statistical estimates. It is not a settled question.

Distance and Time

Having established that operationally defined global consciousness is represented by correlations in the RNG network, we can look for other kinds of structure that might make sense. Two important questions to consider are whether the correlations depend on the location of the RNGs, and whether the correlation strength evolves in time as an event unfolds. Given the complete trial-level description of the data, we can proceed with both spatial and temporal analyses, since the data include, in addition to the trial values, the RNG locations and trial times as parameters.

An immediate challenge is to define appropriate measures for the tests. For spatial structure we might consider where a particular event is located. However, even events with a definite location, such as earthquakes or catastrophic accidents, produce geographically widespread reactions as information about them spreads. The "events" we are assessing, if we think about it carefully, really aren't physically or geographically located. They are something going on in the abstract space of consciousness—they depend on our human reactions wherever we are, and not on our proximity to the place where an event happens.

Fortunately, we have an alternative. The geographical separation of RNG pairs provides a distance measure that is more tractable than assessments of the "distance from the event." The RNG pair separations are known to high precision and provide a useful perspective since any distance dependence of the effect—expressed as pairwise correlations—should lead to a corresponding dependence on pair separation. In ordinary physical systems, correlations tend to weaken as their constituents are separated. Thus, we should predict that the correlation representing GCP effects will decrease as a function of RNG pair separation. The world-spanning GCP network allows us to test this prediction over distances ranging from a few meters to the earth's diameter. If there is a distance effect, assessing the correlation strength as a function of the distance between RNGs should show that pairs that are closer to each other will contribute more to the average correlation.

The geometrical separations of the RNG pairs can be calculated for each of the 10^{10} elements of the primary correlation measure in the event data, providing good statistical leverage. Regression analysis supports the prediction only modestly, with a negative regression slope that approaches but does not reach significance.[78] This applies to the full database as of 2017. It was significant by the usual 5% criterion up to about 2013, but lost some power in the past few years.

But it is more interesting when we look more deeply. The strength of the distance effect turns out to depend on one of the categories discussed earlier, the size or importance of the events. If we divide the database into subsets of large and small events, we find that the small events, which tend to engage people more locally, do show a significant regression on distance. In contrast, the truly global-scale events produce inter-node correlations that remain substantial over global distances. In other words, the inter-egg correlations depend on the distance separating the eggs, but the dependence is clear only in the case of localized events.

Thus, we do have empirical evidence of spatial structure, but it is a function of the distribution of the human population paying attention. Only (or primarily) those RNGs in the general region where people are most engaged become correlated. Pairs separated by great distances show less correlation during the smaller, local events. But that's not the case if the event is truly global, engaging people all around the world. More work is needed to understand the details of distance dependence, for it is complex. We'll need time to understand to what degree it applies uniformly and whether, as these early analyses suggest, it may be important only for certain kinds of events—ones with a small geographic reach.

Temporal structure

While the GCP hypothesis tacitly implies that effects will correspond to the specified events, it does not prescribe the timing or duration of the effects. As the protocol for identifying events developed, it became clear that we had to use inclusive specifications in order to have a good chance of capturing the possible effects. We quickly understood that the event is not just, say, the moment of a devastating explosion; it includes both immediate and spreading reactions to the explosion, and might even include precursor effects. More specifically, we learned that an effect will correlate with the emotional engagement of large numbers of people. Since the experiment does not and cannot independently measure this engagement, we have only an approximate sense of when an effect begins and how long it might last.

We could, in principle, use social media like Twitter trends or Google search terms to quantify widespread shared attention and emotions. But the data history for these social media is short compared to GCP's database, and it turns out that getting relevant and rigorous measures is a non-trivial task. It is a good idea, often suggested, and with major and thoughtful effort I expect it will turn out to be fruitful. I encourage potential analysts to make that effort.

Back to timing: We should expect data correlations that correspond to the human response to events to first grow as an event becomes the focus of global attention, then persist for a time while people attend to the focus, and finally dissipate as attention wanes. The GCP test cases (events) are likely to include sections of null data before or after the anomalous effects because the formally specified periods make generous estimates of the event durations in order to include all or most of the hypothesized effect in the defined event. The temporal pattern we expect to see will thus be periods of correlation during the effect, bracketed by random data.

If this hypothetical picture is correct, intuition suggests ways to characterize the time structure. For example, given two independent correlation measures, the strong C1 and the marginal C2, which show effects during the events and which are both are driven by the same source, we expect correlations between the two measures during the actual effect, but not otherwise. In other words, we think both correlations are driven by the same sources within the defined event, so they should change together. Based on these general considerations, we expect a rise time for noticeable correlation between C1 and C2, a period when it is substantial, and then a decrease back toward random expectation. Exploratory analysis a few years ago, when the strength of the two correlation statistics were comparable, showed this to be a reasonable picture, albeit without robust statistical support. The large variety of event types makes this a difficult analysis because some events are instantaneous, like an explosion, or the stroke of midnight, while others are drawn out over hours. In addition, the weakness of the C2 measure necessarily weakens its potential correlation with C1.

Nevertheless, we can say that on average, it takes some time, perhaps an average of half an hour from the event start time as we define it, for the two measures to display a substantial inter-correlation. The correlation persists for perhaps two or three hours, and then declines toward random, uncorrelated behavior. This is a description of averages, and the exceptions range widely, even including some cases where the effects seem to depart from expectation before the "event" begins. The usual caveat about small effect size definitely applies—we see tendencies that fit a sensible, reasonable pattern, but we cannot yet paint a rigorous picture.

For a serviceable notion, however, it may be helpful to think about timing in human consciousness. We don't perceive the sound of a bell instantaneously when it is struck, but a small fraction of a second later. It takes on the order of a 10th of a second for a flash of light to stimulate the cortical neurons that support seeing that flash. After the bell or the flash, we have a durable experience that lasts until the neural flux dissipates or a new stimulus arrives. We cannot directly observe any such delays, and haven't much control over the duration of perceptions, but it is easy to demonstrate experimentally and to understand. If we take seriously the suggestion that a global consciousness might react and perceive in an analogous fashion, it makes sense to expect an analogous time course. A recent analysis shows that when we average across events with clear effects, the data do in fact show temporal structure that parallels evoked potentials in human cortical activity. There's a major difference, of course. It is clear that a moment in planet-scale consciousness is much longer than the human scale. The proverbial back-of-the-envelope calculation suggests a factor of at least 1000.

Categories, again

There are a number of useful ways to categorize the hundreds of events in the formal series to ask what matters in creating the anomalous effects. This is exploratory work rather than formal analysis, but there is evident structure linked to various categories. For example, GCP event outcomes tend to follow patterns we see in reactions of individuals. One of the clearest examples is that events categorized as evoking strong emotions yield larger than average deviations.[79] At the very least, such explorations indicate that an assessment using well-developed survey and rating tools from the social sciences will be of value.

As noted earlier, criteria such as a separation into major vs. minor events lend themselves to a relatively objective assignment and the opportunity to test reasonable predictions. More important events should yield larger effect sizes, and this hypothesis can be tested by a regression on the estimated number of people engaged by the events. The outcome shows a relationship which is significant at about 2.3 sigma. Similarly, the number of measurement elements, that is, the number of seconds times the number of RNG pairs contributing data for a given event, should correlate with the significance of the effect. This factor also is significant with odds on the order of 100 to 1. Analyses like these are suggested by ordinary physical intuitions; they allow us to ask whether anomalous GCP effects show characteristics of familiar physical variables.

A subset of events showing large deviations in the negative direction suggests that the standard GCP hypothesis, which calls for a positive deviation of the network variance, may be too restrictive. Modeling based on the empirical data indicates that some events do apparently produce "real" negative correlations, and that there are events where a strong negative deviation is not just chance fluctuation.[80] We have yet to determine why, and exactly what kinds or categories of events produce these "backward" outcomes, but it is a good question to pursue. Bryan Williams' analysis identified about a fifth of the formal events as representing global harmony—internally generated events that are typically calm. Even though that category produces a significant positive effect overall, it clearly is a mixed bag, with a substantial proportion showing the opposite outcome. Bryan tested the variance of this subset of scores—how much extreme variation is shown in both directions—and found it is statistically significant: another indication that there might be "real" negative-going events.

In the absence of a robust ability to pre-specify which events might produce negative trends, the original prediction of positive deviation is used consistently throughout the database. It is arguable that if we knew how to make a more precise prediction (accounting for likely negative cases) our bottom line would be more impressive. But we don't know yet how to do that. The finding is valuable, however, because it sets a new question that we know is worth pursuing: What is the general nature of events that produce negative correlations? This of course also implies the corresponding question about positive correlations.

What characterizes the effects?

We can summarize the most salient points revealed by the deeper analysis of the database up to now in a few major points.

1. The primary effect can be usefully described as correlation of the RNGs spread around the world in our network, even though they are designed to be independent, and are separated by large distances.
2. The bottom line statistics show that the network variance or pair-product correlation is shifted from its mean expectation by about 7 sigma. This is strong evidence that "global consciousness" changes RNG behavior.
3. In addition to the simple pairwise correlation, we find modest evidence (~1.4 sigma) of an orthogonal or independent second-order correlation. It is a correlation of the inter-node variance, and it is independent of the network variance (mean-shift) correlation.
4. The primary correlations depend on the distance separating RNG pairs, but mainly in small events with relatively local attention. They do not depend significantly on distance for truly global events engaging people all around the world.
5. The formal trials (identified events) include a substantial amount of null data before and after the anomalous effect (excess correlations). On average the identifiable effect is on the order of 2- or 3-hours duration.
6. There is long-term structure in the complete database, indicating there may be very general, though unidentified, drivers of the inter-RNG correlations, even without "global events."
7. We are able to classify the events into categories that differ according to the estimated degree or level of membership in the category. This works for both objective categories (e.g., counting) and subjective categories (e.g., ascribing emotions).

What else does secondary analysis show?

1. Short events (less than 8 hours) have twice as large an effect as day-long events. This is probably because the "real" effect lasts only a few hours on average, so the long events have

proportionately large null periods before and after the effect proper, or they may have periods of effect interspersed with null periods that dilute the effect.
2. Effects are stronger when we're awake during the local day. The effect strength goes to a minimum at around 3 am and to its maximum around 6 pm local time. This is a common-sense reflection of the difference between the waking and sleeping consciousness. It is strongly suggestive that "global consciousness" depends on, and is an integration of, our personal, individual consciousness.
3. Some events produce negative correlations; strong negative trends may not be just chance fluctuations. Again, a common-sense finding that matches the propensity to separate the events themselves into positive and negative types.
4. There is autocorrelation in the second-by-second network variance measure, C1, which is moderately significant (~2 sigma) and persists over about 6 seconds (that is, 6 trials in the sequence).
5. There is also autocorrelation in the pair-product variance measure, C2. It is also substantial at about 2 sigma, and persists longer, up to about 12 seconds. This lends substance to the reality of the second-order correlation despite that it has apparently weakened over time.
6. The integrated autocorrelation of C1 indicates that the effect is sequentially predictable out to times of roughly 10 minutes. This consistency indicates that whatever is driving the correlations is not instantaneous or momentary, but solidly persistent.

Such findings are instructive, even when they are relatively weak statistically. They suggest good questions to pursue in any new versions of this research.

The data naturally change over time as more formal trials are accumulated, and because our understanding is based on statistical probabilities, it is necessary to keep in mind that the numbers we have are only estimates. Comparisons of current statistics with those characterizing the data a few years ago show that while the primary result (C1, the network variance) has continued to strengthen as the database size increased, another important parameter (C2) seems to have weakened. Variation of parameter estimates is normal, meaning that determination of the magnitude of these parameters is always uncertain though it generally gets better with more data. The framework is clear—there is a strong primary effect, and there are several effective modulators as well as some independent indicators, but they remain estimates with built in variability.

Chapter 21: MODELING AND THEORY

To develop a complete mind: Study the science of art; Study the art of science. Learn how to see. Realize that everything connects to everything else.
—*Leonardo da Vinci*

Before we begin a discussion of theoretical modeling for the GCP effects, we need to set the stage with some general considerations. There is a long history of increasingly sophisticated attempts to explain psi effects, but for a variety of reasons, there is no theory that is understood to be adequate for the empirical evidence. I think one reason for that is that we are conditioned by experience in simpler fields. For example, in classical physics we are accustomed to bare bones causal models that link easily characterized elements. F = M*A says that force is a combination of mass and acceleration—easy to comprehend, easy to measure, and perhaps most important, easy to apply and experience. Even though there are fine details of the real world that render the equation slightly inaccurate in this simple, ideal form, it works well enough.

We don't have anything like that simplicity when we attempt to explain what psi is and how it works, but many of our best efforts are attempts to fit our observations in mind-matter experiments into analogous molds. We need to stretch a bit to deal with intention effects on physical systems, and with group and mass consciousness effects. I won't be able to give a fully satisfying answer to the questions here, but I'd like to argue for opening up to more comprehensive efforts. (It is worth remarking that these statements apply to psychological and social sciences in general. Psi research is not unique in its theoretical intractability.)

No single-source model is capable of explaining the evidence for psi. It is just not that simple, as much as we might like it to be. There is no equivalent to the A or the M in the equation above. Instead are forced to invoke multi-faceted and complex terms in our efforts to nail down how psi works. The experimental data from decades of research provide a range of empirical findings that seem consistent with one or another of several different theoretical approaches, but we have found that none of them covers all the relevant ground.

There is a natural tendency for most people to attribute effects to the nominal source, the psi operator or subject. But some researchers, especially among those who want to develop an explanatory model, propose that the experimenter is the actual source of the effects. As if that alternative view were not sufficiently complex, there's more. In addition to the subject and the experimenter, there are two other general classes of potential influence on experiment outcomes: the nature of the question we ask, and a catch-all I think of as the universe laughing. That is to say we have much more to learn than we realize, and it seems that the odd reversals and unexpected outcomes that show up bear a message: Keep working—stay open to alternatives—you are not there yet and there is still more to learn.

So, after we have excluded all the spurious sources (mistakes, malfeasance, ordinary physical fields, etc.) we need to think about four distinct but partially overlapping sources for psi effects:

1. Nominal Source, the person or agent or group we think we are studying
2. Experimenter Effect, the most interested, responsible person or parties
3. Nature of the Question, how we ask and what perspective we take
4. Universe Laughing, the capricious nature of a hugely complex world

The first two are familiar. Nominal Source is what seems most natural because it is like the standard scientific paradigm. You set up an experiment to capture the effect of a "subject" or an operator. You stroke a billiard ball with the cue stick and it moves. But the Experimenter Effect opens a different possibility, namely that the scientist herself is a source, or even the source of any anomalous effects. Most of us recognize number 1 and, though it is a little surprising, we accept number 2 also with no great difficulty, while number 3 and number 4 take a bit more thought. The Nature of the Question may be understood as similar to the wave/particle duality meme, but also as a relatively mundane result of design choices: selected vs. unselected subjects, good vs. bad environment, changes of critical elements in "replication" efforts, and so on. Number 4, The Universe Laughing, is a symbolic representation of our truly sparse understanding. We have so little knowledge of so many important variables that it should be no surprise that our experiments often don't work, or go backwards, or show displacement effects. The universe laughs to reduce our hubris. This is like the Coyote of Native American traditions, or the Trickster entity in many cultures: a kind of elastic quality to the unknown world pushing back against our efforts to understand and control it.

I think all of these require consideration, and paying attention to such questions can help move us toward understanding of what turns out to be a very complicated territory.

21.1 Modeling based on data

The most direct and in some ways the most satisfying approach to questions of mechanism and efforts to explain the effects is simply to take the data seriously. We have worked hard to gather it and extract its orderly aspects. Recognizing the subtle nature of low signal-to-noise effects, we work toward a sufficient database in terms of size and complexity to create the opportunity to see structure. Going beyond the simple question whether there is an effect, what people call an "existence proof," we seek to characterize the data more completely. The idea is obvious—where there is a change from expectation, it will likely have several dimensions or parameters, and we need to identify them in order to make a clear picture of the phenomenon. This is the path we will need to follow to create a detailed characterization of the data that allows testing various theoretical approaches. In turn, this effort should bring us closer to understanding how the anomalous changes arise and what they mean in a larger context.

The development of multiple measures of structure in the GCP data is critically important for modeling and theory building. If we have clear, robust results representing, for example, temporal and spatial structure in the event data, this complements the formal measure of inter-node correlation as input for theoretical models of the deviations. Ultimately, having several dimensions or qualities of the "signal" we extract from the data gives us a chance to see its nature, leading to better notions of possible explanatory mechanisms. This work is still in progress, but it is possible to give some preliminary descriptions.

Four classes of models to consider are: 1) conventional explanations in terms of physical and electromagnetic fields; 2) conventional explanations in terms of methodological errors or biases; 3) unconventional information transfer via fortuitous selection of events, experimenter intuition, or retroactive influence from future results; and 4) field-like models invoking consciousness or information "fields" sourced in individual human minds, or a complex non-linear field representing a dynamical interaction among minds.

Explanations of the formal experiment based on spurious effects can be rejected for the reasons detailed earlier in descriptions of the formal research program, and on the basis of published empirical studies.[81] Methodological leaks and systematic biases are precluded, respectively, by event specification and registration procedures that effectively blind the analysis, and by resampling controls which find no evidence of effects in the off-event data. Such explanations are also inconsistent with the multiple indications of unexpected data structure described earlier: the independent correlations, effects of distance, temporal structure and diurnal variations, and parametric variation based on category membership.

Proposals based on electromagnetic (EM) perturbations (extra load on the grid, excess mobile phone usage, etc.) are among the most frequently advanced conventional explanations of the GCP results, but they don't work well. Such proposals can be challenged or rejected for a number of reasons. Design features of the RNGs and the network protect the data generation from biases, as previously described. Even if these protections were not in place, it is unlikely that local EM fields could give rise to the correlations we find among the widely separated RNGs. Finally, direct analysis shows no evidence of diurnal variation in the RNG outputs overall, whereas electromagnetic fields arising from the daily cycle of human activity would presumably induce a corresponding variation in the data. We do not see current proposals based on ordinary EM fields as viable explanations for the measured global correlations and data structure, although I wouldn't want to exclude entirely the possibility of subtle EM effects, such as, perhaps, indirect modulations via general field effects on humans. There is reasonably good evidence, for example, that geomagnetic fluctuations may affect performance in some psi experiments, with calm geomagnetic weather apparently conducing to better outcomes. If the GCP correlations arise because of psi-like subtle interactions among people, those might be facilitated by low levels of geomagnetic flux.

Models involving intuitive selection and retroactive information are variants of a theoretical position from parapsychology advanced to explain psi functioning.[82] The general idea is that expectations and attitudes about the experiment play a role in determining the outcome. More particularly, in the data selection case, the key notion is that deviations result from a fortuitous designation of the beginning times and the length of selected events rather than an actual change in the data. The measured anomalies are attributed to the selection of unlikely data excursions in a naturally varying sequence, and the fortuitous selection is assumed to derive from the experimenter's intuition or precognition of the eventual result, which informs the choice of events, their timing and the test procedures.[83] The GCP results have been analytically tested against explicit versions of this model.[84] The tests reject the proposal with reasonably high confidence.

The retroactive information proposal is based on time symmetry arguments. It suggests that experimental outcomes are linked to the future in a manner that is analogous to the apparently causal past. It implicates consciousness directly by claiming that unexpected data correlations can be explained as a desired future actualizing in the present. Retro-causal models are not developed to the point where they can be tested quantitatively against the GCP data, but we note that no simple version could easily explain multiple indicators of structure in the event data.

Finally, we consider field-type models associated with human consciousness. A basic version is similar to ordinary physical models in that it posits a field generated by a distribution of sources—in this case conscious humans. The field dynamics that explain the RNG correlations derive from the coherence of human activity during events. A formal application of this proposal can accommodate all the inter-node correlations and structure seen in the data. It is only a suggestive explanatory model at this point. Although it addresses the structure of the actual data, it is still a phenomenological description, which does not explain how the field arises in terms of underlying principles. But it definitely is a big, promising step toward theoretical explanation. I have to thank my colleague Peter Bancel for his careful work on these modeling efforts. There is more to do, but we have made significant progress toward an understanding of possible mechanisms for GCP effects.

A more complex, yet attractive proposal is that individual minds may be mutually interactive. In this view, interactions among the minds of individuals are responsible for an emergent field or property which depends on individual consciousness but is not reducible to influences sourced in isolated minds. The proposal suggests that dynamic and interactive qualities of consciousness are fundamental and includes also subtle interactions with the physical world. In the proposal these interactions are responsible for certain anomalous phenomena such as are found in the GCP event experiment. It can be construed as embodying in a formal way the ideas of such thinkers as Teilhard de Chardin, describing a "noosphere" of intelligence for the earth,[85] or Arthur Eddington, conceiving a "great mind."[86]

Peter Bancel's work

By far the most complete effort to explain theoretically how the GCP effects might occur is by Peter Bancel, who has done a great deal of analysis to characterize the data. Over the years, he has discovered qualities and defined parameters that make our understanding of structure in the data—which should be random numbers—more complete, adding several other observations to the basic finding that there are anomalous inter-node correlations. These are described elsewhere (for example in the previous chapter), but they form an important background for Bancel's efforts to identify the source of the effects in GCP data. His current model is different from earlier versions, and reaches apparently contrary conclusions about how the effects arise. It is worthwhile to consider what changed in his thinking, and to see whether the more recent model should supplant the earlier version.

A succinct version of the previous view is presented in the abstract for a paper he wrote for the Parapsychological Association meeting in 2013:[87]

> The Global Consciousness Project maintains a long-term experiment which tests the hypothesis that focused attention of large numbers of people during engaging world events will correlate with deviations in a global network of physical random number generators (RNGs). The Project proposes that the correlation is due to a global consciousness field that is sourced in an aspect of shared consciousness which becomes coherent at the time of major events and that the field perturbs the physical behavior of the RNGs. A 14-year replication experiment tests this hypothesis and finds that, during event periods, RNG deviations exceed null expectation by seven standard deviations. However, the formal experiment cannot distinguish between the GCP hypothesis and a hypothesis based on psi-mediated data selection. Thus, the most pressing question the Project faces is whether the experimental result is due to global consciousness or some form of ESP. In this paper I present a model for the ESP hypothesis and develop a model of field consciousness. Seven statistical tests are derived to distinguish the models. All tests favor the field model. Five of the tests allow calculations of precise probability values. The combination of these tests yields a Z-score of 3.98 (P-value, 0.00003) against the selection model, indicating strongly that the GCP experiment measures a true PK effect and is not the result of psi-mediated data selection.

A year later, Peter completed a chapter for a book edited by Broderick and Goertzel[88] in which he presented much the same material. There were small differences in Z and p-values since he was using a slightly different database, but they basically tell the same story. Summarizing the modeling effort, Peter says:

The results of the 6 analyses [including two consistency checks] on the 381 events in the analysis set are shown in this table. *All of the analyses favor the field model.* A cumulative total of the tests suggests fairly strongly that there is evidence to reject the selection model. Cumulative Z-scores using two methods are listed with the corresponding p-values. The p-values are provided as a reference for the reader, but they need to be considered judiciously given that they refer to *post hoc* data analyses. (Emphasis in the original).

Comparison of Field vs Selection Model

Test	Z-score est	p-value
Signal-to-noise	2.68	0.004
Non-standard events	1.65	0.050
Autocorrelation	2.22	0.013
Pair separation	0.73	0.230
Combined Stouffer Z	3.64	0.00014
Fisher's method	3.000	0.00140

Despite such findings, Peter has retreated from his support for a physical, field-like model, based on his inability to see a way for a consciousness field effect to penetrate the XOR barrier which we use to protect the RNGs from spurious sources of influence such as component aging, temperature changes, or ambient electromagnetic fields. In his most recent paper,[89] a chapter for Broderick and Goertzel,[90] he says that while the cumulative result over 17 years and 500 events apparently lends strong support to the proposal of global consciousness, there is an alternate interpretation, namely that the result is due to an anomalous effect associated with persons directly engaged with the experiment.

His paper examines these interpretations and concludes that the data do not support the global consciousness proposal and instead indicate that the GCP result is due to a goal-oriented effect similar to the DAT model proposed by May, Spottiswoode, and Utts.[91] This model explains effects in RNG studies as a consequence of future feedback influencing present decisions; for example, when to "push the button" to initiate a trial. The idea is that all random sequences have unusual excursions, and that an unexpected statistical outcome can be produced by selecting just the right moment to start collecting data for a trial so as to capture the unusual data, which looks deviant although it is just chance fluctuation. Feedback from the future showing the experimental outcome somehow reaches back to influence the participant (or the experimenter) to start the trial or experiment at an opportune time. This proposition is sometimes called retro-causation, and I believe it is considered by many physicists to be plausible because the equations that describe our best understanding of the physical world are time-symmetrical: they work equally well to describe the future or the past.

One of the clear achievements of Peter's earlier work was a test of two models against the GCP data, one representing the goal-oriented idea, namely the DAT model mentioned above, and the other a "field-like model" representing the idea of global consciousness and the thesis that there is an actual physical effect.[92] In that earlier paper Bancel states: "the GCP data reject the DAT model with moderately high confidence. [And] one can show that a similar procedure which tests the…hypothesis of a physical effect accepts that hypothesis as being consistent with the data."

So the new explanatory effort directly contradicts the 2011 and 2013 conclusions, and it is important to understand why. Over the years, Peter worked hard to establish the viability of field-like models. A major focus of his effort was what he called the XOR problem, and he tried to see how the effects of consciousness could possibly penetrate the XOR in order to affect the bitstream. His concern, which some other physicists also express, is that our procedure for eliminating potential physical biases by inverting 50% of the bits (thus automatically compensating any positive bias with an equal amount of negative bias) would also remove or prevent any possible biasing effect of consciousness. What is implicit here is a belief that the only way consciousness can change the outcome is by a physical intervention that changes a bit derived from a voltage level from 0 to 1 or vice versa.

In his new modeling effort Peter makes this issue central, and he explicitly adopts a specific physical model and interpretation. It entails this assumption that physical bits must be inverted, which would in turn require microsecond synchronization of the XOR patterns. We know the latter is not feasible (but we also know inter-RNG correlations do occur at statistically significant levels). He therefore describes the XOR processing as an efficient filter that blocks spurious correlations, and says that RNG-RNG correlations can survive the XOR process only by exploiting a small "loophole" that postulates similarly biased random sequences at two RNGs being processed with identical XOR sequences. Without going into a great deal of arcane detail, the point is that Peter's idea of how things work requires that the RNG data streams must be synchronized to an improbably fine degree with each other and with the imposed XOR sequence. Since microsecond synchronization across the network is virtually if not actually impossible, he concludes there is no possibility that a Global Consciousness "field" could penetrate the XOR barrier and create the correlations we see in the data.

Nevertheless, the correlations do happen, in both of the two major kinds of RNGs, the Orion and Mindsong. Peter examined the degree, and found that correlation strength for the Orion pairs has a Z-score of 3.28, while the Mindsong pairs, which have a more complex XOR pattern, have a less impressive Z-score of 1.17. This difference accords with Peter's conception of the difficulty finding a "loophole" for a consciousness field effect to penetrate the XOR and make correlated changes in the bitstreams. When the crossed pairs are considered we have a surprising result. The Z-score is 5.36, which corresponds to a probability of 0.000053 or chance odds of about 19000 to 1. Using logic similar to that underlying the prediction that the Mindsongs would show less correlation than the Orions, it is hard to escape the thought that the cross-pair result must mean we are looking at a case of asking the wrong question.

Back to the argument that the XOR precludes a field-like PK effect, the question is, if that can't work, but we do have the correlations to explain, what could do it? Well, there is the DAT idea, which says that feedback from future outcomes must influence the decision whether to identify an event for one of our formal hypothesis tests, what analysis to apply, and what exact times to specify for the beginning and end of the event. This may seem unlikely, the more so because the actual data consist of roughly 2000 correlations per second among an average of 65 RNGs. Beyond that complexity, it requires using information acquired from the future in an unexplained manner. But it is nevertheless a model that is favored by a number of physicists who think about psi. As I mentioned earlier, it is no problem for them to regard a model that requires precognition as plausible because time-symmetric equations are intrinsic to the standard model. Whether a model of this nature can accommodate a complex of measures and structure such as the GCP data present is in my mind questionable.

The preference for a goal-oriented experimenter effect model in this case appears to rest on inappropriate physical assumptions about what is needed to create the correlations. There is no substantial reason to believe GCP effects require the raw physical (electrical) bits to be affected, or synchronously "flipped." This is a mechanistic idea that isn't inherent in the system, globally understood, but it looks like an argument for rejecting a field-like model. I think that argument is spurious because it rests on unjustified assumptions and quite pointedly ignores alternatives, e.g., that post-XOR random sequences remain labile; that the anomalous effects are holistic alterations of the statistical output; or that they can be achieved by a "field-like" influence spreading over multiple bits.

Though I respect Peter's scientific acumen, I think excluding a generalized field model based on the assumption of physical bit-flipping is a mistake. This is a common assumption by physicists,[93] but decades of experiments show it is false. Claims made to the effect there must be something wrong with the experiments put the cart before the horse; they do not respect the actual data. Moreover, although some theorists believe all psi effects should be explained by a selection model such as DAT,[94] others, including Bancel himself, show the model does not fit the data from a variety of competent experiments.[95]

Finally, Peter's newly adopted model seems designed to support or embody another assumption, namely that anomalous effects can only be attributed to an intentional source, a mind that knows about the experimental measurement (and has intentions toward it). This reason for preferring experimenter goal orientation over global consciousness is fleshed out in his chapter for Broderick and Goertzel[96] discussing "proto-psi" which he suggests would be the only mechanism for global consciousness to affect the physical world. Since, he says, a global consciousness cannot manifest intention, it cannot be the source of effects on the GCP network.

This idea should be considered in light of Carpenter's discussion of unconscious intention.[97] That may sound like an oxymoron, but Carpenter makes an excellent case that psi is always present in our lives, and manifests in myriad ways without our conscious involvement. In any case, we need to be cautious in claims about entities we can barely conceive, including the deep structure of consciousness and the interconnection of global populations.

Very recently, Peter has produced another argument for the preference of a goal-oriented (GO) experimenter effect model over a field model. Looking at the context around the events, he finds a "signature" for short events showing negative correlation before and after the event, during which there is a positive cumulative correlation. He says this is what should happen if goal orientation is operating to define the analysis parameters with a psi selection process determining the beginning and end of the events. In contrast, a subset of 24-hour events, which have less freedom in the selection of start and end times, don't have the negative scoring before and after the event period.

I found this analysis to be intriguing, so I decided to look into it directly. To make my replication of the analysis efficient and as clear as possible, I chose a subset of events that showed statistical support for the GCP hypothesis, namely all the nominally or marginally significant formal events (positive Z-score greater than 1.50). In contrast to Bancel's thesis, this representative subset of strong results generally do not show negative correlations before and after the events. This is a curious result, prompting us to ask why the GO model does not fit events that provide the best evidence of an effect.

It is unclear that the signature Peter finds for the short events actually implies a GO model. Beyond this, the sorting procedure he describes for this model does not represent what actually was done in the live experiment. In particular, there is a large subset of short events that do not allow choice of start/end points—I would estimate about half of them—because previous events are taken as models. An even larger proportion of events in the database have quasi-arbitrary starting (and ending) points set as convenient points on the hour or half hour preceding the estimated time of the nominal event. The description of the short events' specification is thus off the mark, and the claim that the resulting pattern of deviations is the signature of GO is at best questionable.

It is a clever and potentially valuable analysis, but it should be replicated independently, with *a priori* fixed criteria and methods. The arguments and logic deserve consideration, but they need to be tested. These are *post facto* analyses and there are untested assumptions. I hope they will be replicated by other investigators, because they have the potential to help distinguish the two most compelling models for GCP effects.

One further observation: The "signature" Peter describes, if transformed to raw data, is virtually identical with that of evoked potentials in neurophysiology. Using repeated measures and signal averaging, researchers find that a visual or auditory stimulus produces a consistent variation in EEG potentials, generally a strong peak preceded and followed by a somewhat weaker deviation in the opposite direction. We observe similar patterns in signal-averaged GCP event data, which suggests that the structural form of a response in the domain of global consciousness may parallel what is found in psychophysiological research on humans and other animals. The time-course is counted in hours rather than milliseconds, but the pattern is remarkably similar.[98]

Contrasting views

I would not discount Peter's view, based as it is on a deep understanding of the data. On the other hand, it is essential to remind ourselves of factors that contribute to a more inclusive picture that suggests the field model cannot be discarded just yet. Much of the broader view comes also from Peter's work, and somewhat ironically, it is sharply in contrast to the goal-oriented or experimenter effect view.

Most of the elements in a more comprehensive view are discussed elsewhere,[99] but I will list some of the more important ones here, in the context of the question whether a goal-oriented model is to be preferred over a field-like explanation for the effects. The common feature of all these elements is that they are discoveries from secondary analyses addressing questions that had not been asked in the original experimental design. They are the result of looking for more structure in the data than the simple standard measure could reveal. Most of the questions have been formulated only in the last few years, and being *post hoc*, were never part of any experimenter's intentions or expectations (as the goal-oriented model would require).

In addition to the primary correlation of RNGs across the network, there is a suggestive second-order correlation of the variances across the network. This is an independent measure, and while weak ($Z \sim 1.4$), it is of the same nature as the original measure—except that it was not part of the conceptual structure of the experiment.

The design of the RNG network implied some questions which, although they weren't intended as part of the hypothesis, were of interest as potential contributors. Both temporal and spatial parameters could be examined to see if they revealed any further structure. Again, though it wasn't part of the design, it was natural to ask about the time-course of any effects, and also natural to ask whether the spatial separation of the RNGs had any effect on the correlations. Various explorations led to the general conclusion that both of these parameters do matter.

The time-course is very much what one would expect from physical considerations; that is, it is like what might happen for an ordinary influence like turning on a stove to heat water. There is a slow buildup of water temperature to a constant, and then when the heat is removed, a gradual decrease. For the GCP event tests, it appears that on average it takes on the order of half an hour for the cumulative deviation to peak, with an hour or two of steady state and then a decline. As mentioned before, there is a similarity to ordinary brain activity and cognition, though the time-scale is very different.

Distance also matters, but the way it manifests is certainly different from my ingoing expectations, as well as those of other professionals in psi research. Most of us have come to regard psi as a nonlocal phenomenon, essentially unaffected by distance. When designing the GCP network, I realized there would be an opportunity to ask the question scientifically since we would have nodes at global distances from each other. This allowed us to ask whether separation or distance modulates the correlations. The answer is a complicated yes—during relatively small, relatively localized events we do see a decrease in correlation strength as the separation increases. This is counter to the original expectations held by any of the experimenters or analysts. For large events with truly global interest and engagement, the tendency for separation to matter is weak. In retrospect, these findings make sense, but they obviously are not compatible with an experimenter (or analyst) goal orientation model.

One of the most persuasive "new" findings in this context is the discovery a couple of years ago that the effect size is a function of time of day.[100] There is a clear pattern across all the events, where the effect is largest in the local afternoon, and smallest in the middle of the night. In other words, it seems to depend on whether people are awake or asleep. This is another item where most of us will say, "of course, why would we think otherwise?" But in the context of identifying the source of effects, it seems terribly unlikely that this result could be an experimenter effect. Or, perhaps it is the analyst—in this case Peter Bancel. But we really can't postulate that everything one finds in the data, whether it is bizarre or utterly logical, is only there because of experimenter or analyst intention. Such *ad hoc* accommodation to the analytical findings would be perilously close to unfalsifiable theory making.

There are more points that are similarly incompatible with an experimenter effect/goal orientation model. Effect size scales with the number of eggs, and if we are looking at a field we should see such an effect. The trial data are autocorrelated, meaning the next few trial values are predictable given the current value. This wouldn't be unreasonable for a goal-oriented model if the goal was to produce or find autocorrelations. But that was never a hypothesis we intended to test in the first instance. It was a reasonable analysis to make in order to learn more about the structure that appears in the nominally random data, but definitely not a "goal" of the experiment.

For a field-like model, these and the other late arriving results of continuing analysis fit naturally. If there is a "field" affecting a trial value, it is an easy and obvious step to predict it will affect adjacent values. The distance findings and the temporal aspects of the effects also are readily accommodated by a field-like model. A small event would be the source of a small field we might expect to weaken with distance. A globally engaging event, on the other hand, should produce a field of global dimensions with little or no attenuation as RNG separations increase. And a time-varying field effect associated with awake and aware human beings makes sense, while attributing that variation to experimenter intention is problematic.

Looking at the question from a broader perspective, there are several more considerations that present difficulties for an experimenter/goal-orientation model. Although it is possible to argue that the "experimenter" might include several of my colleagues, and perhaps even all the people who know or think about the project when a likely event comes up, the simplest straightforward version of the experimenter/goal-orientation model would be with Roger Nelson as the source of the anomalous effects. The following notes take that perspective.

Examining the Formal Hypothesis Register reveals that less than 200 of the 500 formal events were primarily identified by me (Nelson) and of these, many are "repeats," which have their parameters largely or completely determined by the previous version. So, logically, I would have had to tap into the future feedback not just for one, but for two or more events separated by months or years.

Of course, I am ultimately responsible for the registration of all the events, which is to say I know something about all of them—what kind of events they are, and when they happened or will happen. But I can say that although I am interested on a general level, my investment is usually minimal beyond ensuring that everything is being done according to protocol. Only for a small minority of events do I feel engaged beyond the needs of the record keeping. But even then, my interest isn't about getting a positive result in the GCP data. Instead I'm thinking about or responding to the event as most people do. I would guess that for that minority of events that hold my attention, I am joined by millions of others whose interest and focus is similar to mine. There is a difference of course—they don't know about the experiment and I do—but when the tsunami happens, or the mine explosion, or New Year's, for that matter, my attention and connection to the event is like that of the rest of the world. I feel the deep compassion, or the joy of celebration—I don't consciously "intend" that there be an effect on the GCP network. The idea is foreign to my concept of the experiment. I may harbor all kinds of unconscious intentions,[101] but I see no logical way to avoid the conclusion that should apply equally to the possible mass consciousness we are talking about.

On the global level of the experiment as a whole, it could be said that my intention is clear. I do want to learn something, and I have expectations that will be tested against the data. But can that be construed as an intention to mold (via a postulated goal orientation that accesses the future) the experimental outcome to match my hopes and desires? Could my intention to learn how things work be satisfied by reaching into the future to see the experimental outcome so I could apply it to my choices for setting the GCP's specific hypotheses? I don't think so. Instead, thanks to my respect for science as a set of tools, I am deeply opposed to using or, more correctly put, to misusing those tools to support preconceptions or cherished notions. Logically, I could not satisfy my intention to learn something about the world by manipulating it to provide "desired" results.

Put in concrete terms, the idea that experimenter psi of this sort (pretty much the same as DAT[102]) can explain the broad array of facts and findings in the GCP database seems unlikely. It seems a bit much to expect from any individual (especially one whose documented performance as a participant in the PEAR experiments was at the modest end of the scale). For the small group of people who know the experiment and helped identify events, my guess is that their energies were, like mine, typically engaged in the social and personal event as it transpired—not in an attempt to get or even to hope for a particular outcome.

No, although the experimenters' influence on the experiment is without question more likely than that of people who don't know it is happening, it seems virtually certain to be about aiming the instrument rather than dictating or influencing its readings. As I've mentioned elsewhere, the determinants of subtle phenomena like those we study in the GCP are multiple—the nominal source of mass consciousness; the experimenters deciding where to point the instrument; the question, whose nature necessarily influences its answer; and the universe, playfully and curiously forcing us to think deeply, and then to think again.

21.2 Speculative Notions and Models

Something unknown is doing we don't know what.
—Sir Arthur Eddington

We have little real understanding of the mechanisms that might underlie the anomalous correlations found in the GCP data. The mathematical modeling we have done is more useful in establishing constraints on what might work than for describing any particular mechanisms. Here we offer some speculations that may be helpful in thinking about possible models. There are several more-or-less scientific notions, and though none can be presented as a finished, competent explanation, I think they are interesting ideas, and in any case they are thought-provoking.

Many questions are asked that relate to underlying mechanism, such as whether there is an optimal speed or frequency for data collection, or whether the number of bits that are momentarily in play will matter. The short answer is that these and similar questions may harbor assumptions that aren't correct. It appears that the domain for most of the effective variables is not mechanics or physics but psychology, not matter but mind. So, counting the elements or measuring the speed at which things happen are not necessarily relevant unless the counts and measures are in the non-physical realms we usually leave to poets and musicians.

So we often disregard the wisdom of the ancients, and of other cultures than that of modern Western science, which Ken Wilber calls a monocultural flatland.[103] He shows, for example, that the modern Western view is shallow at best, a "flatland" incapable, because of its narrow focus on what can be located and what can be counted, even of asking the questions we know we must be able to ask about consciousness and spirit.

The GCP analyses are based on canonical statistics, and while some argue that this cannot provide "real" evidence, only correlations, the implications of statistical measures can be profound. Though we don't know how an RNG's behavior can be altered by thoughts and emotions or intentions, we know empirically that the effects touch upon information theory and imply entropy reduction, and we think that resonance and coherence are good metaphoric descriptors for the necessary conditions. Most important, there is a correlation between a history of meaningful events and variations written in our data.

After one and a half decades of experience with the GCP data, looking at the varieties of correlations and the factors that seem to matter, I begin to see a "mechanism" for the GCP effects. I don't yet know how to express it in clear scientific/mathematical terms, but the substance is that *correlation is something*. There is a real entity in the world whose nature appears to be relationship and pattern—and it is not just an idea or an abstraction, but a "Ding an sich" that can be touched upon in various subtle experiments. There is a clear, albeit intuitive linkage of this idea with the insights of Carl Jung on meaningful coincidence, or synchronicity, as well as the powerful structures represented in fundamental statistics. But there is a particular dimension or quality that isn't developed in canonical statistical science.

The core defining quality of the correlations in GCP data, as we see also in our search for explanation of other psi effects, is meaning. To see why, consider that we would never see the subtle data anomalies in GCP data without having posed the question about correlation of our data with big, human-centric, meaningful events on the world stage. It is obviously necessary to accept and explore psychological factors that we cannot describe in physical terms in order to describe and ultimately explain the GCP findings.

We find some useful points in models based on David Bohm's notion of active information[104] (which I'll summarize below), and in Brian Josephson's article on String Theory, Universal Mind, and the Paranormal.[105] One of the most coherent approaches to evidence demanding thoughtful extensions of physical models is Rupert Sheldrake's description of Morphic Fields.[106] Abraham Boyarsky argues that any theory of mind is better than none, and uses the language of nonlinear dynamical systems and ergodic theory to present a theoretical framework for the study of mind.[107] For a lively and insightful look at the physics of consciousness (with consciousness as primary, the ground of all existence) look up Amit Goswami's writings.[108] This is just a small sampling of efforts to make sense of a world in which consciousness is obvious to everyone, but fails to make an appearance in our useful, generally accepted models.

GCP correspondents have over the years suggested a variety of explanatory models and made potentially useful comments. In this border area it is difficult to know what will turn out to be the most viable ideas, and it is worthwhile to keep an open mind. Still, at this point most of what can be said is speculative, and not immediately helpful for understanding the empirical data. We do not know how a mental state such as an intention or emotion is able to inform a physical system so as to affect its behavior. In addition, all of the robust measures we have that provide evidence for the anomalous effects are statistical in nature, and the signal-to-noise ratio is extremely low. This means that we typically cannot be sure that the "signature" of an effect in any individual analysis is actually driven by the hypothesized influence of consciousness. The details written in the data from single instances are more likely to be chance fluctuations than consciousness effects. Only in larger concatenations, gathering the weak signals from many separate events, can we be satisfied that trends and structure represent the hypothesized effect.

After all the caveats, however, we can say that the evidence for an effect of consciousness on RNGs is strong. We are driven (here I should say "I am driven" because, as we have seen, some of my very bright colleagues have other ideas) by that evidence to infer that something like a "consciousness field" exists, and that intentions or emotional states that structure the field are conveyed as information which is absorbed into the distribution of samples from labile physical systems.

The bottom line is that the output distribution of data from the RNGs differs from what would be expected without the influence of consciousness. Two major questions should be kept in mind to help focus our speculations:

1. What is the physical meaning of the statistically unlikely patterns that appear in our random data?
2. What is the bio-social meaning of the correlation of such patterns with events of importance to humans?

The Active Information Field

I have from the time I first encountered it felt an affinity to David Bohm's idea of an implicate order—which he thinks is the fundamental background and source of physical reality. The following is my summary of Bohm's thoughts on a particularly important aspect, the active information field. Quite recently I found a beautifully direct presentation in a 5-part interview with Bohm on YouTube.[109] What he says is remarkably close to what we find the GCP data to be saying.

His friend and colleague Basil Hiley remarked that, from a very early age Bohm felt that there was a deep "interconnectedness" in nature that went far beyond the primitive notion of particles (or fields) in interaction. This was a fundamental conviction he worked to express consistently. In Bohm's own words, "First of all, we note that the universal interconnection of things has long been so evident from empirical evidence that one can no longer question it."[110]

If we look for alternatives to Wilber's suggestion that Western science is a flatland we see some good news. Among the ordinary tools of modern physics, there are some effective expansions and some questions that begin to distort the flatland into more dimensional forms. One of the most promising models I have found for thinking about the GCP data is based on a generalized application of the "active information" proposed by Bohm as the core of the quantum potential or pilot wave which is fundamental to his theoretical approach.

If we look at evidence from studies of the far reaches of consciousness, we are impelled to envision a metaphorical equivalent to the fields that link physical objects (EM fields). But to deal with psi data, this conceptual framework needs to be applied to the non-physical, to the experienced world of ideas, structures, relationships. We need a well-defined equivalent to EM fields that can accommodate interconnections in a more subtle realm, something that integrates the effective interactions of a field with the meaningful implications of directed mental interconnection. A viable starting framework can be found in an extension of Bohm's efforts to link the sensible world with the implicate order. The remaining step is to take seriously the notion of active information, which is virtual but can be actualized, and consider that it is a field linking us universally to our world. Let's call this an active information field (AIF).

The proposed model builds on the idea that consciousness or mind is the source or seat of a nonlocal, active information field or AIF. Each of us is centered in an extended mental or consciousness presence, which has some of the character of a field analogous to, though not the same as, those we are familiar with from radio, television and electromagnetism. The AIF is not a standard, well-defined physical construct, but an operational metaphor intended to help create useful questions for the empirical research.

For example, such fields should interact, usually with random phase relationship and no detectable product. When many consciousness (information) fields are driven in common, or for whatever reason become mutually coherent and resonant, they interact in phase, and create a new integration on a higher level: a structured information field. The RNG has an informational aspect (entropy) and a completely undetermined labile future. That is, there exists no description or determination of the next element in the RNG output. I speculate, following Bohm, that the RNG, with its unknown next moment, manifests a "need for information" which allows or guides the actualization of the virtual, active information sourced in human consciousness, including group or global consciousness. With this, the RNG's next moment is brought into existence; it is determined.

Most simply put, I think consciousness is a source of active information, and that the objects of attention for consciousness can be sinks that attract and hence actualize the information. When we give attention to a situation, this mental act creates a subtle change, opening it to relevant information. It is thus possible for it to absorb the information inherent in intentions and emotions that relate to the situation. A simple example: If we discover a mutual attraction with another person, we each are informed in subtle, unconscious ways that make us different from our previous state. We fall in love, perhaps, or become life-long friends, bonded by the mingling and merging of the active information each of us expresses and absorbs. If this description sounds unfamiliar, it is because we don't generally have any way to perceive the process—it is entirely automatic and unconscious. Yet it is quite beautiful, and the source of poetry that embodies our deepest understanding.

The qualities of active information make the concept of an AIF richly supportive of the otherwise inexplicable connections we see linking mind and matter. The AIF is non-local and thus has universal dimension and accessibility. It is virtual, and hence not amenable to observation, unless it is actualized by a need for the structure or formative influence that comprises its nature. It is thus both the manifestation and the generative source of a universal interconnectedness. Its nature comprises both the creation and the application of form and meaning.

Interacting fields

The evidence for something new arising out of the interaction of consciousness or information fields requires us to think more deeply. Even the simple electromagnetic fields we know about generally just interpenetrate without interaction, but physical models of EM may offer some insight. We know that a single particle, an electron or a photon, even a long way from its neighbors, is never alone in field theory. This is true even in classical electrodynamics, where the electron sources the electromagnetic field from which it can never escape. This is a picture that appears to be apt for information or consciousness as well. Our research shows that here also there is no ultimate separation, even over great distances. This is the meaning of entanglement, and as stressed by Dean Radin[111] it seems applicable to consciousness as well as to quantum objects.

An analogy might suggest that interactive consciousness arises from local excitations in the information field. We need to take care in choosing useful analogues, however. In simple free field theories particle excitations can be seen, but the particles don't interact with each other. To represent the situation that interests us, where fields do influence each other, more complicated theories that include interaction terms must be used. These higher order terms or coefficients in a field model are called coupling constants. The coefficients condition what happens as time passes, and serve to maintain stability within weakly coupled, interacting fields. It should be fruitful to consider what the dimensions of coupling constants for interacting information fields might be. This is beyond the reach of this book, but it is an interesting, important challenge for the science of consciousness.

Other interesting models

A variation on my Active Information Field approach comes from Lian Groza, who offers ideas (personal communication) that touch the same themes, but attempt to keep a strong link with familiar physical models:

> Let's imagine that we have a fifth, non-physical field (see Bohm's quantum potential, or Sheldrake's morphogenetic field) and let's call it IF (information field). The information carried by it is, as Bohm describes, encoded in the form of the wave rather than its amplitude, hence it is independent of the field strength (distance independence).
>
> Now, let's imagine this IF as being related to the EM field in the same way electricity and magnetism are mutually dependent: in the same way a magnetic field is created by an electric current moving inside a wire, an IF signal can be created by certain configurations (patterns) of EM waves, and vice-versa (IF signals can perturb and modify the EM-coded bioinformation of a target organism, producing a healing effect or, as the case may be, being registered as EM thought patterns in a telepathy experiment).
>
> Another intriguing possibility is that this hypothesized

EM/IF interplay may account for the target identification/specificity that such phenomena display. If one views a target's identity as being encoded by a unique EM signature, then a long-range IF signal might act as a scanner/matched filter that would first need to "resonate" with the target's EM signature before "delivering its message". (Of course, this is all highly speculative and I haven't got a clue as to what would constitute a unique EM signature for a person or location.)

In this scenario, then, the practice of yogic asanas, samadhi, etc. would serve to enhance one's ability to develop and sustain the necessary EM signal to create a coherent (resonant?) IF wave, while normal consciousness would be equivalent to a plurality of weak, non-resonant, mutually destructive IF signals.

Entanglement

Among the possibilities presented by current physical theories that attract the attention of people trying to explain psi effects is entanglement. Dean Radin has developed this idea to the point where it can be conceptually applied to many of the conundrums in psi research. His book *Entangled Minds*[112] is an excellent introduction not only to the topic of anomalous interactions, but to the physics. Here is a brief summary of the idea:

> When a physical system is separated into components there remains an entanglement that exists even over great distances. The result is that if one element changes, a measurement on the separated component will show it has undergone a correlated change. The fundamental notion is that once connected, there is always a connection between nominally separable elements. In the context of our consciousness, the extension of the entanglement construct suggests that there is an underlying connectivity between people and between us and the physical environment which is tantamount to a permanent nonlocal linkage. As always, the devil is in the details, but this approach is promising and attractive as a possible explanation for anomalous interconnections.

M5 model

A different, yet related perspective is taken by Bob Jahn and Brenda Dunne in their "Modular Model of Mind/Matter Manifestations," which looks deeply into the sources of both the physical and the experiential world. They urge a more "cogent representation of the merging of mental and material dimensions into indistinguishability at the deepest levels of their interactions." A description of the model was published in the *Journal of Scientific Exploration*.[113] Here is a brief note on what I think is an insightful core idea that helps to think about how mind or consciousness may have effects in the physical world.

> The most crucial interface in our model, that between [the unconscious and the intangible], is the least sharply defined. Indeed, if the contention of several authors regarding the indistinguishability of mental and physical phenomena at the deepest levels of these two domains is valid, there can remain no interface there at all, only a pre-distinction continuum bearing only vestigial characteristics of the Cartesian divide that forms above. We are proposing that it is this homogenized lowest layer of [the unconscious and the intangible] that provides the tunnel for anomalous passage of information from the mental side to the material side or vice versa, or perhaps more aptly, that it provides the gestation site for some embryonic "pre-information" commodity that subsequently will emerge into both tangible events and conscious experiences. Given their common origin, these events and experiences will inevitably display intrinsic correlations, and these comprise the apparent mind/matter anomalies that bemuse our conscious minds.

First Sight Theory

Another rich and helpful perspective on the anomalous effects of consciousness is First Sight Theory, described by Jim Carpenter.[114] To start, he says the effects aren't anomalous at all, but always present. We only need an adjustment of perspective on what consciousness is and how psi effects are part of it.

In the First Sight model, several almost universal but implicit assumptions about psi are changed: Psi is not an ability, ESP is not knowledge, PK is not action. Psi is a natural and normal part of our makeup. It is unconscious and ever present, somewhat like gravity, which shapes our existence as water does for a fish, or the social matrix that contributes so much to our being.

Perhaps the most important new assumption is that psi is not an ability. Psi events are implicit indicators of unconscious connections. It is not a rare and special attribute, but a universal characteristic of living organisms, a basic feature of their being-in-the-world. It is a fact that we are all unconsciously and perpetually engaged in a universe of meaning that extends far beyond our physical boundaries in space and time.

This sounds very much like what must happen to create the correlations we see in the Egg data. Nobody perceives or feels them happening. But interconnections do occur at deep levels of our consciousness, and they make themselves known in the data.

Future models

This is a brief survey of possible models and theories reaching for descriptions of the anomalous findings in experiments like the Global Consciousness Project. They fall short of the ideal of understanding and explanation. To go forward with that goal, what we need are testable, falsifiable models. The models we have in hand are steps toward understanding, and although they do not establish an accepted scientific explanation of the subtle effects of consciousness on the physical world, they can guide experiments and help to formulate better questions.

There is only so much to be gained from further data collection even if it consolidates our gains in confidence that there is a real phenomenon to explain. We can be quite convinced that human consciousness has direct effects in the world, but we want to know how, and we'd like to go one step further and find out why. What is the purpose served by these intriguing aspects of mind, which are old in poetry, but new in science? It seems essential to know how this works, because it can be seen as an important part of our lives, a set of tools we've never learned to use intentionally even though we've been praying and wishing for all of human history.

We obviously have more work to do. Perhaps we need to lean back in a meditative way, open and ready for inspiration. The first step has been taken, so we know there is a question begging for answers. The next step will be to refine that question to the point where it bears within it the answer it needs. This sounds like our conception of "Active Information" again. The challenge is to create a well-formed need that can actualize the implicate potential for understanding.

But at this point I will leave the question of advanced modeling to others whose natural inclinations and skillsets are up to the task. There are real challenges here, in search of mastery.

Part Four: Interpretation and Meaning

The concepts which now prove to be fundamental to our understanding of nature...seem to my mind to be structures of pure thought,...the universe begins to look more like a great thought than a great machine.

—*James Jeans*[115]

Evidence for Noosphere

The GCP response on 9/11 was so powerful and persuasive that it brought out the entrepreneurs, who saw a chance to make big bucks on "terrorism detectors." They interpreted suggestions of a precursor response, with the data making a strong inflection several hours before the first plane hit the towers, as a tool for predicting other disasters and giving a warning to allow prevention or mitigation. There were even some immediate efforts to patent such systems—which as far as I know did not work out. I did what I could to be sure there was a public awareness that even if our GCP system were to show a surge of correlations, the only workable message would be that a major event might be coming soon. Interest waned when the entrepreneurs finally understood that a big spike in the data might reflect either positive or negative happenings, and even if it was huge, unmistakable, we would have absolutely no idea what it represented, or where it might be. The detector flurry was quite a good example of the difficulty we have dealing with wishful thinking, which so often overwhelms objective evidence. But this over-optimistic response to the data was actually a distraction from much more potent implications. The results hold important messages about interaction and interconnection.

Setting the wild and exciting extrapolations aside, it's clear that while we are not finished asking questions and seeking answers in further analyses of the data, we should be comfortable with some straightforward interpretations of the evidence, which touch on the early inspirations for the EGG project.

I originally envisioned a faint, developing interconnection among people, which would be global in scope, and which might be shown by effects on RNG data. It seemed reasonable to refer to this as a "global consciousness" (GC) even though it was (and remains) unlikely that we could be aware of the necessary interconnections, and even less likely that the GC would be actually "conscious" in the normal usage of the term.

For us as individuals, the existence of this inchoate entity and our possible participation in it would be unconscious and inaccessible. For this new global entity, an actual consciousness would be similarly unlikely and unmanifest, at least in any way we might perceive or even envision. Nevertheless, the search for evidence of something in this domain seemed worth pursuing, and the resulting 17-year experiment has yielded plenty of food for thought. Some of the implications are quite clear, while others remain speculative or tentative, but it is worthwhile to list some that seem most prominent. Without much in the way of explanation, here are some reasonable statements about what this research implies. These ideas and conclusions are supported by other research in various ways, but I see them as directly evident from the EGG Project work.

> Consciousness has presence in the world.
> Consciousness is extended and non-local.
> Humans are connected at a deep level.
> Mind can have effects we have not imagined.
> Cooperative intention has consequences.
> When we are coherent, we create a Noosphere.
> It is time to accept oneness as modern wisdom.

It is worthwhile to consider these ideas from the grand perspective expressed by Carl Jung in his correspondence with Wolfgang Pauli. They are thinking deeply about synchronicity or meaning-correspondence, as Pauli liked to think of it:

> I would now like to propose that instead of 'causality' we have '(relatively) constant connection through effect,' and instead of

synchronicity we have (relatively) constant connection through contingency, equivalence, or 'meaning.'

Sometimes it seems to me that such conversations, with their deep and honest intensity, need to continue, or to resume. Indeed, I imagine that is happening because there is so much interest in how things work for us humans, and what it means to be conscious. A look at social media with the relevant questions in mind reveals a flood of commentary and questioning that touches on exactly the same questions I am addressing. Each time I publish or post a new analysis or comment on the Global Consciousness question, there is an immediate return of equally poignant and purposeful questions from other people wishing to understand more, and to do more with the understanding. We've talked about the difficulty finding a really good model to explain our results, but in the end we have to respect the tentative place we occupy on the way to knowing how things work. The effects in the GCP data are hard to see in terms of causality, but their meaning is immediate and transparent. That means, surely, that the real questions to address are about doing the right thing with what we have learned, putting our insights to work, getting on with the business of being human.

Chapter 22: EXTRACTING MEANING

As our unconscious links mature, humans will grow into a role like neurons in a global brain, creating an intelligence for the earth—a global mind.

—*Gunnar Rog*

To start the interpretive process, we need to consider some of the more difficult definitions and procedural issues we had to deal with in developing the project. These need careful description because the language (words like consciousness, for example) often is misunderstood, or taken to mean something we don't intend. I'm mindful of such difficulties, described cleverly in a little wall plaque given to me by my brother:

I know you think you understand what I said, but I'm not sure you realize that what you heard is not what I meant.

—*Anonymous*

A useful observation generally, but critically important in science. Our hypothesis testing depends on being quite specific about things that have names or use words that are in common parlance, but often used with different meanings. One of the first questions an interviewer may ask me is, "What is consciousness?" It seems to most folks to be a good question since the project name includes it. A little careful thought makes clear that this is a complicated word and a complex topic that depends utterly on the context for the discussion. One good answer is that consciousness is what allows us to ask such questions. But that doesn't help with what the interviewer meant to ask. What does help is to explain that we create a definition by specifying what we do. I've described this earlier, but it bears repeating.

To establish our formal series of rigorous tests, we first identify and delimit a "global event" that meets criteria we have set to select occasions when large numbers of people are synchronized in their thoughts or emotions. We want to look at moments in time when a substantial number of people, in most cases many millions, become coherent or resonant with each other, sharing an experience that evokes deep emotional responses. Second, we specify an analysis that will be applied to the corresponding GCP data to quantify deviations from expectation. We work to simplify our data and create a focused summary we can test for correlation with that coherent moment.

These two operations define what we mean by "global consciousness" in this special experimental context. If the data depart from expectation, we identify the deviation as a moment of global consciousness. It's abstract, but a practical and consistent way to tell what we mean. The concatenation across repeated tests like this, each addressing a similarly defined specific hypothesis, ultimately provides evidence for or against our general hypothesis: focused attention and emotion shared by large numbers of people will affect our GCP instrument. If that happens, we can say we have captured a moment of global consciousness.

Defining a global event and specifying when it begins and ends is a bit arbitrary, but there are many cases that most people will agree upon, and there are effective ways of assessing the data to see if there is any anomalous structure. The results are based on correlating these carefully chosen moments, mostly drawn from world news headlines, with data taken at the same time by the EGG network. When we assess the correlations, we find a tendency for the data to be changed from what is expected, leaving only a few possibilities to consider.

It may be that the interest and desires of the people in the EGG project produce what is called an "experimenter effect" that is registered by the detectors. It is probably the case that the nature of the question we ask somehow shapes the outcome, and there may be subtle contributions from other sources. The results are remarkable in any case, but it is fair to say that the pattern of correlations shows a primary influence that looks most like a shared human response to events. Overall, it seems most consonant with the complex of results to interpret the anomalous structure as evidence that there is something like a mass consciousness, or what we're calling global consciousness, which exists in a faint but detectable form.

With our limited detection capabilities, we cannot be certain whether it is momentary and fluctuating or instead may be persistent. If we could make that distinction it would tell us the difference between a few flickers of intelligence or something like Teilhard's noosphere. The series of formal events can be thought of as 500 independent probes looking for correlated activity and interconnection.

What is also interesting in this context is that when we look at all the data as a continuous sequence over months and years, we see statistically significant long-term trends that might be interpreted as effects of a weak, continuing mass consciousness. But the evidence from such exploratory analysis, though tantalizing, needs rigorous support. Whether the source of our anomalous correlations is persistent or not is an important question we need to ask in future work to learn more about a global presence of mind.

Beginning interpretations

We are sure these results represent a genuine anomaly, but at this point it is not possible to offer a definitive explanation. There are suggestive interpretations that might begin to explain these effects, which are correlated with great events via what we have called global consciousness. But these remain speculative although we have made progress on models that accommodate the structure found in the data. The kinds of explanations that are viable are a limited set; some possibilities can be excluded while certain explanatory directions are favored.

An important conclusion we could draw from mathematical modeling of the first 10 or 12 years of data is that the effects are physical, not merely fortuitous selections from fluctuating possibilities. In other words, the effects are "real" changes in the behavior of the RNGs, so the kinds of theoretical descriptions we need could be usefully constrained. More recently, Peter Bancel's analyses have suggested that conclusion needs to be tempered and that some kind of goal-oriented experimenter effect may be operative, as described in Chapter 21. Nevertheless, I am confident that the data are affected by something about the mass consciousness created by major events. The experimenters are certainly part of the picture, but I think we act as a focusing lens, while the light that creates the scene comes from deep-lying human interconnections brought forth by synchronous and coherent reactions to intense moments with widespread impact.

It seems clear that the mechanism we are looking for embodies information in a particular mode (closely related to meaning). In a metaphoric if not actual sense, information is absorbed into the network of RNGs and changes the sequence of bits. This does not require an electrical pulse or a physical push, only a decision—a bit of information.

A small number of these bits—whose future identity, we recall, is not fixed or predictable—change from what they would have been. The probabilities for a 1 or 0 change very slightly, and this happens in concert across the network. To actually say the words feels like an exaggeration because the correlations between pairs of RNGs are so very small. But something changes, and when we patiently test for the possible change, we find it. Over the course of dozens of events, the statistics build to persuasive levels. They show that changes in the RNG network have taken place. Some of my colleagues may object, saying such changes aren't required to produce the anomalous effects; it could be that precognition of future results influences the fortuitous selection of a moment with unusual deviations. That idea, as I have argued, won't wash because it fails to accommodate so much real structure in the data.

How can we explain the results? One of the most promising physical models for the anomalies we see in this work is drawn from David Bohm's concept of active information, which I described in Chapter 21. In his terms, information (and concomitant meaning) can be nonlocal, extending indefinitely throughout space and time. Active information may be envisioned as a potential field interaction that guides developing manifestations in the physical world. Active information is virtual, but when a "need" for it exists, the need actualizes the information by creating or being a repository for it to manifest.

In such a model, the question we ask in the EGG project plays the role of the need for information, making it possible for the inchoate meaning of global consciousness to manifest. I'll repeat that in other words. When we set up and monitor the RNG network, the GCP instrument, we are implicitly asking a question creating a need for information of a particular sort. Shared, coherent mental and emotional activity in millions of people is a potential source of such information, and our experiment is designed to link the need and the source.

It should be clear that I am invoking metaphor. I intend it to be a first approximation, and trust we will find a more finely tuned, satisfying answer to the question how the GCP effects arise.

Suggestions like those made in many intellectual and cultural traditions, that there is an Earth consciousness, appear to have a modicum of scientific support in the GCP results. Similarly, the idea of a large-scale group consciousness, potentially engaging whole populations, gains credence. At the very least, these results are consistent with the idea that a subtle linkage can exist among widely separated people, and that we may be linked on a grand scale by something like a consciousness field. The sequence of unlikely "chance" events leading to the EGG project has brought us the means to examine questions like this by looking for distortions of chance itself, apparently wrought by consciousness reaching out to connect our minds and to touch the material world. We seem to have captured a faint indication that Teilhard de Chardin's vision of our destiny is beginning to manifest.[116]

Global Mind?

If we read the great books and poetry, or look and listen to the arts generally, it is clear that humanity has long since begun to exhibit its global destiny. Even though we cannot easily see it, there is an intertwining golden braid of great beauty that links our cultures. We have a poetic history, and that is where we will find our future. We need to appreciate our human qualities, and the nearest, richest source for that is what we call art. As Lewis Thomas said, if we want to know about consciousness, we ought to listen to music.[117] More specifically, he said listen to Bach. But each of our major cultural streams has its own Bach, and at this moment in history these streams are mingling and we are on the verge of understanding how much alike we all are. It is a small step to begin a global dance. We still need the communication channels of electronics and airplanes, but these are creating a common language and bringing us face to face with ourselves.

Perhaps the data from the far-flung EGG network ought to be viewed through an artistic lens too, and thus seen with the more perceptive heart. Though we start with a scientific attitude and maintain the clarity of purpose necessary for objective evaluation, it seems very important to open up the field of view to another, more creative eye, that of the subjective mind. After all, we wish to touch this new possibility of mind, which the heart sees as an awesome, albeit immature gathering of potential, lying gossamer across the world. So, for a deeper understanding, we ought to make music with the numbers, and allow harmonies that might be hidden in the correlations sound out. And we should paint pictures and weave webs of meaning from the not-quite-random values sent by GCP eggs in Europe and Africa, and Asia, and the South Pacific, and the Americas. We want to mix these as sounds and colors, and combine them with the poetic insights that frame and sketch the design of an imagined global consciousness, just waking. In the meantime, science, with its highly developed objective methods, succeeds in drawing some elegantly instructive graphs as pictures that turn the data into insights, and give a high perspective on the questions. These have their beauty too, and they show structures where there ought not to be any—unless it is created there by some faint stirring of a global consciousness.

Orderly mind stuff—the beginnings of a theory

We are, in the most personal sense, orderly mind stuff. The aspect of myself that "I" refers to is made of something different from matter and molecules. This is a personal, experiential fact, and it deserves attention because we don't quite know what to make of it; we don't yet see how to benefit from knowing what mind is—and is not. But for the moment, talking about and studying the greater mind of global consciousness, it is enough to know that this orderly mind stuff can interact, not only with other mind stuff, but with our curious machines. The random event generators create a roughly textured page on which the mass mind can impress a message. We would like to understand this too, and have a theory to explain Orderly Mind Stuff, but that must wait, for we still have to learn much more to formulate an adequate question.

An obvious question for many people is, "Well, what do you mean by the term, consciousness? Don't you have to define that first before presuming to study it, the more so if you want to study something you call global consciousness?" I have already touched on this, but let's look at it more deeply. It is a fair question, though I think we have to recognize the slippery nature of definitions, at least those put into words. Why? Because, as Wittgenstein suggested, "Language bewitches intelligence." He meant that when we put language on some object we think we have captured it and properly defined it—but we don't recognize the fact that what I hear you say may be and usually is affected by my personal experiences and motivations. In other words, I can only hear something that fits my understanding, which is surely different from yours. Simply put, naming an object does not define it.

We need more, and in science, where precision is important, the best we can do, usually, is an operational definition. As described earlier, this is literally the procedure for our research, a description of what we do to study the object of interest. The result is exact and understandable, and though it might not satisfy in the way a literary definition can, it is transmissible and testable. At the level of experimental science, this is what we need.

On another level, we want to talk about the presence of something interesting in the world. The operational approach is necessary, but not necessarily satisfying. So we want to supplement it with a definition closer to common experience, hoping at the same time to keep track of the connection to an operational characterization. Ultimately, the two perspectives should complement each other, and allow extrapolations from the experiment to a world of implication and interpretation.

Let's look at a "literary" attempt, which may ring some bells, or on the other hand, may seem so far afield as to be meaningless. Either way, we will probably want more, and for scientific purposes, more precision will certainly be necessary.

Consciousness seems to result from a coalescence of connections among the elements of brain and mind. (And what is mind? Already we sense difficulties with the wordsmithing approach.) Consciousness is created (or perhaps it finds a place to touch down) when coherence develops in an otherwise chaotic, random flux of subtle chemistry and faint electrical signals. Ordering influences may be external agents and operators, and they also may be internal, self-organizing principles.

The essence is order, pattern, structure, and, ultimately, meaning. The metaphor can be extended in most any domain. Consciousness can be small and simple, like what we would imagine for mice, birds, snails, bacteria. It can also be stretched mightily, to help think about forests, oceans, flocks, herds—and groups of people. And, of course, it can be extended to the world, where we can apply the metaphor on multiple levels, ranging from crowds and cultures, to all living beings—to Gaia herself. In human terms, consciousness is usually associated with being awake and aware, possibly even self-reflective. Because we are here looking at a broader set of possibilities, our usage necessarily implies also the unconscious and subconscious aspects of the organized activity that defines the mental world.

Putting consciousness together

Is it possible, even without a fully satisfactory definition of consciousness, to go beyond the individual and speak of combining or melding together two or more minds? In personal experience and poetry, there is certainly a likely candidate. When two people meet and share a kind of recognition that develops into what we call love, they create something new. The two become one in many ways which are recognized by others as well as by the couple themselves (itself?). There are many mundane ways for this shared consciousness to manifest, and in addition there are some that suggest interconnections that operate at a level we can't access normally, even though we may perceive something of their effects.

Let's consider more than two—groups of people who may be functioning with a common interest and focus. When we're part of a group that really comes together and begins to resonate and become coherent, there is a change that only becomes apparent if we step back. Of course, doing so interrupts the coherence in some measure. Indeed, the observation of group consciousness when it is powerful or profound is typically retrospective. We say that was a really good meeting, looking back to see it was creative and collaborative to an unusual degree. We shared in a new thing, an independent group mind, for a while. This is a subjective and personal observation, but it seems to be confirmed in data from the FieldREG protocol that was a stepping stone leading to the EGG project. Data recorded when people feel they are part of a group that becomes deeply integrated shows some structure. Actively creative groups, ritual activities in sacred places, truly captivating music, any deeply engaging shared moments tend to manifest departures from expectation in what should be random data.

Group consciousness produces small, but significant changes in the data. The mental coherence of a group appears not to be confined to the individuals, but to bind them together and even to include somehow aspects of the environment. We find structure that is evidence of coherence within the data sequence in the form of small but detectable correlations, which are shifts away from purely random behavior. The changes are strongest when the group is most integrated and most completely absorbed.

Global consciousness?

The next level, with participation by large numbers of people in a shared experience, is even more difficult to define. And yet, although we haven't much ability to recognize that we are part of a mass consciousness, it isn't hard to grasp the notion. Just as we can reflect on the group consciousness experience and retrospectively note its power, we also do see the common emotions and sharing created by great tragedies. I think we are even able to identify the potent connections based in emotions like compassion, linking us to vast numbers of fellow humans we don't know and will never meet. When the news is full of a major earthquake, or yet another suicide bombing that brings great suffering to people, there is an outpouring of deep feeling, of connection with the people who have lost loved ones. Even without thinking, we shift a part of our consciousness to their tragedy, and we give them unspoken love and shared sadness for their troubled time. That movement of thought and emotion is profoundly human. We are creatures of compassion and thus we are interconnected in our unconscious responses and reactions—and that interconnection is worth our attention, for it is a defining human quality.

The idea of a great composite mind exists in virtually all cultures and times, but it isn't a viable scientific construction. So, in working toward research that might reveal something of a possible global consciousness, our working definition was general: we predicted correlated deviations in our random data during moments we could be sure would inspire synchronous collective emotion shared around the world.

And that is what we have found: departures from expectation, which happen just when we come together sharing experience and emotions, becoming one great organized consciousness, a global consciousness. The next step for us is to take this oneness, which is at this stage essentially accidental, mostly driven by events, and turn it around to be intentional, collaborative, creative, and effective. We are just at the edge of becoming evolutionary entrepreneurs, ready and able to decide what future we will have, what we will become.

Theoretisch, ja, aber praktisch (Theory is ok, but be practical)

Do synchronized emotions touch the physical world? Let's do a recap to look for an answer. Based on laboratory and field experience, we built an experiment to gather evidence of mind-matter interactions on a global scale. The idea was to create a monitoring system that could register consciousness effects using random number generators in a network with nodes around the globe. We collect the data sequences, which are tested for deviations and correlations, and also gather information on what matters in producing or modulating the statistical effects. The material becomes a basis for models that can lead to a theoretical understanding and to practical applications.

The results in the experiment show that what we're calling global consciousness is linked to small, but ultimately significant correlations among the RNGs in the network. This is an anomaly, because these devices are designed to be truly random, and moreover are separated by great distances. But they do become correlated. The odds against chance for the GCP's composite result are more than a trillion to one. In addition, an ongoing program of deeper analysis and modeling reveals several more measures of structure in the data, including two orthogonal correlation measures (analogous to mean and variance), and variations in secondary parameters including distance and time. The data also show that effects are larger when people are awake, which is an unpredicted but eminently reasonable result.

In addition, categorizing the events by quantifying some aspect or by rating the presence of some quality yields sensible differentiations. The number of people engaged by the event (which is related to its importance) definitely matters, with events judged to involve millions of people showing stronger effects than those at the other end of the scale. Few formal events have really small numbers, but we have a good sample that have just a few thousand or tens of thousands of people involved. In non-formal explorations, I have looked at data for events that are important to just a few people, for example, the passing of a loved one. My mother died in 2002, and I looked at the GCP data as if it were a global event. Although this was a deeply meaningful event personally, the network variation was too small to say it was beyond chance fluctuation. Important to me, yes, but evidently not on the global scale.

Direct comparison shows that large events have stronger effects and that the difference is significant with 1000 to 1 odds against chance. The number of trials collected in an event also seems to matter, with somewhat more robust statistics when more eggs and hence more pairwise correlations are available over the period set for the event. These factors show how we might refine the "instrument" by giving it more capacity and by applying it to the biggest, most global events. They also suggest or confirm there is power in numbers. This is a practical pointer for our actions. Two heads are better than one, and a million minds manifesting one intention are a power to reckon with.

More subtle and subjective issues can also be addressed with reasonable clarity. We can ask about the level or strength of emotions characterizing the event, and we see, not surprisingly, the higher the level, the stronger the correlations in the data. We can go further in this direction to test the power of various particular emotions. One of the best examples is compassion. People can reliably rate the events as embodying or evoking compassion, and when we calculate the associated effect size, the result is clear. Compassion is a powerful determinant, so that events characterized as strong on this dimension produce significantly greater correlation. This is an informative finding, because the defining quality of compassion is a local and familiar model of what we hypothesize might be the source of the GCP correlations. Compassion is by definition an interaction, an interconnection, between two and sometimes many people. Compassion happens when people share deeply, touching each other emotionally and melding together around a felt commonality. This is a good description as well of the interconnection generated by events that produce the correlations we see in the GCP data. The implication is immediate: Cultivate compassion.

While there is room for different interpretations, for me the meaning of our slight departures from expectation in data that should be random is quite clear—human interconnection happens. Mostly this goes unnoticed, however. We are usually much too busy with our individual stuff, the things that make our lives "real" even if we are somewhat unconscious of it. We are usually preoccupied, captured by what needs to be done, or by entertainments brought to us by media and sought by us in games and theaters and sporting events. But sometimes it is very different. Once in a while we are taken by surprise out of the regular run of activity and into a common path with others, by a great catastrophe or an accident that rouses broadly shared attention and emotions like compassion. Or we go deliberately with millions of others into a shared celebration, or a ritual observation of a moment or a day. In these "different" moments shared with great numbers of other humans near and far, we escape the personal and enter the common ground of our fundamental nature. This is our future destiny, if we collectively choose it.

A singular perspective

Although I claim to be an empiricist and not much given to theoretical speculation, people ask how it all fits together, and it turns out that I do have some well-established opinions. Of course, I have been thinking about formulating good questions in this difficult border domain of intellectual inquiry for a long time, more than 35 years. I have a collection of personal experiences like those of many people who meditate and people who have surprising personal episodes of "anomalous" communication and striking runs of "luck." In addition, I've been doing hands-on research developing a broader view of human consciousness since 1980 in the company of bright and thoughtful people. I don't have any doubt about the phenomenology we're touching here, because of direct engagement in the entire process of experimental design, data collection and processing, and interpretation of results.

The work I'm describing here is an effort to capture some faint indications of a true global consciousness. The purpose is to examine subtle correlations that appear to reflect the presence and activity of consciousness in the world. Just as the biosphere is composed of all the organisms on Earth and their interactions, Pierre Teilhard de Chardin postulated that the noosphere would be composed of all the interacting minds on Earth. What he encouraged us to envision is a trans-human consciousness emerging from our interactions to become a guiding intelligence for the planet.

Evolution starts with particles that coalesce to become atoms and then gather as molecules that become progressively more complex. These become life-building blocks from which smaller and then larger animals emerge and eventually you have us: self-aware animals. While that has been quite a run, it's not over. There is at least one more stage, in which we become a new organ of consciousness for the earth, evolving into something analogous to the cerebral cortex in humans. We can, and to survive, I think we must, engage in conscious evolution to decide and then to create what the future will be.

Evolutionary theorists are looking beyond the idea, encapsulated by the "selfish gene" metaphor, that genes are definitive. Instead, they suggest that organisms play active, constructive roles in their own development and that of their descendants, so that they impose direction on evolution.[118]

My favorite picture is that we are all already participants in a giant interaction, similar to that among the neurons in a brain. The neurons don't know anything about the mind or the questions we ask, or what consciousness is, but they participate anyway by doing perfectly what neurons do. I think we are participating already in something that is a higher level of consciousness and that, for all we know, could even be conscious and self-aware already. Like the neurons, we don't need to know anything about this; we only need to be developed humans doing our job, manifesting our humanity.

Consciousness has a creative, productive, generative role in the world such that what we wish for is more likely to be than if we hadn't wished for it. We have good evidence that this is true. What we envision together will manifest in the world in a subtle way. This means that we have an enormous, untapped (or at least uncontrolled) capability of changing the future. The corollary is that we also have a responsibility. Succinctly put, we have both the capability and the responsibility for changing the world so that the future is brighter. Doing so depends on coalescing into a greater consciousness.

When rain falls on a mountaintop it creates rivulets that flow together and become streams. Then they wind down the mountains and join to become rivers, and the rivers eventually get to (and form) the sea. The Global Consciousness project is such a rivulet. Each of us in our way is such a rivulet, and sometimes we even feel the power of joining others in a stream—of thought, of prayer, of intention. What would it be like to have most people on the earth join in a conscious intent?

The ancients talk about 24,000-year cycles where consciousness wakes up and then goes to sleep, wakes up and then goes to sleep. I think this is a framework in which the global consciousness idea might make sense. We can use it as a mirror to look at ourselves in a different way, allowing us insight into the ride we are taking on the universal wave of consciousness. To be clear, the idea is that we are on the verge of the peak of the wave, the waking part of the long cycle. To take advantage of the moment, we need to become doubly self-reflective—to watch ourselves learning to see our destiny. Our task is to observe and in observing, to foster our coalescence into consciousness.

The truth is, most of the time we are asleep. But we can wake up a little bit. That is the promise of global consciousness.

Chapter 23: AND THEN?

The Age of Nations is past. The task before us now, if we would not perish, is to build the Earth.

—Teilhard de Chardin

So what?

A friend and faculty colleague of mine who was a businessman was appointed as Undersecretary for Education in Reagan's administration. He was a wonderful, charismatic, no-nonsense guy who I liked though we were very different. I visited him when I was in Washington for a conference, and I described the new research I was doing at Princeton. A very smart guy, he understood the experiments, and he took in the results showing human attention could change the behavior of a random number generator. After a little pause, he said quite simply, "So what?" I was taken aback for a moment, but that was Wayne's style—cut to the chase: Yes, that is a very interesting finding. Now what is it good for? What can be done with it? Of course, he was right. We do need to think about implications and applications. This is startling stuff, but it is of little lasting interest until and unless it becomes part of what we do in the bigger world. Wayne was by no means the only person asking this kind of question.

A very recent example is a correspondent hoping to create applications based on the GCP. More correctly, he was hoping to find a way to monetize the technology and the findings by constructing a mobile app to do something useful—like creating an alert or warning about some event about to happen. He asked, "Of all your anomalies identified by the GCP, such as 911, which ones do you believe have had the most significant result supporting Consciousness, the Sixth Sense, etc.? If you have any more specific thoughts as to using Consciousness to identify life-threatening situations, I'd love to hear them!"

My response:

That's complicated. On the one hand, the protocol and the question asked in the GCP is of a different sort than you have in mind. My guess is that you are extrapolating from the apparent "premonition" showing in the variance analysis for 9/11, which many people think is powerfully persuasive. This is an important piece of information, but I don't take it as a model of what the GCP network does. On the contrary, that particular *post hoc* finding is basically outside the territory we know how to interpret. The GCP does not have a way to identify future threats.

What it has is anomalies that coincide with big, engaging events with either negative or positive valence. We don't have any predictive capacity for threats. You can see how unlikely the "warning" capability might be by considering the next question after seeing a "spike" in the data. OK, we have a huge deviation! Something is about to happen! OK, what sort of thing is it of the thousands of things it might be? And where is it on our rather large planet? I'm afraid the most it could do for us is to say, "Be afraid." That's not of much value.

What's valuable about the GCP is that it points to extremely important qualities of the human being, and to capacities we have and ought to learn to use. At the end of the day, the GCP says we are interconnected. The evidence is good, and it urges us to learn more about the deep-lying links that show up when we are stimulated by powerful events, or when we decide to share a moment in time with millions of others. We are not usually conscious at all of our connections to other people, to the trees and birds and animals all around us, but those connections exist. My intention for the GCP data is to use it as a vehicle to help more people become intentionally conscious of the matrix of life and mind in which we are swimming as a fish swims in water. I hope I can help people see and feel the water, the matrix that sustains us. I believe we are capable of conscious evolution toward our potential, and moreover, I think that capability implies a profoundly important responsibility. We can, and we must move with as much consciousness as we can muster toward becoming fully human.

It isn't what you had in mind in asking my thoughts on using consciousness to identify life-threatening situations, but that is exactly what I see—we are in a life-threatening moment now, and what we do in the next months and years, individually but also as families and communities and cultures, will either destroy our future or make it bright. We're sitting on a very sharp edge, and we have to make decisions for the ages. What will our grandchildren—what will the seven generations have left to them? It can be bright and beautiful, but I believe that will happen only if we act together in shared wisdom, with love and charity and benevolence that crosses the spaces that appear to separate us.

Chapter 24: IMPLICATIONS OF THE EVIDENCE

A new scientific truth does not triumph by convincing its opponents and making them see the light, but rather because its opponents eventually die, and a new generation grows up that is familiar with it.

—*Max Planck*

It's such a small effect

What would be the value of showing that there is a tiny effect of mind on matter, so small we can't ordinarily see or use it, and so elusive that most scientists can't believe there is good evidence for it? What would be the value of a subtle interconnection of minds, so delicate that we seldom can be sure we actually touch each other?

It isn't for making money, but for understanding better who we are, and how we belong to the world. Most of us who look seriously at our situation as we move into the next few decades think we are plunging into deep and dangerous waters. There are many voices saying we need to change our way of being, to include more compassion and respect for each other and for our environment. Our only home is beautiful, but threatened by forces we can control only if we understand our role and our capacities.

This book describes a unique research project that reveals an extraordinary dimension of human existence. The basis is scientific, but the implications touch upon the realm of poetry and mysticism, where we allow ourselves to believe in deep interconnections. Ancient wisdom traditions all speak in one voice about unity, and poets in every language say that two who love become one. Science, while it is one of the most remarkable tools we have for looking at the complex world around us, has almost nothing to say about the most important qualities in our lives. Love, compassion, the creative impulse—these are not explained in textbooks.

But it is time, and as a bit of old wisdom says: Time is of the essence. It is all we have in the world. Timing isn't everything, it is the only thing.

I think we can take some encouragement from the work of the GCP. It is a unique scientific project that has for more than 17 years been gathering data which seem to show a great earth mind just born, or just awakening. Though that may be hyperbolic, it is symbolic of our need for more wisdom about living together on this beautiful planet and keeping it safe from our own tragic tendencies. There are many threads now being woven into a guide for recognition of the problems we have created, and many efforts aimed toward constructive measures to solve them. The presence of a true global consciousness in our midst, and literally in ourselves, may be the metaphor we need to encourage our best efforts to create a richer and more beautiful picture of the future of the earth.

The Global Consciousness Project, beginning with the sources and inspirations that brought people from richly varied backgrounds together, ultimately created a scientific instrument to illuminate our most subtle social imperatives. We became an international collaboration joining many others, including the readers of this book, who are not satisfied with the accumulation of stuff. We are asking what is our purpose as humans, and what shall we do with our intelligence and will? Poets and storytellers of all cultures speak of a unity out of which we come and to which we always belong. Personal experiences of interconnection, such as falling in love or losing ourselves in the beauty of a sunset, remind us all that we are not alone, imprisoned in our skin and skulls. As conscious beings, we love the state of sharing directly with each other, becoming one in our feeling and perceptions, and magically creating something new and lovely. Now, just at a time in history when it appears to be essential for us to work together, we see evidence of a shared consciousness beginning to appear on our planet.

The technical foundation of the formal, scientific research of the EGG project is fascinating, touching, as it does, on the presence of randomicity and chance in our lives. It is about discovering ways to extract signals from noise, to read messages that may be buried in a confusing background. Perhaps these discoveries apply, and not just metaphorically, to our self-perceptions. We live in a very noisy world, and it can be hard to extract what is important and meaningful from the chaos of news and chatter that surrounds us.

The GCP data come from a world-spanning network of what

we might call resonance detectors, responsive to coherent or resonant information from human consciousness. Subtle structure in the data allows us to paint pictures of a chaotic global mindstuff which becomes focused and coherent at special times when great events focus the world's attention.

When we allow the artist's eye and the poet's heart to enhance the rigorous view of the scientist, the global mind begins to have a richer presence, and even in its nascent form speaks hauntingly in a language we begin to understand.

Isn't it time?

The GCP is approaching the age of majority—and getting ready to vote. We have made a case for the existence of correlation between big events in human consciousness and changes from expected random behavior in the GCP network of random number generators. As my business friend said to me, "I understand the result. The next question is, "So what?"... "What comes next?"

The answer has multiple branches.

1. Understand the data. Search for structure using new analyses and sophisticated tools in aid of the next item in this list. Be creative and adventurous because these data are an opening to unknown but important territory.

2. Modeling and theory. Testing models against data structure, testing theoretically-based hypotheses. Why? Because this uses the empirical data to develop understanding and explanation, and to know more about our consciousness.

3. Aesthetics. Make art pieces, visual, kinesthetic, musical, beautiful, for art's sake, and to host applications. The purposes are broad, from simple appreciation to directed action. Art can inspire, and it has great power because its language is not words or even ideas, but the emotional beating heart.

4. Applications. Develop the implications of GCP findings for individuals and society. Create social presence. Many

organizations and individuals are working on common problems, with the same goal, to create a brighter future. Connecting them is the most obvious growth mode to promote healthy, pleasant and productive living. What we struggle to imagine becomes obvious and inevitable when we interconnect and truly become one.

All of these areas are rich with possibility for more discovery and deeper understanding. I hope that what we do with the GCP findings can benefit society and help foster a future that promotes wellness and is mindful that we are responsible, but also gifted with capabilities we only need to recognize. The recipe for this is clear but not yet broadly known. It can most simply be expressed as "conscious evolution." That pair of words might sound innocent, but think about it: Being conscious is more than being awake, and evolution is more than a random process.

Mind is not isolated inside the skull

We are swimming in a consciousness field that we cannot detect by any of our normal senses. We do get hints and subtle suggestions of this ocean in which we live our lives, but more often from poets and musicians and the seers who make it their mission to tell us about ourselves.

This shared matrix of life and consciousness is made of many interacting fields, and it is mostly quite chaotic because the components are normally uncoordinated. Now and then, one of the many factors influencing the structure and rhythm of the individual fields may become a common influence to many parts of the array, and this can produce something like a resonance or coherence—the ripples overlap and build on each other and make a ringing chord of shared, coherent activity. We think and feel the same thing in concert, and the result is a new creation for the moment, a group consciousness that is at once independent of us, and on the other hand surely dependent for its existence and nature on our being. When our cohesion dissipates, the common field will weaken and fade away as well, though there is a trace of it remaining in the universe. A template remains to allow it to more readily form again.

Over time, maybe eons, such collective construction will grow stronger and more used to itself, and we can expect it to develop self-reflection, just as in the distant past our forebears gradually adjusted to their own remarkable awareness, and began to see themselves as observers.

There is little doubt that a remarkable presence comes into being in the world in response to connecting, collectivizing events. It is born and nurtured by things that draw focus and hold it to the exclusion of personal reflection, at least until later after the attracting event has lost its ability to hold our attention. What is so deeply intriguing about this is that we can create those moments—we have the ability and we are accumulating experience bringing communal consciousness into being.

From ancient times we humans have come together in deliberate intentional moments, using ritual and song and ceremonies. This is the deep grounding of true religion, and remains an important part of religious gathering, even now when so much that isn't spiritual has been added. Churches and temples and mosques remain centers of focus for ritual gathering and the creation of community. I wish I could say those centers invariably contribute to a growing global consciousness, but we haven't grown into our destiny far enough for that to be so. Nevertheless, the example is important. What we need is the good fortune to see it shifting toward a future of inclusion and generosity of spirit. That can be our vision and goal.

Local fields

It is possible, and perhaps natural to conceive local fields of consciousness—fields that represent and affect just our personal surround, and I know that most people who think about it have that as their first image, born of experience with ordinary actions and responses to forces in the world. But once we embark on the idea of fields, it is difficult to find sensible ways to limit the extent they might have. A field in physics is a construct that represents forces acting over distance, allowing interactions of separated objects with each other. Magnets attract iron filings, the moon lifts earthly tides, electric motors run because of induced forces which are understood as fields. This description of interactions is relatively new in history, with early versions from Newton and Mach, and more formalism from Maxwell, leading to clear and broadly applicable expression early in the 20th century at the hands of Einstein and the founders of QM. Fields provide conceptual links between objects and in mathematical form embody the forces that constitute physical interactions. It may be that interactions in the realm of consciousness, thoughts, and emotions will benefit from an analogous effort.

What we need to explain is very similar, structurally. We have separated entities, two people between whom some anomalous, non-sensory communication appears to occur, or one person and some physical system such as a random number generator in a PK experiment. There is no direct contact, and no ordinary physical force or field to carry the information that shows up as evidence of an interaction. Yet, just as the moon manifests its presence through a field called gravity, there is a need for a field description that can formalize the effect of intention to change a random number sequence, or communicate information about an artwork I'm enjoying, which somehow appears in a distant sleeper's dreams.

The science of consciousness fields is still young, and we don't yet know if they might conform to the model of physical fields where potency diminishes with distance. A good part of the evidence shows no indications of this decline of effect with distance, and there is reason to suspect that consciousness effects may be nonlocal in time as well as space. In any case, there is as yet no formal model for it, but we are beginning to see and feel the presence of mind. When we can write the equation linking energy and information, we will be on the verge of discovering equations that make the mind more available to itself.

Personal field

We each find ourselves centered in a kind of personal universe, sometimes very small, and at other times so expansive as to include the whole natural world. If I have a toothache or an itchy mosquito bite my consciousness shrinks down to a fine focus for the moment. But if the door opens and a friend comes in, my world grows double or more, and if she says, "Come outside, there's an eagle over the meadow. It's beautiful. Come see!", my functional consciousness grows to include so much more. I become part of a natural world. Without thinking about it or trying, my isolation simply disappears, replaced by interconnection. The I becomes we, with shared space and time, mutual interests and reactions, and a complex of connections to the contextual world—none of which we usually give a second's thought. It is clear when you think about it this way that your consciousness and mine are not enclosed in our heads. It feels like there is a kind of center "here" but an extension outward in space and time so your consciousness field and mine will overlap and interpenetrate. And sometimes these fields will interact and build something more because circumstances or influences synchronize and harmonize us, make us resonate to the same music or to our mutual delight in the beautiful curve of an eagle's wing.

Group field

As with two, so also with more individuals gathered with common purpose or shared focus. These ideas are tools we can use for our personal work and for our contributions to right actions. Some meetings, perhaps for mundane planning or problem solving, perhaps for more obviously creative purposes, turn into remarkable experiences for the people involved. They say afterward, "That was a great meeting." But they don't notice it as it goes on because they are fully engrossed, and they and everyone else become parts of a group consciousness. It is time to become more mindful of these interactions—they are a defining part of being most human. There are ways to work on this, beginning with the intention. We do have to get out of our own way in such matters, but if we invite ourselves to look for the group, letting go of the personal for the moment, we learn to become one with each other. By its nature the process is gradual, but conscious intention helps the process to mature into its own nature. We have this experience when we sing or play music in a group, when we dance and when we are part of a sports team. Extending the experience to social and cultural gathering is a natural step.

A concert that captivates the audience, a charismatic speaker, a celebratory moment... these are examples where the fields of individuals, which normally just interpenetrate, become partially coherent. The interacting fields produce harmonics because they are driven by the context—the beauty or fascination—to share some fundamental rhythms. In the imprecise but evocative current expression, we are "on the same wavelength," or we pick up the "vibes" of others sharing the same experience. These common expressions may seem to be mere metaphors, but there is more to it. Experiments like the GCP indicate that the linkages we feel have subtle manifestations that can show up in physical data. The coherence and resonance we experience can have a direct presence in the world. We can create these experiences deliberately and with purpose to change the way the future develops. We have that capability in principle, and there's no question we can manifest it in practice.

Time for a hug

A GCP colleague, Hans Wendt, sent a link to an article by Rebecca Kessler, who assembled research on the length of basic physiological events and certain nervous system functions.[119] Natural actions like goodbye waves, musical phrases, and infants' bouts of babbling all last about 3 seconds. Her article, "Hugs Follow a 3-Second Rule," asks how long a hug lasts. The answer is about 3 seconds. The more profound discovery is that this is about the same time as many other actions and neurological processes, and this supports a hypothesis that we go through life perceiving the present in a series of 3-second windows.

We had earlier noted that it takes about a 10th of a second to become aware of a sensory input, and compared that to the rise time for GCP effects, which is thousands of times longer. Most of us are aware that the passage of time for the earth, or for evolutionary changes is very different from the scale of our personal experience. We say of such changes that they are "glacial," meaning that the movements are imperceptible, just as is the flow of a glacier. We know it is progressing, but we cannot directly see any change until we create a systematic history, a technical time-lapse view of the great ice masses.

If we see through a personal 3-second window, what would that suggest about a moment in time for our hypothesized global consciousness? It is clear that if there is a global consciousness, its movement through time is very slow by our standards. Teilhard understood this when he suggested it would be thousands of years before humans would fully inhabit the next phase of evolution. When we take the question seriously, the GCP data suggest that the nascent global consciousness perceives in approximately 2- or 3-hour windows. Simple arithmetic says our perceptions and cognitions operate 1000 to 10000 times as fast as Mother Earth.

But she has been at it for such a long time that we still have a long way to go to catch up. Our task is to become conscious of this path we are on, so we can shape our efforts toward a collaboration that can shorten the way. We have a long journey ahead, and yet, because we are conscious, we have the capacity to change the pace of our evolution. It is within our power to take on the mantle of the noosphere. If that becomes our intention, it will happen in a planet-scale trice. How many of us would it take? The answer is to start gathering our intentional forces—we'll find out.

Chapter 25: REFLECTIONS

Until you make the unconscious conscious, it will direct your life and you will call it fate.

—Carl Jung

My friend Jim Deneen, whom we lost a year ago, was a wise and highly intelligent man. Though it came out of a different intellectual realm from his, he was interested in and understood the GCP data, and was not resistant to the idea that we were looking at a real manifestation of consciousness. But he had questions, very good ones like this: Why would a "global event" that actually was important or known to only a small portion of humanity register? What about all the minds engaged in everything else?

I suggested that what we are seeing is a response to a "field" that is usually random, but which sometimes may be pushed slightly toward structure that affects the REG devices. That occurs when there is a "coherence" among many minds, even if not all minds. The coherence is like the shared quality that induces resonant interactions of piano strings with a singer's pure tones. If a great event captures the imagination or attention of the world, in fact only a small fraction of us, 5 or 10% at the most, might know or care, and for most of what the GCP identifies as global events an even smaller number likely would be the source of coherence. In an important subset we've examined (organized meditations), the numbers of people are probably in the hundred thousand to a few million range, and yet there is a consistent effect. It seems that a comparatively small "dose" of resonance, especially if it represents high coherence, can register in our detection system.

While the Global Consciousness Project focuses mainly on doing the science well, it is appropriate also to think about the implications of our work. We are seeing clear indications of human interconnections which, though subtle, are very important. We see pointers about where we should focus. For example, we are urged to push toward peace because peace is the necessary condition for creativity. Large numbers of people and groups are doing that, as you will discover if you have that question in mind when you go to the web. There are hundreds or thousands of organized efforts to bring us together. Most are small and many arise and disappear in a brief time. But many are large and persistent, though in the scale of the earth and evolution they are still just glimmers of possibility.

It is possible that we will soon see this glimmering become a glow, and if we somehow get organized, the light will increase to the point where it illuminates a truly bright future. We don't have a clear picture of how to accomplish this, but it surely is worth paying attention and giving some of our best creative thought—or better yet, our creative action.

The other side of the fence

Here is the question I face most often when I think about working to improve the situation. Assuming we have an understanding that speaks to useful goals, we need to communicate it and recruit help. But there is a persistent problem: How can we speak to those who are not in the choir? What means are there for bringing political and business and financial movers into a picture of healing for the planet? We need their help, and we need to find ways to go completely around the blocks of blame and accusation.

Cooperation? Yes, but how? Why should a hedge fund manager think for a second about turning away from money to help forge eudemony—well-being—for everyone else? Seems simple to you and me perhaps, but it isn't simple. A big part of the reason for that is the huge but seldom considered differences between ourselves and others. We know (and select) our friends, but what of the people we don't know—most of the world? A moment's reflection shows big differences we can't explain. Why do those "others" vote for the "wrong" person? Why do so many love baseball or soccer, while others seldom think about sports? How is it that anyone can still be racist? Where does religious fundamentalism that separates us so profoundly come from? Why don't those "others" see things as I do?

It is enormously complicated to match motivations and perspectives. This is the challenge of this time of change. It will define the new calendar that must follow if we are to need any calendar at all a hundred years from now.

Words of beauty and wisdom

We have lots of help from our friends, and from our shared cultural treasures. Examples abound, and I will collect here and in the next chapters a few special gems from a great library of quotations, wisdom, and poetry I've come across that express some of our feeling for the earth and our possibilities on this beautiful planet. If you explore the web looking for inspiration and ways to contribute to a healthy planetary future, you will see that there is a growing and increasingly coherent network of people with related motivations to honor our only home. You may find connections important to your needs, and without doubt you will find enjoyment looking through these riches.

Quotes and illuminations

> *There is one thing that is stronger than all the armies in the world, and that is an idea whose time has come.*
> —*Victor Hugo*

An idea whose time has come is that we are interconnected at a deep level. When we bring this up to awareness we will have the power to change the world; we will be co-creators in a bright future. Intentional evolution needs only communication, cooperation, and creativity.

> *If a man could make the right choices, then he could significantly alter the course of the possible future. No man, then, should feel insignificant, for it only takes one man to alter the consciousness of mankind through the Spirit-that-moves-in-all-things. In essence, one thought influences another, then another, until the thought is made manifest throughout all of Creation. It is the same thought, the same force, that causes an entire flock of birds to change course, as the flock then has one mind.*
> —*Grandfather Stalking Wolf*

Our brothers and sisters who met us when we came from Europe knew their world, and they told us how it and they were interconnected. They hoped then, and hope still, that we could see ourselves as another integral part of the natural world.

Conscious evolution

Often it seems my interests and activities, especially those relating to the GCP, are driven by remarkable and surprising links, so much so that my favorite chapter title is "Design by Coincidence." Here is a mild example:

I decided to send out one of my occasional GCP/EGG Update notes before going to Kazakhstan, but I waited too long and was unable to send it because of technical issues I had no time to resolve. But the meeting was so rich with experiences and ideas that it turned out to be good timing because when I got back I could give a little report, fresh off the press.

I didn't know much about Kazakhstan, nor about the meeting, but it was somehow clear I should accept the invitation. Wise decision, because it was a gathering of people from around the world all interested in the conscious evolution that must be our future. Noosphere—the sheath of intelligence predicted by Vernadsky and Teilhard—was not a foreign word among the delegates, even though there were dozens of languages spoken by 500 people from 70 countries. A major discussion centered on a well-developed Noospheric Constitution.[120] The event was the World Forum of Spiritual Culture, and was the work of organizers from several countries, supported directly by the President and the government of Kazakhstan.

A sample of those I met: The Children of the Earth[121] were there—literally, via the presence of several young people who travel the world helping to inspire and unite young people for peace worldwide; the leaders of the Goi Peace Foundation,[122] who have distributed 400,000 "peace poles" around the world; Representatives of institutions like the World Council of Religious Leaders,[123]; people from the Alianza de Civilizaciones,[124] and so many more.

Because I, like many others at the meeting, feel that while the talk and sharing is of some value, we really must be doing and working, it was a special pleasure to learn of the International Simultaneous Policy Organization.[125] It's an organization in the UK promoting a mechanism that is a likely game changer, with the potential to mitigate the impasse of international competition that prevents wise evolution. The plan operates through ordinary political systems to encourage Simultaneous Policy (Simpol), changes on matters such as desperately needed regulations and more equitable wealth distribution. Their website describes the Simpol idea clearly and includes links to YouTube pieces by John Bunzl, the businessman and social entrepreneur who is the driving force.

R. Buckminster Fuller

According to a Sufi friend, Himayat Inayati, Fuller passed me Baraka during a presentation in Washington, one of his last speeches. Whether or not that is so, he was a hero whose insight and wisdom comes even more into focus these days. His lifework is an application of global thinking. He was a truly global consciousness. Following are excerpts from an article in U.S Politics Today[126] by its editor, Joe Rothstein, describing interesting examples of Bucky's continuing impact:

> A wise old friend of mine used to define an optimist as "a scientist who believes the future of humans of Earth is still in doubt." By that definition, Buckminster Fuller was one of the world's most prolific optimists. He knew, and often said, that we are at a decision point in human history. The decision could go either way.
>
> With only a sliver of the resources otherwise devoted to war, pollution and planet degradation [could be washed away.] A lot of ingenious people around the world are working hard to develop evolutionary strategies and products that are culturally, ecologically and economically viable.
>
> Fuller liked to say that we are in the midst of humanity's final exam. The Buckminster Fuller Challenge grant provided by the Institute that is his legacy is doing its best to help us pass.
>
> His was direct wisdom: "You never change things by fighting the existing reality. To change something build a new model that makes the existing model obsolete."
>
> "And never forget, no matter how overwhelming life's challenges seem to be, that one person can make a difference in the world. In fact, it is always because of one person that all the changes that matter in the world come about. Be that one person."

Earth embedded Noosphere

Some time ago I recommended reading Ode, a wonderful magazine for optimistic social observers. (Ode recently became the online Optimist Daily.[127]) An early issue had an interview article with the Dalai Lama saying, "War is old-fashioned." Every day they bring informative and often inspiring articles—something to balance the tilted world of mainstream news.

In Denver I discovered another magazine with a similar perspective in a fresh and very young mode. It was called Elephant, with the subtitle, "It's about the mindful life." It has disappeared or morphed, but in the issue I read they interviewed Bill McKibben, who says,

> Our great shortage in this country is community. Connection. We've become a hyper-individualist, self-obsessed society, the likes of which the earth has never seen.
>
> And in the process we're changing the earth in unbelievable ways....
>
> But the good news is that...we may finally be in a place where, if we get the message, we could begin to think about changing.

That is good news, and it will be better when we "individually" recognize how powerful we are when we engage and become a community. We are connected, and that's beautiful. It appears (if you squint) that we are changing and that trust in our interdependence is growing. It may be too subtle to see, but the evidence is good that it's real.

We have in our midst wonderful spokesmen and spokeswomen for the efficacy of such connection, created by compassion and love. Sometimes they surprise us, coming from parts of our public world that often represent our dark side. Perhaps that context makes a person of deep sensibility more vulnerable to the influences of our better nature.

Chapter 26: WHAT WE CAN DO

I want the brightest minds on the planet in one circle working as a team, toward the same end, which is the enlightenment of the noosphere.
—Glistening Deepwater

Sometimes it seems our leaders in politics and commerce act in a latter-day manifestation of the stance taken by Louis XV. His last words were "apres moi le deluge" ("after me, the deluge"). It is our task and our responsibility to the future to re-educate ourselves, to overcome this terrible egocentrism.

At present most men still merely understand strength, the key and symbol of violence in its most primitive and savage form of war. But let the time come, as come it will, when the masses will realize that the true human successes are those which triumph over the mysteries of matter and of life. At that moment a decisive hour will sound for mankind, when the spirit of discovery absorbs all the momentum contained in the spirit of war.
—Teilhard de Chardin

How can we help hasten that time? What applications can be devised to exploit what we learn by looking for global consciousness? We see the world as deeply divided into haves and have-nots, powerful and weak, rich and poor, loved and lost, blessed and bereft. What would better balance do for the world? The answers have become terribly important, and it is time to look for the questions that will elicit applications to redress pain and cure the diseases of power and corruption, repealing and replacing lust and unconscionable greed. No one can promise a rose garden, but the will of a global consciousness can surely move masses to insist on change and literally to create change, just as we see in the GCP data that the compassion of millions brings patterns into being from the material of chaos.

As the GCP has grown more mature, while the world around us changes faster than ever, we receive more emails from young people asking for suggestions about what to do to help make the world they are inheriting brighter and more humane. It is encouraging to see the seriousness and intent they bring to the question.

The best answers are actually quite simple: connection and collaboration. We need each other, and we already are participants in a complicated matrix of influences and motivations. We are already on the dance floor, and the music is playing. Even if it seems a bit discordant, the thing to do is touch hands, start moving together in rhythm. Soon enough the band will take up the harmony. When we're all aware and intentional, it will be quite a party.

Let me suggest a few groups for you to consider joining. The list could be very long, and each of us will have different needs and tastes, so what I can suggest is just a hint of the possibilities. Look locally for groups aligned with your feelings about the world. Look globally as well, because there are beautiful connections to be made across the borders and distances that (only seem to) separate us. Touching another's hand and watching his or her eyes makes true connection and collaboration easier, but we're blessed with powerful modern communication tools, and they will also work, especially if we understand that direct person-to-person contact is the model we should follow, even though the medium we use is a phone call, a text, or some online service like Facebook or Twitter. The important point is to connect—to stay focused on something more than just entertainment or a way to pass time. (Why do we ever want to "pass time" anyhow? It is precious stuff, and we'll never get any more.)

Not to be too serious about it, because it is a pleasure to become part of a group of people with common interests and a shared goal of looking toward a future with more love and compassion. Here are some possibilities to look up which appeal to me. You will find what you need by simply having the intention—putting the question "out there" and waiting confidently for your connections to become clear. If you are ready, opportunity appears. An unforgettable movie put it this way, "Build it and they will come."

What to do

Joining and volunteering—so many groups and organizations need you. The cool thing is they give back. Being of service, giving your time creates connections that help others while putting you in touch with really nice people and a deeper layer of yourself.

> The Institute of Noetic Sciences (http://www.noetic.org/)
> Global Coherence Initiative (www.heartmath.org/gci/)
> America Meditating (http://www.americameditating.org/)
> Changemakers (http://www.bemagazine.org/changemakers-directory/)
> Goi Peace Foundation (https://www.goipeace.or.jp/en/)
> The Shift Network (http://m.theshiftnetwork.com/main)
> Unify.org (http://peace.unify.org/)
> Uplift (http://upliftconnect.com/)
> Global organized meditations (www.thegreatsilence.org/)
> Focus on peace (http://pathwaystopeace.org/culture-of-peace-initiative/)

These are just a small sample. For a longer list and broader coverage, please see the GCP website links page at http://global-mind.org/links.html. Beyond my collection, there are endless possibilities you can find with good search terms on the web.

Many hundreds, probably several thousand groups have come together in recent years with the intention to contribute to a desirable future. They are focused on peace and harmony, on well-being, on protecting the environment, fostering equality, conservation, creativity, conscience, and honoring love as the measure of our value as human beings.

I think the common quality is that everyone recognizes the challenges we face and the absolute imperative of working together. I hope you will find your group, looking near home and far afield. You will likely find lots of opportunities to connect to groups with the essential shared understanding that nothing is more important than to create our future together. Without that, we will have sadness, loss, and suffering. But with that creative gathering of resources, we will generate beauty that no one has ever seen, and peace and love greater than we could have imagined.

Chapter 27: POETIC HISTORY

Approach love and cooking with reckless abandon.

—The Dalai Lama

We experience the world with beautiful immediacy, and with a quality of direct participation that seems completely natural. And yet it is quite magical. We take meaning from music, we know our loved ones from afar, and we leap in thought to the stars. Sometimes we sense that we have dissolved ourselves into a group or a larger whole. And we always have prayed as if it could make a difference.

Even when building what was to become the Global Consciousness Project was difficult, it was fun. It turns out that we have necessary and often surprising allies to help make matters including paradoxes and contradictions understandable. There are dreams,[128] for example, and ancient wisdom like that of the I Ching,[129] to help us stay on the path with a heart. There's modern wisdom too, as some simple recommendations attributed to the Dalai Lama[130] help us see. Indeed, we can touch the perennial wisdom.[131] Or consider A Congressman's Prayer,[132] by Dennis Kucinich (D-OH). And what could be more natural than a poem[133] to ask a deeper question?

> *Nothing is harder, yet nothing is more necessary, than to speak of certain things whose existence is neither demonstrable nor probable. The very fact that serious and conscientious men and women treat them as existing things brings them a step closer to existence and to the possibility of being born.*
>
> —*Hermann Hesse*

For some years my email signature has been: Mitakuye Oyasin. It is from the Lakota and speaks to our interconnectedness, declaring we are all related. A colleague's is from the Maya: in lak'ech ala k'in—I am you and you are me. The original peoples of the Americas beautifully said that we are really one.

This is a critical time in history. We face the necessity to transform our civilization into one that is conscious of its potentials and responsibilities. We have the ability to choose cooperation and collaboration over dissension and strife. The result will be a flowering of culture and a reversal of trends that threaten to destroy a world we love yet which we take for granted.

We do have models, and they are both beautiful and workable. Père Teilhard de Chardin's *Phenomenon of Man*[134] is, as are his other writings, filled with poetic expression, even for simple and scientific understandings.

> *Man can be understood only by ascending from physics, chemistry, biology, and geology. In other words, he is first of all a cosmic problem.*
> —Pierre Teilhard de Chardin

Our most prodigious thinkers have seen us, humanity, as the culmination of creation, and this may be an acceptable view if we somehow fulfill our creative destiny. But there may be very little time, really, for growing up and reaching for the best we can be. The Earth, the beautifully balanced ecosystem, is seriously damaged already from our point of view (whenever we look beyond the ends of our material noses to our future). Ironically and sadly, all the responsibility for the damage is ours—we have grown too quickly capable and too slowly wise—and rescue and repair are up to us, entirely.

We are not, thank goodness, utterly without insight. A small number of voices have always spoken out to teach, and to urge necessary actions. A poignant and striking, utterly clear description of where we are and what we must now do, is presented as Four Prophecies[135] given in 1920 by the American Indian medicine man, Stalking Wolf. When I read his striking description, given 100 years ago, of the rolling tragedy of modern life, it seemed also to be a description of the opportunity we have to help the earth—and ourselves—by becoming more conscious. He said we could change the course of nature by prayer and a joining of minds. When we decide to change our ways and rid the Earth of all unnatural pollutants she will heal, and our home will become once again welcoming.

Buckminster Fuller maintained, eloquently, that we have the power to think about and understand where we live, and ultimately to organize the materials of our world so that there is plenty for all of us, even for more of us if we intelligently decide that's what we want.

> Take the initiative. Go to work, and above all co-operate and don't hold back on one another or try to gain at the expense of another. Any success in such lopsidedness will be increasingly short-lived. These are the synergetic rules that evolution is employing and trying to make clear to us. They are not man-made laws. They are the infinitely accommodative laws of the intellectual integrity governing universe.

He offered a serious warning:

> If humanity does not opt for integrity we are through completely. It is absolutely touch and go. Each one of us could make the difference.

Ultimately, Fuller said:

> I'm not trying to counsel any of you to do anything really special except dare to think. And to dare to go with the truth. And to dare to really love completely.

So many say the same things, a rich trove of wise counsel telling us how to live together on a small planet. As Fuller says, once we ask a good question the answer is embedded in it. The global consciousness that we have seen glimmering faintly shows more brightly in the presence of profound emotions shared across the distance and boundaries that only seem to separate us.

Perhaps we are asking a good question. The evidence is showing that we are all connected in a subtle way. The next task is to exercise and strengthen that elusive possibility with intention. It is a practical challenge, but it is also a spiritual opening with rich possibilities. Albert Einstein, as always quotable, says that the most beautiful and profound emotion we can experience is the sensation of the mystical:

It is the sower of all true science. He to whom this emotion is a stranger, who can no longer wonder and stand rapt in awe, is as good as dead.

To know that what is impenetrable to us really exists, manifesting itself as the highest wisdom and the most radiant beauty, which our dull faculties can comprehend only in their primitive forms—this knowledge, this feeling, is at the center of true religion.

And then there is Dee Hock, a businessman who practically invented the credit card industry. Definitely a pragmatic person, he nevertheless wholly agrees with the ancient wisdom traditions, and with Stalking Wolf's and Albert Einstein's picture of the scientific and spiritual journey that is before us:

> Beyond all else, it is a story of the future, of something trying to happen, of a four-hundred-year-old age rattling in its deathbed as another struggles to be born—a transformation of consciousness, culture, society, and institutions such as the world has never experienced. We must try.
> —Dee Hock [136]

Imagine

Imagine there's no Heaven
It's easy if you try
No hell below us
Above us only sky

Imagine there's no countries
It isn't hard to do
Nothing to kill or die for
And no religion too
Imagine all the people
Living life in peace

You may say that I'm a dreamer
But I'm not the only one
I hope someday you'll join us
And the world will be as one

Imagine no possessions
I wonder if you can
No need for greed or hunger
A brotherhood of man
Imagine all the people
Sharing all the world

You may say that I'm a dreamer
But I'm not the only one
I hope someday you'll join us
And the world will live as one"

—John Lennon

After a few years in the communication network that is the Global Consciousness Project, it became beautifully clear that there are many centers of conscious intention to effect necessary changes in culture. They are beginning to flow together and I am hopeful the effects will mature in time. To foster this flow, we need to become more compassionate and less self-serving, and we need to laugh together! Most of what I write is rather too serious, but I know as most of us do, that humor is a wonderful connector. Laughing together is a magical way to connect.

Human intelligence grows much faster than human wisdom. We are quick to develop technologies that give us power over nature, and slow to understand the implications and unintended consequences. How shall we change this?

> Each time a man stands up for an ideal, or acts to improve the lot of others, or strikes out against injustice, he sends forth a tiny ripple of hope, and crossing each other from a million different centers of energy and daring, those ripples build a current that can sweep down the mightiest walls of oppression and resistance.
> —Robert Kennedy, Capetown, 1966

Let's take just one more vision from the Poetic History of which I believe Global Consciousness is a part. Again, the early people who lived on and honored the American continent speak clearly of the attitude we can take. They had a special relationship with the earth and all living beings, which served them well over a long history. It is one we must try to understand in its depth, for it is one that will serve us well in creating a future for our children and grandchildren.

Message from the Hopi Elders

We have been telling the people that this is the Eleventh Hour.
Now we must go back and tell people that THIS is the hour.
And there are things to be considered:
Where are you living? What are you doing?
What are your relationships?
Are you in right relation?
Where is your water?
Know your garden.
It is time to speak your truth.
Create your community. Be good to each other.
And do not look outside yourself for the leader.
This could be a good time!
There is a river flowing now very fast.
It is so great and swift that there are those who will be afraid.
They will try to hold onto the shore.
They will feel they are being torn apart, and they will suffer greatly.
Know the river has its destination.
The elders say we must let go of the shore,
Push off into the river.
Keep your eyes open,
And your heads above the water.
See who is in there with you and celebrate.
At this time in history, we are to take nothing personally, least of all ourselves.
For the moment that we do, our spiritual growth and journey comes to a halt.
The time of the lone wolf is over. Gather yourselves!
Banish the word struggle from your attitude and vocabulary.
All that we do now must be done in a sacred manner and in celebration.

We are the Ones we've been waiting for.

Andrew Revkin connects a vision of extraordinary human power with the growing recognition of our responsibility to use it consciously and wisely:

> Nearly 70 years ago, a Soviet geochemist, reflecting on his world, made a startling observation: through technology and sheer numbers, he wrote, people were becoming a geological force, shaping the planet's future just as rivers and earthquakes had shaped its past.
>
> Eventually, wrote the scientist, Vladimir I. Vernadsky, global society, guided by science, would soften the human environmental impact, and earth would become a "noosphere," a planet of the mind, "life's domain ruled by reason."
>
> Today, a broad range of scientists say, part of Vernadsky's thinking has already been proved right: people have significantly altered the atmosphere and are the dominant influence on ecosystems and natural selection. The question now, scientists say, is whether the rest of his vision will come to pass. Choices made in the next few years will determine the answer.

It's difficult for me to conceive a more elegant expression of noosphere than Teilhard's (he was a poetic writer). But it is time to integrate the astounding new material elements of communication and what he would identify as forces of societal compression. Most people who think about these things find the actual "noosphere" that Teilhard and Vernadsky described, to be just metaphoric, but we have now substantial evidence that it is an actual phenomenal presence in the world. It can be likened to the mind that arises when neurons interconnect. But in the case of the noosphere, there are no chemicals in synaptic junctions. Yet there is an interconnection, and a mutual influence matrix that can be observed only indirectly (and rarely) by our rather primitive tools. The future of our work is to seek better instruments, and to sharpen the tools we have, and ultimately to foster the integration of the material infosphere and the ethereal noosphere. That will happen of course as the future arrives, but to the degree we become aware of the process we can both accelerate it and benefit from the powers conferred by a global consciousness.

> *In becoming planetized humanity is acquiring new physical powers that will enable it to super-organize matter. And, even more important, is it not possible that by the direct converging of its members it will be able, as though by resonance, to release psychic powers whose existence is still unsuspected?*
>
> —*Pierre Teilhard de Chardin*

It will in the end be songs, or beautiful photographs, that give some feeling for this quest to create a meaningful link to Mother Earth in the shape of scientific work. Artists and writers, and indeed nearly all people do have a deep though inchoate understanding that we are connected, in many ways. It is in our poetic arts that some expression can be given to the heart's knowing.

There will be time, and there are endless possibilities, to add more material of this nature, with the purpose of making a backdrop in poetic form that can express the sources, and the mostly unconscious understanding of a world in which a global consciousness is possible. For now, these are just a few examples of the thin places[137] where we may touch on other possibilities.

Chapter 28: LOVE TO THE EARTH

My relatives say it is over 133,000 years that we have been here, the time period of human mind development upon this land. There have been four creations before this, and now we are in the Fifth Creation, the Fifth World. The Fifth Creation, like the fifth tone in music, is the opportunity to go into yet another realm. We can come now to the Beauty Path, the path of right action, of good relationship, of clear intention. That is a choice we make as this fifth cycle ends.

—Dhyani Ywahoo, *Cherokee keeper of wisdom*

The GCP is an experiment that asks fundamental questions about human consciousness. Are we isolated or interconnected? Can there be true group consciousness? Can we identify indications of mass consciousness? Might it be possible to see the beginnings of a noosphere-like global consciousness?

I am comfortable with the idea that we are touching on deep truths about human consciousness. Our findings suggest that some aspect of our ethereal consciousness is a source of real effects in the material world. This is a provocative notion, but convergent evidence for human interconnection enriches our understanding of consciousness.

In sum, the evidence points to an interdependence and interaction of consciousness and the environment, although the mechanisms for this remain obscure. Much work remains before we can provide a sound theory explaining how consciousness relates to and drives the experimental RNG results. Our findings do not at this point fit into scientific descriptions of the world, but facts at the edges of our understanding can be expected to direct us toward fundamental questions. As Richard Feynman remarked, "The thing that doesn't fit is the thing that is most interesting."[138]

Ultimately, indications of a global consciousness require us to ask deeper questions about our relation to the world and each other. Might we find that the best model resembles a coherent, extended consciousness akin to Teilhard de Chardin's aesthetic vision of a noosphere? While this is a possibility that is beyond the supply lines of our scientific position, the experimental results are consistent with the idea that subtle linkages exist between widely separated people.

What should we take away from this evidence of interconnection? If we are persuaded that the subtle structuring of random data does indicate an effect of human attention and emotion in the physical world, it broadens our view of what consciousness means. It implies that our attention matters in a way we may not have imagined possible, and that cooperative intent can have subtle but real consequences. This is cause for reflection about our responsibilities in an increasingly connected world. Certainly, our future holds challenges of planetary scope that will demand both scientific clarity and mutual cooperation.

We want to manifest a vision of that future time when we take control of the passions that drive us and choose what we want to be. We are at a critical time in history. We face the necessity to transform our civilization into one that is conscious of its potentials and responsibilities. We have the ability to choose cooperation and collaboration over dissension and strife. The result will be a flowering of culture and a reversal of trends that threaten to destroy a world we love but take for granted. The GCP has a role to play by illuminating our deep interconnections to each other and to the earth. It is one of a myriad of thought-provoking streams of insight that are converging into greater understanding of who we really are and how we may become conscious stewards of our destiny. When these streams reach the ocean of truly reflective and integrated consciousness, we will manifest our highest potentials.

> "We think the world apart." said educator Parker Palmer. "What would it be like to think the world together?" The philosopher Teilhard de Chardin had a word—unfurling—to describe that "infinitely slow, spasmodic movement toward the unity of mankind." He saw education and love as the twin pillars of progress. At this amazing point in history, we have the opportunity to get things right
>
> —Mary Pipher, *Nebraskan*

MITAKUYE OYASIN: WE ARE ALL CONNECTED

From the Lakota
An invocation at the end of each morning prayer

Acknowledgments

The Global Consciousness Project would not exist except for the contributions of Greg Nelson and John Walker, who created the architecture and the sophisticated software that is the project's backbone. Dean Radin, Dick Bierman, and others in the planning group contributed a richness of ideas and experience. Paul Bethke ported the software to Windows, thus broadening the network, and has been our go-to networking guru. Rick Berger created a comprehensive website to make the project available to the public. Its most recent incarnation is courtesy of Marjorie Simmons. Much of the sophisticated data analysis is the work of Peter Bancel, whose skill and dedication have yielded deep insights. From the early days, Stephan Schwartz and Larry Dossey have given moral support, believing in the importance of this work. We have also profited from the robust skeptical view represented by Ed May and James Spottiswoode.

Thanks to Marilyn Schlitz, the GCP is affiliated with the Institute of Noetic Sciences, and IONS is our non-profit home. Our scientific home is the continuing legacy of the PEAR lab at Princeton University, created by Bob Jahn and Brenda Dunne. Our financial support has come from individuals including John Walker, Richard and Connie Adams, Charles Overby, Tony Cohen, Reinhilde Nelson, Marjorie Bancel, Michael Heany, Alexander Imich, Richard Wallace, Anna Capasso, Michael Breland, Joseph Giove, J. Z. Knight, Hans Wendt, Jim Warren, Alex Tsakiris, and the Lifebridge Foundation. We also gratefully and gladly acknowledge online donations from many individuals.

Finally, the project has been completely dependent on the commitment of time, resources, and good will from all the hosts of network nodes. They are all listed in the Appendix and listed with complete technical details at http://global-mind.org/egghosts.html.

Appendix: GCP EGG HOST SITES

The data sources for the Global Consciousness Project are referred to as Eggs and comprise a hardware random number generator (REG or RNG) attached to a computer running custom software. A Google map on the GCP website, accompanied by a detailed version of this table shows all eggs that have contributed data, including those that are no longer active.

The map and table displaying the egghost sites was originally developed by Fernando Lucas Rodriguez to replace a simple listing. It was updated in April 2012 by Oliver McDermott, and brought into modern form by Marjorie Simmons in September 2014.

The listing below shows all Eggs in the order they came online, the location and the Egg hosts. Many have been in the network for two decades; others contributed data for shorter periods. We are grateful for all the time and energy given to the GCP by so many individuals.

Number	Location	Host
1	Princeton, NJ, USA	Roger Nelson
2	Neuchatel, Switzerland	John Walker
3	Princeton, NJ, USA	Roger Nelson
4	Neuchatel, Switzerland	John Walker
5	USA Knoxville, TN, USA	Greg Nelson
5	Rocky Hill, NJ, USA	Greg Nelson
6	Amsterdam, The Netherlands	Dick Bierman
7	San Francisco, CA, USA	Steven Foster, Jim Fournier, Doug Piercy
8	Santa Clara, CA, USA	Mike Cheponis
9	Braunschweig, Germany	Reinhard Caspary, Udo Unrau
10	Durham, NC, USA	Richard Broughton
10	Durham, NC, USA	John Palmer, Bob Bourgeois
11	Edinburgh, Scotland	Paul Stevens
12	San Antonio & Austin, TX, USA	Gary Heseltine (was Rick Berger)
13	Wien, Austria	Peter Mulacz
14	Suva, Fiji	Robin Taylor, Simon Greaves
15	Black Forest, CO, USA	Bdale Garbee

Number	Location	Host
16	Laguna Niguel, CA, USA	George deBeaumont
17	Rochester, NY, USA	Ryan Tucker
18	Edmonton, AB, Canada	Ed Boraas
19	Freiburg, Germany	Jiri Wackermann
20	Chennai (Madras), India	Chino Srinivasan, Anand Krishnan, Srikanth
21	Auckland, New Zealand	Barry Fenn, Bryan Roberts
22	State College, PA & Cincinnati, Ohio, USA	Doug Mast
23	Jakarta, Indonesia	Jeroen Martinot
24	Auckland, New Zealand	Sze Tan
25	Sao Jose' dos Campos & Sao Paulo, Brazil	Pedro P.B. de Oliveira, Carlos Cecanecchia Neto
26	Wien, Austria	Robert Pucher, Alexander Nimmervoll
27	Paris, France	Mario Varvoglis, Laurent Briois, Gregory Gutierez, Pierre Macias
28	Richmond, CA, USA	Loren Carpenter
29	Bangalore, India	Chino Srinivasan, Srikanth, Kishor
30	Grahamstown, South Africa	Richard Ragland, Chris Stones, Jacot Guillarmod
31	Malmouml, Sweden	Isak Johnsson, Peter Eriksson ('til 2005)
32	Soeborg to Valby, Denmark	Klaus A. Seistrup to Christian Andreasen
33	Oconomowoc, WI, USA	Paul Bethke
34	San Jose, CA, USA	Dean Radin, Dick Shoup
35	San Antonio, TX & Strongsville, OH, USA	Rick Berger
36	Sydney, Australia	Anand Kumria, Christian Kent
37	Toulouse, France	Pierre Macias
38	Wellington & Auckland, New Zealand	Ross George, (was Miles Thompson)
39	Mogi das Cruzes, Brazil	Agostinho Serrano de Andrade Neto
40	Asheville, NC, USA	Richard Wallace
41	London, England, UK	Sina Morawej
42	Chicago, IL, USA	Fred Bosick
43	London, Ontario, CA	Robert Downie, transfer Quinn

Number	Location	Host
44	Beer-Sheva, Israel	Yubal Masalker
45	New York City, NY, USA	Lisette Coly, Nancy Zingrone, Ian Clarke
46	Gibsonburg, Ohio, USA	Nick Reiter, Lori Schillig, Trevor Reiter
47	Vasterhaninge, Sweden	Henry Blom, transfer Thorsbro
48	Mississauga, Ontario, Canada	Clifford Roche
48	Halifax, Nova Scotia, Canada	Chris Hynes
49	Hessdalen, Norway	Erling Strand
50	Juno Beach, FL, USA	Norman Hirsch
51	Boulder Creek, CA, USA	Tom Beckman, Mike Atkinson
52	Nairobi, Kenya, Africa	Luke Ouko, Odhiambo
53	Walla Walla, WA, USA	Michael Breland, Martin Manny
54	Tokyo, Japan	Masato Ishikawa, Hideki Matsuzaki, Tatsu Hirukawa, Takeshi Shimizu
55	Copenhagen, DK	Brian Peter Thorsbro, was Henry Blom
56	North Pole, AK, USA	Michael Walker
57	Shanghai, China	Jammy Xie
58	Moscow, Russia	Sergey Medvedev, Ramil Yafizov
59	Vladivostok, Russia	Oleg Avchenko
60	Vancouver, Canada	Frank Ogden, Jim Semenick
61	Porto, Portugal	Hugo Ferriera
62	KihiKihi, New Zealand	Duanne McMahon
63	Manila, Philippines	Mike Mangubat, Beth McDonald, Chris Remoto, Jojo Jimenez
64	Soest, The Netherlands	Lex Sjoerds
65	Koh Samui, Thailand	John Robarge
66	Cologne, Germany	Johannes Hagel, Margot Tschapke
67	Cayenne, French Guiana	Olivier Guin
68	Athens, Greece	Panos Axiomakaros
69	Seoul, Korea	Yong Hwan Kim, Hojun Na
70	Havana, Cuba	Carlos Delgado
71	Prague, Czech Republic	Vadim Petrov
72	Cluj-Napoca, Romania	Adrian Patrut
73	Los Angeles, CA, USA	Ian Cook

Number	Location	Host
74	Moscow, Russia	Vasiliy Malyshev (was Dmitriy Kulikov)
75	Irvine, CA, USA	Dr. Jes
76	Adelaide, Australia	Graham Andrew
77	Belo Horizonte, Brazil	Joao Vicente Dornas
78	Verona, Italia	Matteo Mion
79	Klenci pod Cerchovem, Czech Republic	Dalibor Bartos
80	Vuollerim, Sweden	Annchristine Anderson, Audun Otterbech, Anders Y Larsson
81	Kaneohe, Hawaii	Michiel Schotten, Karen Maruska
82	Peyia, Cyprus	Linda LeBlanc, John Knowles, Geoff Rudge
83	Izmir, Turkey	Inci Erkin, Mustafa Haznedaroglu
84	Athens, Greece	John Piliounis
85	Brampton, Ontario, Canada	Steve Quinn
86	Lisbon, Portugal	Jaime Machado
87	Apex, NC, USA	David Hinson
88	Cuauhtemoc, Mexico	Natalie Larrode
89	Tallinn, Estonia	Henri Laupmaa
90	Penampang, Sabah Malaysia	Arthur Eeckart
91	Bogota, Colombia, South America	Sergio Carvajal
92	Buenos Aires, Argentina, South America	Andres Kievsky
93	Hamilton, Bermuda	Walter Cooke
94	Hsinchu, Taiwan	Phillip Adam Ward
95	Hsin Chu City, Taiwan	Tong-Miin Liou
96	Seville, Spain	Anonymous
97	Rochdale, England, UK	J. Miles Heaton Cooper
98	Sandton, South Africa	Aurelian Duarte
99	Santiago, Chile	Fernando Erbetta Doyharcabal
100	Quepos, Costa Rica	James Lindelien
101	Beijing, China	Peter Sallade
102	Buenos Aires, Argentina	Kristen Neiling
103	Novosibirsk, Russia	Ivan Avdeyev
104	Lima, Peru	Vasco Masias, Yoel Celis Chlimper
105	Helsinki, Finland	Jyri Hovila

Number	Location	Host
106	Irvine, CA, USA	Chris Heiner
107	Saint John, NB, Canada	Cheryl Horgan
108	Varna, Bulgaria	Filip V. Filipov
109	Buenos Aires	Maurice Taslik
110	Kapaa, Hawaii	Michele Zina, Andre Zina
111	San Francisco	Scott Ciliberti, Rich Glintenkamp
112	Ripley, Tennessee	John Todd
113	Eden Project, UK	Lisa Cronin, Nick Argent, Martyn Fellows
114	Northcliff, South Africa	Brett Cave
115	Muenster, Germany	Florian Gruenert, Tilman Schoeps
116	Singapore	Kartik Budhraja
117	Ottawa, Canada	William Treurniet
118	Lakeside, Montana	Jimmie Sue Reneau, Danae Hanson
119	Marabella, Trinidad and Tobago	Randall Maharaj
120	Islamabad, Pakistan	Abdulsamad Khan
121	Little Rock, Arkansas	Larry Flaxman
122	Cairo, Egypt	Dr. A M Fahmy
123	Warszawa, Poland	Krzysztof Kasianiuk
124	Boulder Creek, CA, USA	Mike Atkinson
125	Kauai, Hawaii	Scott Berrett
126	Al Hofuf, Saudi Arabia	Mike Atkinson
127	Lewes, East Susses, UK	Mike Atkinson
128	West Fork, AR, USA	David Bercaw
129	Kamuela, HI, USA	Christian Veillet, Kanoa Withington
130	Tsukuba, Japan	Takeshi Shimizu
131	Edmonton, Alberta, Canada	Gordon Nelson
132	Tokorozawa, Japan	Takeshi Shimizu
133	Capetown, South Africa	Oliver McDermott
134	Perth, Western Australia	Simon Collins
135	Thanedhar, India	Kartik Budhraja
136	Flagstaff Hill, SA, Australia	Brett Burford
137	Valkenswaard, Nederland	Ruud Verwimp
138	Coronation, Alberta, CA	Mike Atkinson
139	Madrid, Spain	Carlos Gacimartin

Number	Location	Host
140	Peria, North Island, New Zealand	Mike Atkinson
141	Bangalore, India	A. John

Endnotes

1. David Bohm, *On Dialogue*. (London: Psychology Press, 2004).
2. Pierre Teilhard de Chardin, *The Phenomenon of Man*. (New York: Harper & Row, Publishers, 1959).
3. Elmer Green, *Beyond Biofeedback*, 1st edition. (New York: Delacorte Press/S. Lawrence, 1977).
4. Roger D. Nelson, "GCP Webpage: Home Page," The Global Consciousness Project, accessed February 6, 2017, http://global-mind.org/index.html.
5. Carl G. Jung and Sonu Shamdasani, *Synchronicity: An Acausal Connecting Principle*. Trans. R. F. C. Hull, with a new foreword by Sonu Shamdasani. (Princeton University Press, 2010).
6. Pierre Teilhard de Chardin, *The Future of Man*. (Image Books/Doubleday, 2004).
7. J. B. S. Haldane, "The Origins of Life," *New Biology* 16 (1954): 12–26.
8. Charles Tart, "Experimental Design," Personal communication, 2016.
9. "GCP: REG Design," accessed February 8, 2017, http://teilhard.global-mind.org/reg.html.
10. Roger D. Nelson, "Multiple Field REG/RNG Recordings during a Global Event: Gaiamind," *Electronic Journal Anomalous Phenomena* (eJAP) 97.2 (1997), accessed February 8, 2017, http://global-mind.org/ejap/gaiamind/nelson_eJAP2_gaia.html.
11. Roger D. Nelson, "Multiple Field REG/RNG Recordings during a Global Event, Princess Diana," *Electronic Journal Anomalous Phenomena* (eJAP) 98.1 (1998), accessed February 8, 2017, http://global-mind.org/ejap/diana/nelson_eJAP.htm.
12. "Autodesk | 3D Design, Engineering & Entertainment Software," accessed February 25, 2017, http://www.autodesk.com/.
13. John Walker, "Fourmilab," accessed February 8, 2017, http://www.fourmilab.ch/.
14. Dean Radin and Roger Nelson, "Evidence for consciousness-related anomalies in random physical systems," *Foundations of Physics* 19, no. 12 (1989): 1499–1514.

15. Julie Milton, "Meta-Analysis of Free-Response ESP Studies without Altered States of Consciousness," *The Journal of Parapsychology* 61, no. 4 (December 1, 1997): 279.
16. Dean Radin, *Entangled Minds: Extrasensory Experiences in a Quantum Reality*. (Simon and Schuster, 2009).
17. Pierre Teilhard de Chardin, *The Phenomenon of Man* (Lulu Press, Inc, 2015).
18. David J. Chalmers, *The Character of Consciousness*, 1st edition (New York: Oxford University Press, 2010).
19. Robert G. Jahn and Brenda J. Dunne, *Margins of Reality: The Role of Consciousness in the Physical World*, 1st Edition. Harcourt Brace Jovanovich, 1987. (Reissued in 2009 by ICRL Press.)
20. R. D. Nelson et al., "FieldREG Anomalies in Group Situations," *Explore: The Journal of Science and Healing* 3, no. 3 (May 1, 2007): 278.
21. R.D. Nelson et al., "FieldREG II: Consciousness Field Effects: Replications and Explorations," *Journal of Scientific Exploration* 12, no. 3 (1998): 425–454.
22. "Chief Seattle Quotes," BrainyQuote, accessed February 8, 2017, https://www.brainyquote.com/quotes/quotes/c/chiefseatt104989.html.
23. David Bohm, *Wholeness and the Implicate Order*, Reissue edition (London: New York: Routledge, 2002).
24. Helmut Schmidt, "Observation of a PK Effect under Highly Controlled Conditions," *Journal of Parapsychology* 57, Dec. 1993.
25. Dean Radin and Roger Nelson, "Meta-Analysis of Mind-Matter Interaction Experiments: 1959-2000," *Healing, Intention and Energy Medicine*. (London: Harcourt Health Sciences, 2003, 39–48.)
26. Robert G. Jahn, "The Persistent Paradox of Psychic Phenomena: An Engineering Perspective," *Proceedings of the IEEE* 70 (1982): 136–70.
27. Russell Targ and Harold E. Puthoff, "Information Transmission under Conditions of Sensory Shielding," Letters to Nature. *Nature* 251, no. 5476 (October 18, 1974): 602–7.
28. Brenda J. Dunne, Robert G. Jahn, and Roger D. Nelson, Precognitive Remote Perception. Princeton Engineering Anomalies Research, PEAR Technical Report,1983.
29. Brenda J. Dunne and Robert G. Jahn, "Information and Uncertainty in Remote Perception Research," *Journal of Scientific Exploration* 17, no. 2 (2003): 207–41.

30. Brenda J. Dunne, Roger D. Nelson, and Robert G. Jahn, "Operator-Related Anomalies in a Random Mechanical Cascade," *Journal of Scientific Exploration* 2, no. 2 (1988): 155–79.
31. York H. Dobyns, "Overview of Several Theoretical Models on PEAR Data," *Journal of Scientific Exploration* 14, no. 2 (2000): 163–94.
32. Roger D. Nelson, "Wishing for Good Weather: A Natural Experiment in Group Consciousness," *Journal of Scientific Exploration* 11, no. 1 (1997): 47–58.
33. G. Johnston Bradish et al., Apparatus and method for distinguishing events which collectively exceed chance expectations and thereby controlling an output, US5830064 A, filed July 19, 1996, and issued November 3, 1998, http://www.google.com/patents/US5830064.
34. "GCP: REG Design," accessed February 8, 2017, http://teilhard.global-mind.org/reg.html.
35. R. G. Jahn et al., "Correlations of Random Binary Sequences with Pre-Stated Operator Intention: A Review of a 12-Year Program," *Explore: The Journal of Science and Healing*, 3, no.3 (May 1, 2007): 244–53.
36. Ibid.
37. Jessica Utts, "Replication and Meta-Analysis in Parapsychology," *Statistical Science* 6, no. 4 (November 1991): 363–78.
38. Roger D. Nelson et al., "FieldREG Anomalies in a Group Situation," *Journal of Scientific Exploration* 10, no. 1 (1996): 111–41.
39. Roger D. Nelson, "FieldREG Measurements in Egypt: Resonant Consciousness at Sacred Sites." Princeton Engineering Anomalies Research, PEAR Technical Report, 1997.
40. R.D. Nelson and A. Apostol, "A Repeated Measures FieldREG Application: Dowsing Biolocation at Devils Tower." Princeton Engineering Anomalies Research, PEAR Technical Report, 1996.
41. R.D. Nelson, "FieldREG Measurements in Egypt: Resonant Consciousness at Sacred Sites." Princeton Engineering Anomalies Research, PEAR Technical Report, 1997.
42. Dean Radin, *The Conscious Universe: The Scientific Truth of Psychic Phenomena* (New York: Harper Collins, 1997.
43. D.J. Bierman, "Exploring Correlations between Local Emotional and Global Emotional Events and the Behavior of a Random Number Generator," *Journal of Scientific Exploration*, 1996, 363–374.
44. R.D. Nelson et al., "FieldREG II: Consciousness Field Effects: Replications and Explorations," 1998, *J. Scientific Exploration*, 12, No.3, pp.425-454.

45. B.J. Dunne, "Co-Operator Experiments with an REG Device." Princeton Engineering Anomalies Research, PEAR Technical Report, 1991.
46. P. Teilhard de Chardin, *Le Phénomène Humain*, written 1938–40; translation, *The Phenomenon of Man* (Paris: Éditions du Seuil, 1955).
47. V.I. Vernadsky, *The Biosphere*, first published in Russian in 1926. English translations: Oracle, AZ, Synergetic Press, 1986.
48. Frank Waters, *Masked Gods: Navaho & Pueblo Ceremonialism*, 1st edition (Athens, Ohio: Swallow Press, 1950).
49. "GCP Registry of Formal Specifications for Global Events," accessed February 12, 2017, http://global-mind.org/pred_formal.html.
50. Roger Nelson, "Multiple Field REG/RNG Recordings during a Global Event, Princess Diana." *Electronic Journal Anomalous Phenomena* (eJAP) 98.1 (1998), accessed February 8, 2017, http://global-mind.org/ejap/diana/nelson_eJAP.htm.
51. "GCP Registry of Formal Specifications for Global Events," accessed February 12, 2017, http://global-mind.org/pred_formal.html.
52. Roger Nelson, "GGP Webpage: Egghosts," accessed February 12, 2017, http://global-mind.org/egghosts.html
53. E.C. May and S.J.P. Spottiswoode, "Global Consciousness Project: An Independent Analysis of the 11 September 2001 Events," (Laboratories for Fundamental Research, Palo Alto, California, 2002).
54. P.A. Bancel and R.D. Nelson, "The GCP Event Experiment: Design, Analytical Methods, Results," *Journal of Scientific Exploration* 2008, no. 22 (n.d.): 309–333. (Also in Roger Nelson and Peter Bancel, "Effects of Mass Consciousness: Changes in Random Data during Global Events," *Explore: The Journal of Science and Healing* (New York, N.Y.) 7, no. 6 (December 2011): 373–83.)
55. Anthony Freeman, *Consciousness: A Guide to the Debates* (Santa Barbara, CA, ABC-CLIO, 2003).
56. "Bertrand Russell Quotes," accessed February 12, 2017, http://cswww.essex.ac.uk/CSP/library/Russell.html.
57. Roger D. Nelson, "GCP Webpage: Formal Results," 2017, http://noosphere.princeton.edu/results.html.
58. Desmond C. Ong, "A Primer to Bootstrapping and an Overview of Bootstrap Resampling" (Department of Psychology, Stanford University, August 22, 2014).
59. P. Bancel and R. Nelson, "The GCP Event Experiment: Design, Analytical Methods, Results," *Journal of Scientific Exploration*, Fall 2008, Vol. 22 Issue 3, 309–334.

60. Roger Nelson, "GCP Webpage: Egg Number 1," Global Consciousness Project, accessed February 12, 2017, http://teilhard.global-mind.org/pear196.html.
61. "GCP Registry of Formal Specifications for Global Events," accessed February 12, 2017, http://global-mind.org/pred_formal.html.
62. Roger Nelson et al., "Correlations of Continuous Random Data with Major World Events," *Foundations of Physics Letters* 15, no. 6 (2002): 537–550.
63. "InfoPlease 'Year in Review,'" December 2000 through November 2001, 2002, http://www.infoplease.com.
64. D.I. Radin, "Exploring Relationships Between Random Physical Events and Mass Human Attention: Asking for Whom the Bell Tolls," *J. Scientific Exploration* 16, no. 4 (2002): 533–548.
65. Adam Curry, "Entangled: The Consciousness App," accessed January 26, 2017, http://www.consciousness-app.com/.
66. Roger D. Nelson and Peter A. Bancel, "Anomalous Anticipatory Responses in Networked Random Data," AIP Conference Proceedings, vol. 863, 2006, 260–72.
67. Bryan Williams, "GCP Global Harmony Note," accessed January 30, 2017, http://leyline.org/papers/GCPGlobalHarmonyBW.pdf.
68. Jessica Utts, "Replication and Meta-Analysis in Parapsychology," *Statistical Science* 6, no. 4 (November 1991): 363–78.
69. Edwin May and James Spottiswoode, "The Global Consciousness Project, Identifying the Source of Psi: A Response to Nelson and Bancel," *Journal of Scientific Exploration* 25, no. 4 (2011),
70. Roger Nelson, "Emotional Nature of Global Consciousness," in 7th *Symposium of the Bial Foundation: Behind and Beyond the Brain*, vol. 7th (Fundacao Bial, 2008), 97–114.
71. Ibid.
72. P. Bancel and R. Nelson, "The GCP Event Experiment: Design, Analytical Methods, Results"; Nelson and Bancel, "Effects of Mass Consciousness"; Peter Bancel, "Reply to May and Spottiswoode's 'The Global Consciousness Project: Identifying the Source of Psi,'" *Journal of Scientific Exploration* 25, no. 4 (2011).
73. R. D. Nelson and P. A. Bancel, "Effects of Mass Consciousness: Changes in Random Data during Global Events," *Explore: The Journal of Science and Healing*, 7, no. 6 (December 2011): 373–83.

74. P.A. Bancel and R.D. Nelson, "The GCP Event Experiment: Design, Analytical Methods, Results," *Journal of Scientific Exploration*, Vol. 22 Issue 3 (Fall 2008): 309-334.
75. Ibid.
76. Ibid.
77. R. D. Nelson and P. A. Bancel, "Effects of Mass Consciousness: Changes in Random Data during Global Events," *Explore: The Journal of Science and Healing*, 7, no. 6 (December 2011): 373–83.
78. Ibid.
79. R. D. Nelson, "Emotional Nature of Global Consciousness," in 7th *Symposium of the Bial Foundation: Behind and Beyond the Brain*, vol. 7 (Fundacao Bial, 2008), 97–114.
80. P.A. Bancel and R.D. Nelson, "The GCP Event Experiment: Design, Analytical Methods, Results," *Journal of Scientific Exploration*, (Fall 2008), Vol. 22 Issue 3, 309–334.
81. E. May and J. Spottiswoode, "Global Consciousness Project: An Independent Analysis of the 11 September 2001 Events," (Laboratories for Fundamental Research, Palo Alto, California, 2002); Bancel and Nelson, "The GCP Event Experiment: Design, Analytical Methods, Results," *Journal of Scientific Exploration*, Vol. 22 Issue 3 (Fall 2008): 309–334.
82. E.C. May, J.M. Utts, and J.P. Spottiswoode, "Decision Augmentation Theory: Toward a Theory of Anomalous Mental Phenomena," *Journal of Parapsychology*, 59(3), 195–220, (1995)
83. E. May and J. Spottiswoode, "The Global Consciousness Project, Identifying the Source of Psi," *Journal of Scientific Exploration*, Volume 25, Number 4, (2011)
84. P. Bancel, "Reply to May and Spottiswoode's "The Global Consciousness Project, Identifying the Source of Psi," *Journal of Scientific Exploration*, Volume 25, Number 4 (2011).
85. Pierre Teilhard de Chardin, *The Phenomenon of Man*, (New York: Harper & Row, Publishers, 1959).
86. A.S. Eddington, *The Nature of the Physical World*, (MacMillan, 1928).
87. Peter A. Bancel, "Is the Global Consciousness Project an ESP Experiment?" Paper for Parapsychological Association Meeting, (Affiliation: Institut Métapsychique International Paris, France, June 10, 2013).
88. Damien Broderick and Ben Goertzel, *Evidence for Psi: Thirteen Empirical Research Reports* (McFarland, 2014).

89. Peter A. Bancel, "An Analysis of the Global Consciousness Project," in *Evidence for Psi: Thirteen Empirical Reports*, Eds. Broderick & Goertzel (McFarland, 2014).
90. Damien Broderick and Ben Goertzel, *Evidence for Psi: Thirteen Empirical Research Reports* (McFarland, 2014).
91. E. May, J. Utts, and J. Spottiswoode, "Decision Augmentation Theory: Toward a Theory of Anomalous Mental Phenomena." *Journal of Parapsychology*, 59(3), 195-220 (1995).
92. P. Bancel, "Reply to May and Spottiswoode's "The Global Consciousness Project, Identifying the Source of Psi," *Journal of Scientific Exploration*, Volume 25, Number 4 (2011).
93. J. D. Scargle, "Was There Evidence of Global Consciousness on September 11," *Journal of Scientific Exploration*, Volume 16, Number 4, 571-577 (2002).
94. E. May, J. Utts, and J. Spottiswoode, "Decision Augmentation Theory: Toward a Theory of Anomalous Mental Phenomena," in E.C. May and S.B. Marwaha, eds., *Anomalous Cognition: Remote Viewing Research and Theory* (Jefferson, NC: McFarland, 2014).
95. York H. Dobyns, "Selection versus Influence Revisited: New Method and Conclusions," *Journal of Scientific Exploration*, 1996, http://www.global-mind.org/papers/pear/selection.influence.pdf; P. Bancel, "Reply to May and Spottiswoode's "The Global Consciousness Project," *Journal of Scientific Exploration*, Volume 25, Number 4, (2011).
96. P. Bancel, "An Analysis of the Global Consciousness Project," in *Evidence for Psi: Thirteen Empirical Reports*, Eds. Broderick & Goertzel (McFarland, 2014),
97 James C. Carpenter, *First Sight: ESP and Parapsychology in Everyday Life* (Rowman & Littlefield Publishers, 2015).
98. Roger Nelson, "Evoked Potentials and GCP Event Data: Parallel Structures" accessed January 11, 2019, http://teilhard.global-mind.org/papers/pdf/event.data.vs.evoked.potentials.pdf
99. Roger Nelson, "The Global Consciousness Project: Subtle Interconnections and Correlations in Random Data," in *Evidence for Psi*, ed. Damien Broderick and Ben Goertzel, vol. Vol. 1 (McFarland, 2014).
100. P. Bancel, "An Analysis of the Global Consciousness Project," in Evidence for *Psi: Thirteen Empirical Reports*, Eds. Broderick & Goertzel (McFarland, 2014),

101. James C. Carpenter, *First Sight: ESP and Parapsychology in Everyday Life* (Rowman & Littlefield Publishers, 2015).
102. E. May, J. Utts, and S. J. Spottiswoode, "Decision Augmentation Theory: Toward a Theory of Anomalous Mental Phenomena." *Journal of Parapsychology*, 59(3), 195–220 (1995).
103. Ken Wilber, *A Brief History of Everything*, 2nd edition (Boston: New York: Shambhala, 2001).
104. David Bohm, *Wholeness and the Implicate Order*, Reissue edition (London: New York: Routledge, 2002).
105. Brian Josephson, "String Theory, Universal Mind, and the Paranormal," arXiv:physics/0312012 V2, no. 2 Dec (2003), https://arxiv.org/html/physics/0312012.
106. Rupert Sheldrake, *A New Science of Life: The Hypothesis of Formative Causation* (Los Angeles, Boston: J P Tarcher, Inc., 1982).
107. Abraham Boyarsky, *Theory of Mind* (Gordon and Breach Science Publishers, 1999), http://teilhard.global-mind.org/papers/pdf/boyarsky.theorymind.pdf.
108. Amit Goswami, *Creative Evolution: A Physicist's Resolution Between Darwinism and Intelligent Design*, 1st Quest Ed edition (Wheaton, Ill: Quest Books, 2008).
109. Roubiere, Interview with Physicist David Bohm (Part 1/5), 2008, accessed February, 2017, https://www.youtube.com/watch?v=SvyD2o7w24g.
110. David Bohm, *Causality and Chance in Modern Physics*, Reissue edition, pg 143 (Philadelphia: University of Pennsylvania Press, 1971).
111. Dean Radin, *Entangled Minds*, (New York, Paraview Pocket Books, 2006)
112. Ibid.
113. Robert G. Jahn and Brenda J. Dunne, "A Modular Model of Mind/Matter Manifestations (M5)," *Journal of Scientific Exploration* 15, no. 3 (2001): 299–329.
114. James Carpenter, *First Sight: ESP and Parapsychology in Everyday Life* (Rowman & Littlefield Publishers, 2015).
115. James Jeans, *The Mysterious Universe* (New York, Cambridge, Eng.: Kessinger Publishing, LLC, 2010).
116. Pierre Teilhard de Chardin, *The Future of Man*. (Image Books/Doubleday, 2004).
117. Lewis Thomas, *The Medusa and the Snail: More Notes of a Biology Watcher*. Reprint edition (New York: Penguin Books, 1995).

118. Kevin Laland, "Evolution Evolves: Beyond the Selfish Gene," *New Scientist*, accessed March 25, 2017, https://www.newscientist.com/article/mg23130920-600-evolution-evolves-beyond-the-selfish-gene/.
119. Rebecca Kessler, 2011, and Pm, "Hugs Follow a 3-Second Rule," *Science | AAAS*, January 28, 2011, http://www.sciencemag.org/news/2011/01/hugs-follow-3-second-rule.
120. Jose Arguelles, *Manifesto for the Noosphere: The Next Stage in the Evolution of Human Consciousness* (North Atlantic Books, 2011).
121. "We Are All Children of the Earth | Children of the Earth," accessed February 21, 2017, http://www.coeworld.org/.
122. "The Goi Peace Foundation," accessed February 21, 2017, https://www.goipeace.or.jp/en/.
123. "The World Council of Religious Leaders," accessed February 21, 2017, http://www.millenniumpeacesummit.org/.
124. "Portada—Nexos Alianza," accessed February 21, 2017, http://www.nexosalianza.com/.
125. John Bunzl, "Simpol.org—Campaign Concept," accessed February 21, 2017, http://www.simpol.org/index.php?id=8.
126. Joe Rothstein, "Hang On, Planet Earth, Help is on the Way (Joe Rothstein's Commentary)," EIN Newsdesk, June 4, 2010, accessed February 21, 2017, http://uspolitics.einnews.com/article_detail/57081276/_s1Pjw-HDKRJAjEU.
127. "The Optimist Daily," accessed February 21, 2017, https://www.optimistdaily.com/.
128. Roger D. Nelson, "Birthing a Lion," accessed February 21, 2017, http://teilhard.global-mind.org/liondream.html.
129. Roger D. Nelson, "The I Ching," accessed February 21, 2017, http://teilhard.global-mind.org/iching.html.
130. "Dalai Lama, 2005," accessed February 21, 2017, http://teilhard.global-mind.org/dalai.lama.2.html.
131. Roger D. Nelson, "Perennial Wisdom," accessed February 21, 2017, http://teilhard.global-mind.org/perennial.wisdom.html.
132. Dennis Kucinich, "A Congressman's Prayer," 2002, http://teilhard.global-mind.org/kucinich.html.
133. Tom Sawyer, "Dreaming the Dimension of Random Sight," accessed February 21, 2017, http://teilhard.global-mind.org/poem.tom.html.
134. Pierre Teilhard de Chardin, *The Phenomenon of Man.* (New York: Harper & Row, Publishers, 1959).

135. Tom Brown, Jr., "Four Prophecies," accessed February 21, 2017, http://www.leyline.org/~ghn/prophecies.html.
136. Dee Hock, *Birth of the Chaordic Age* (San Francisco: Berrett-Koehler Publishers, Inc, 1999).
137. Roger Nelson, "CAOL ÁIT," accessed February 21, 2017, http://teilhard.global-mind.org/thinplace.html.
138. Michelle Feynman, *The Quotable Feynman* (Princeton University Press, 2015), http://press.princeton.edu/titles/10540.html.

Index

9/11, 138-139, 144-149, 165, 186, 202, 205, 207, 209, 257, 276
911, 275

Adams, Richard, 94, 313
ancient wisdom, 14, 107, 128, 279, 299, 302
Anderson, Brad, 94, 123
anomalies research, 63, 97

Bancel, Peter, 94, 119, 147, 168, 189, 190, 201, 205, 206, 217, 220, 234-241, 243, 263, 313
Bethke, Paul, 94, 313, 316
Berger, Rick, 50, 94, 313, 315, 316
Bierman, Dick, 42, 89, 93, 94, 122, 313, 315
Bohm, David, 13, 57, 247, 249-250, 252, 264
Bradish, John, 66-67
Brainpainting, 124
Burton, Jim, 125

celebration, 16, 41, 48, 54, 69, 104, 105, 117, 134, 153-158, 162, 168, 171-172, 186, 210, 214, 245, 272, 305
ceremony, 48, 87, 122, 195
coherence, 10, 25, 35, 41, 51, 83, 84, 89, 97, 103, 104, 123, 130, 141, 154, 163, 175, 194, 233, 247, 267, 268-269, 282, 286, 289, 297
compassion, 12, 18, 30, 34, 42, 105, 127, 133-134, 149, 152, 158-159, 166, 209, 211, 213-214, 245, 269, 271-272, 279, 294, 295, 296, 304

Dale, 94, 121, 122
deBeaumont, George. 94, 101, 137, 153, 163, 316
deterministic, 57
Devils Tower, 86-87
Dobyns, York, 67-68, 81, 84
Dunne, Brenda, 62-63, 66, 82, 85, 161, 254, 313

earthquake, 23, 102, 105, 121, 133, 149-152, 190-191, 209, 221, 269, 306
EEG, 14, 16, 43, 93, 124, 141, 241
Egypt, 85, 87-89, 319
Electroencephalogram, 43
Electrogaiagram (EGG), 16, 43, 93
evolution, 12, 23, 30, 33, 90, 273, 276, 282, 287, 290, 291, 292, 301

flood, 21, 89, 133

Groza, Lian, 252

India, 49, 156-157, 166, 175, 316, 319, 320
Institute of Noetic Sciences (IONS), 297, 313

Jackson, Taylor, 94, 122
Jahn, Robert, 61-63, 65, 66, 161-162, 254, 313
Jung, Carl, 15, 30, 95, 247, 258, 289

Kumbh Mela, 105, 156-158, 172, 198

Laghleigh, Kevin, 94
Lettieri, Arnold, 69

Mandela, Nelson, 160-161
Mast, Doug, 94, 118, 316
May, Ed, 155, 201, 203, 237, 313
McDermott, Oliver, 94, 124, 315, 319
meditation, 17, 37-38, 42, 85, 87-88, 105, 133, 171, 174, 175-176, 186, 187, 194-195, 210, 214-215, 289, 297
Meyer, Mike, 94

Nelson, Greg, 43, 94, 313, 315
nonlocal, 42, 43, 44, 164, 243, 250, 253, 264, 284
noosphere, 12, 13, 24, 30, 33, 44, 45, 49, 91, 94, 96, 234, 257, 258, 263, 273, 287, 292, 294, 295, 306, 309-310

Obama, Barack, 168-170, 186, 187, 191194, 206-207

Princeton Engineering Anomalies Research (PEAR), 56, 60-62, 63, 64, 66-69, 71, 72, 76, 77, 79, 81, 80, 84, 89, 90, 103, 161-162, 197, 198, 245, 313
prayer, 17, 25, 39, 53, 57, 133, 171, 187, 194-195, 210, 274, 299, 300, 311
pseudo-random, 73, 109, 117, 145, 146, 157, 182

Radin, Dean, 10, 42, 89, 93, 94, 143, 145, 148, 154, 155, 168, 251, 253, 313, 316,
random event generator (REG), 72, 76, 96, 140, 266
random number generator (RNG), 16, 25, 27, 37, 38, 47, 56, 57, 60, 61, 72, 73, 79, 109, 118, 119, 185, 218, 235, 270, 275, 281, 284, 315
religion, 22, 27, 120, 283, 302, 303
resonance, 83, 84, 85, 93, 95, 96, 167, 247, 281, 282, 286, 289, 307
ritual, 25, 40, 48, 82, 83, 84, 85, 88, 162, 172, 195, 269, 272, 283
Rodriguez, Fernando, 94, 124, 315
Roffey, Leane, 94, 125
Ruuward, Jaroen, 94, 122

Schlitz, Marilyn, 43, 93, 94, 313
Schwartz, Stephan, 94, 313
Scott, Bill, 124
Shaman, 15, 28, 87
Simmons, Marjorie, 50, 94, 313, 315
Singh, Nishith, 94, 122
skeptic, 13, 25, 68, 80, 198, 313
soccer, 89, 133, 158, 167-168, 290
sports, 133, 187, 285, 290
Spottiswoode, James, 155, 168, 201, 203, 237, 313
Srinivasan, Chino, 94, 316
standard analysis, 101, 107, 108, 113, 119, 162, 166

Teilhard de Chardin, 12, 13, 21, 24, 29-30, 33, 35, 37, 44, 45, 90, 94, 95, 234, 263, 265, 273, 275, 287, 292, 295, 300, 306, 307, 309, 310
terror, 9, 16, 23, 105, 133, 134, 135, 138-143, 166, 186, 202, 209, 214, 257
Treurniet, William, 94, 319

volcano, 86

Walker, John, 43-44, 51, 94, 121-122, 313, 315
war, 23, 28, 30, 41, 48, 133, 134, 135, 137-138, 165, 192, 210, 293, 295
well-being, 30, 195, 290, 297
Wendt, Hans, 94, 286, 313
what is consciousness, 12, 29, 261
Williams, Bryan, 187, 194, 210, 225
World Cup, 133, 159, 167-168

Yifang, 126

www.ingramcontent.com/pod-product-compliance
Lightning Source LLC
Chambersburg PA
CBHW070935230426
43666CB00011B/2444